ACTIVATE THE THIRD SPACE

How to Align, Communicate and Lead
in a Hyper-Competitive World

Bill Cornwell & Michael Switow

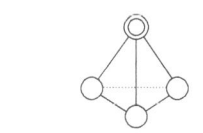

CASCADE CONSULTING
SWITOW MEDIA

Copyright © 2022 by Bill Cornwell and Michael Switow.

Published by Switow Media LLP and Cascade Consulting Pte Ltd. All rights reserved. No part of this publication may be reproduced, distributed, or transmitted in any form or by any means, including photocopying, recording, or other electronic or mechanical methods, without the prior written permission of the authors, except in the case of brief quotations embodied in critical reviews and certain other noncommercial uses permitted by copyright law. For permission requests, write to the authors at michael@switowmedia.com with "Attention: *Activate the Third Space* — Permissions Coordinator" in the subject heading.

Name(s): Cornwell, Bill, 1949-, author | Switow, Michael, 1967-, author.
Title: *Activate the Third Space: How to Align, Communicate and Lead in a Hyper-Competitive World* / Bill Cornwell and Michael Switow.
Description: First edition. | Singapore: Switow Media LLP and Cascade Consulting Pte Ltd [2022]
Identifier(s): ISBN 979-8-9870817-0-9 (hardcover) | ISBN 979-8-9870817-1-6 (case laminate) | ISBN 979-8-9870817-2-3 (paperback) | ISBN 979-8-9870817-3-0 (ebook)

Portions of this book are memoir. The writing reflects the author's present recollections of experiences over time. Some names and characteristics have been changed, some events have been compressed, and some dialogue has been recreated. Although the author and publisher have made every effort to ensure that the information in this book was correct at press time, the author and publisher do not assume and hereby disclaim any liability to any party for any loss, damage, or disruption caused by errors or omissions, whether such errors or omissions result from negligence, accident, or any other cause.

Cover design, layout and typesetting by James Eric Jones, kasimir.fr

To my father, Wheeler Cornwell,
who tolerated and answered most of my
questions growing up,

and

to my wife Tina, my greatest advocate,
without whose encouragement and support, this book
would not have seen the light of day.

Contents

FOREWORD	7
INTRODUCTION	17
THE FIRST SPACE	
CHAPTER 1: Rethinking Hierarchy	27
THE SECOND SPACE	
CHAPTER 2: Proactive Self-Leaders	43
CHAPTER 3: Human Capitalists	61
The Leadership Driving Range	79
THE THIRD SPACE	
CHAPTER 4: The Third Space	97
CHAPTER 5: Cascade Trading	135
THE ELM FIELD GUIDE	
The Model	154
For Leaders	160
For Proactive Self-Leaders	166
For Human Capitalists	177
For the Organization	188
Guidelines for Operating in the Third Space	195
Tools & Resources	197
THIRD SPACE DIALOGUES	
Career Conversations	203
Team Discussions: Assessing a New Initiative	209
The Bottom of the Funnel	216
Additional Scenarios	219
FREQUENTLY ASKED QUESTIONS	229
SUGGESTED READING	236
ACKNOWLEDGEMENTS	239
NOTES	243
ABOUT THE AUTHORS	250

Foreword

*How the Enterprise Leadership Model Saved My Ass
and Can Transform the Inner Workings of a Global Brand*

BY SANDEEP SETH

IN 2018, two years before what should have been the start of the Tokyo 2020 Summer Olympics, my team at SK-II, a business unit of Procter & Gamble, was in the throes of planning one of the most ambitious projects we had ever undertaken. We wanted to create a whole new shopping experience for our consumers, no longer relying on traditional distribution methods, but instead creating experiential pop-ups and an immersive online experience, unlike anything SK-II had ever done.

Whatever we created would be tied to the Tokyo Olympics; our parent company Procter & Gamble was a top-tier, global corporate sponsor. Moreover, the project was personal for SK-II, as our roots are in Japan. SK-II was launched in the 1980s following an intriguing quest to answer a quintessential Japanese question about beauty: why did elderly saké brewers have wrinkled faces, but extraordinarily soft and youthful-looking hands? Researchers discovered the Secret Key (SK), an ingredient called Pitera, that's part of the saké fermentation process. The saké brewers were constantly in contact with it.

Some 40 years later, we had an opportunity to return to Japan, to show our support for the country as it hosted the world's biggest sporting event and to highlight the brand philosophy that is at the heart of SK-II's multi-billion-dollar business. Destiny, we believe, is not a matter of chance, but a choice. Inspired by true stories, #CHANGEDESTINY sheds light on the pressures women face and the universal "box" they are put in to be perfect in society's eyes.

We were trying to create something for which there was no benchmark, and I must say that I couldn't be prouder of the outcome.

Let me describe it for you: **SK-II City** is an animated, virtual community situated alongside Tokyo's iconic Shibuya crossing. When you first enter this metaverse, each street presents a different choice. Down one crossing is the Andy Warhol X SK-II Arcade. Inside, there are fun, futuristic, retro games (think *Space Invaders*) that offer messaging about recycling and factoids about SK-II products.

Back at the main SK-II City crossing, visitors can choose to enter #CHANGEDESTINY Street. There are flower sellers and kimonos, a 13th-generation confectioner and a soul food cafe selling premium, healthy Koshihikari rice balls. Despite the diversity of offerings along this animated pedestrian side thoroughfare, the shops share one key element: each is run by an inspiring, real-life female entrepreneur. Visit #CHANGEDESTINY Street and you are invited to listen to their stories while they exercise their crafts in a series of marvelously produced SK-II Studio videos.

There's more: we also created a virtual cineplex of SK-II Studio's work. The marquee attractions are six short films portraying decorated Olympic athletes confronting their inner demons. The Japanese call them *kaijus*, which literally means "strange beasts." We mix animation with behind-the-scenes footage of Simone Biles and other Olympic champions in this VS Series (pronounced "Versus Series") as each athlete faces off against a real-life, contemporary challenge: online trolls, self-doubt, society's obsession with appearance, restrictive cultural norms and more. Along the way, we worked with world-renowned filmmakers, animators, musicians and content creators; John Legend and China's Lexie Liu even contributed original music. I really encourage you to check out the VS Series. The production is top-notch and the messages pertinent and profound.

On top of all this, we created experiential pop-up stores to bridge the retail and storytelling experiences and enable visitors to immerse themselves in the VS Series cinematic universe.

As you can imagine, this was not a straightforward project and success was far from assured.

WHEN I FIRST MET BILL CORNWELL, my team and I were in the thick of this massive project, but we had not yet coalesced around a solution. Procter & Gamble's human resources department introduced Bill to support me in my leadership development. There were some things I needed to polish up. From our first conversation, in which we assessed each other to see if he wanted to coach me and if I wanted him to be my coach, I could tell that Bill's questions and insights would bear fruit, though, at the time, I had no idea how much impact he would have, not just on my career, but on my entire unit's ways of communicating and working.

LET ME TAKE a step back. My leadership style has always been to challenge the status quo. "If it ain't broke, break it," I tell my team. This start-up mentality has been a key factor in our success, as we challenge the norms of our business segment and seek new ways of doing things very differently.

At the same time, SK-II's fast pace of growth, while a source of pride, was also beginning to take a toll on me and the team. "How do we create a model and culture that can sustain high growth over the long term?" we wondered.

This is the context under which we were operating, as my team and I strived to create a new shopping experience in line with SK-II's brand and the Tokyo 2020 Summer Olympics that was outside the realm of anything we had tried before.

WHEN WE FIRST STARTED WORKING on the Olympics initiative, before I met Bill, SK-II was extremely hierarchical. We operated under a traditional "waterfall model," where the leadership team provides a clear brief with clear objectives, the working group implements, and at each stage of the project, the leader inspects their work to verify that they are achieving the required deliverables, before proceeding to the next phase.

Not this time, though. We had a North Star, an experience we wanted to create, but we were not at all clear about how to get there or even what it looked like. As a result, we went through multiple iterations and kept returning to the drawing board. My team was getting frustrated.

"There were months when people were confused and going around in circles," Mayu Arao, my #2, shared with me as we looked back on the project. "They felt that their work was not meaningful, especially junior members of the team. We had so many comments on the execution of the project that they felt micromanaged."

Truth be told, I was hands-on, but I didn't know any other way. As CEO of a prestige brand, I thought I needed to be involved at every step to ensure that the user experience lived up to our strategy. This often felt overwhelming. Not only did success or failure ride on my shoulders, but it seemed like every decision along the way did as well. At the same time, my team thought, "Tell us what you want us to do, and we'll do it." But this was not possible since we did not have a clear grasp of the final product yet.

"Guys, I also don't know where we're going, but I'm with you," I told the team several times. "We've got to figure this out together. Don't worry, I have you covered. If this fails, it's mine. But I need you to help me. I'm learning about this at the same time as you. So, how do we move together?"

I had a core group of a few super-charged team members who were up for the challenge, but that wouldn't be enough to pull this off. It takes a village. The question then becomes, "How do you bring along the village in this environment?"

SEVERAL MONTHS INTO our coaching sessions, Bill told me about the Enterprise Leadership Model. I think he was hesitant to do so, at first, because he knew that P&G has set ways of working and that the organization might even show him the door for introducing something so "radical." But he also recognized that I value innovation and that, frankly, our team needed help.

"Look, I have something that I can show you, a model that I've developed, that will get people to take personal responsibility for their own areas of work and for the organization," he told me. "It will slow things down for you. As they take on responsibility, you'll have time to be more strategic."

Bill proceeded to draw the methodology on the whiteboard of our meeting room.

"You tell people what to do because you want to move things along," Bill explained. "Let's shift this around. If you allow your team members to flourish in their own areas of leadership, and raise your expectations of them, they will make more effective decisions without coming back to you all the time. They'll become motivated to tell you what they're doing; then, you can react to it."

His model had an elegant simplicity. I quickly grasped the possibilities and decided we should share them with my team. Bill joined us at a company retreat, and one of the first things I discovered was how incredibly out of sync we were. What I was saying about the Olympics project, or at least what I thought I was saying, was not what my team members were hearing, and vice versa. Even though we were several months into the planning, we had very different perceptions of the outcome. To succeed, we needed to come into alignment, and to do this, we implemented three major changes that were rooted in Bill's Enterprise Leadership Model.

Transformation #1: Proactive Self-Leaders

FIRST, leadership of this project would no longer be based on hierarchy. Forget salary bands and job titles; they did not matter. Instead, we looked at expertise and recognized that each phase of a project required different skills and know-how. Leadership would be skill-based, but it would also shift from one person to another. Defining the vision, at the beginning of the project, would be led by myself or another senior team member, but as the project advanced, leadership would move around as well.

No longer would one person or team simply hand over their work to someone else. In fact, I banned the term "handover." At every stage, we would remain connected and have open conversations about where we were headed. We created a culture of working together from start to end, co-creating and owning the success collectively. We each agreed to stay engaged throughout the process.

What did this mean in practice?

More people were involved in this project than any other we had undertaken. It was also the most significant investment in our brand history. Design was playing a key role and it was clear that we needed a global design leader, based in our Singapore headquarters, to helm the work, as well as someone in Japan to support them and ensure seamless execution.

Delphine Buttin was an associate marketing director and one of our top brand managers, always coming up with great content and new ideas. We chose her to oversee design and to lead the project. We paired Delphine with YoeGin Chang, SK-II's Business and Brand Leader for Japan. They were natural, albeit unconventional choices, particularly Delphine. She was more junior than the others, but had the best skill set to take this forward. We all agreed that Delphine would be the project boss and we would report to her.

"There were at least ten big components related to the Olympics project — video assets, on-the-ground activities, an Olympic pavilion — but we were all very clear," recollects Mayu, whose leadership helped ensure our success. "Each of us, myself included, might be a leader of a particular subset of the project, but we needed to keep Delphine and YoeGin informed, so they could maintain an overall view and guide us."

"We said, 'No one else is above Delphine on this project,'" adds YoeGin. "Of course, we gave stripes, but it came with responsibility."

Delphine immediately rose to the task. Without being asked, she put together a team charter to detail how we would work together, both internally and with external agencies and partners, to deliver this enormous undertaking. Despite being a junior member of the team, she demonstrated excellent management skills and enrolled the entire team in her leadership. Delphine was taking personal responsibility for success, just as Bill had suggested.

Transformation #2: Human Capitalists

AS WE SHIFTED to skills-based leadership within SK-II, we needed our partners in Human Resources to play new roles as well. Not only would they be required to recruit the right people, which in large organizations with strict processes can be more challenging than you think, HR would also be responsible for upholding SK-II's innovative brand culture and setting the tone for the organization. This strategic change was the second transformation to ensure SK-II's success.

What did this mean in practice?

For one thing, HR helped SK-II break out of functional silos. They worked with us to identify and quantify needed skillsets, then to assess and leverage individual strengths, as well as to provide opportunities and training for members of the team. Instead of boxing people into roles, HR asked, "How do we unleash the potential of each individual?" As team members took on new hats, HR guided them. Instead of managing people as resources, we looked to grow our human capital.

As an example of this new approach, consider the reorganization of SK-II's marketing department. Traditionally, we would hire brand managers, assistant brand managers, etc. But in today's world, where data and social media are integral to a business, we needed different mindsets and skillsets. So, we began looking for "hipsters, hackers and hustlers."[1]

Hipsters ensure the final product is cool, hackers (often coders) have the toolbox of tech solutions to make it happen, and hustlers can package it up in just the right way to generate sales and partnerships.[2]

To find hipsters, hackers and hustlers, we began recruiting in places outside P&G's typical hiring grounds, such as companies like Facebook and Microsoft. We also brought some roles in-house, like a creative director and computer programmers, that agencies and external partners would have previously handled. Human Resources even forged a connection with a technology school to create a pipeline of interns.

None of this was straightforward. How do you determine salary bands or career paths, for example, for people whose roles are so different from our traditional kind of work? Out-of-the-box hires typically require the approval of the home office in Cincinnati, which can take time, but our HR partners deftly navigated the process.

SK-II's Human Resource business partners also organized innovative, new events, like a week-long hackathon to help us strategize and create new initiatives. Picture this: we flew 250 people into Singapore. The majority, around 200, were employees of SK-II; the rest were either P&G personnel or YouTubers from outside the company. We booked a massive studio for the event, a big open space. The energy was fantastic, as were the outcomes.

We divided participants into groups of three to four and each team had to define a business problem. How should SK-II build? How do we entice first-time consumers to fall in love with our brand? What's needed for the public to see and appreciate SK-II's core values and not just the product itself? Teams tackled over fifty issues. One great initiative that came out of this hackathon was Nourish Our World (NOW), a sustainability and customer loyalty program that empowers shoppers to easily contribute to a good cause.

Without question, HR was at the center of defining and enabling success, and as it did so, it grew and unleashed the power of our human capital.

Transformation #3: The Third Space

THE THIRD MAJOR CHANGE that enabled us to get SK-II City and other significant initiatives back on track was the creation of what Bill calls "The Third Space," a nonhierarchical, psychologically safe environment to listen, promote understanding and discuss issues. It was thanks to the Third Space that I discovered how incredibly out-of-alignment we were, several months and many dollars into planning for the Tokyo Olympics.

However, once we learned to create a safe space to candidly discuss projects, ideas, challenges, risks and anxieties, we quickly came into alignment. The team felt fully engaged and everyone enjoyed a sense of ownership of the project, even though we initially had different directions in mind. If we had not had a Third Space dialogue, it would have been tough to bring the team together again; everyone would have pursued their own vision, rather than a collective one.

"You can talk about things and move forward in the Third Space," reflects Fu Shuqi, who led SK-II's global brand communications. "Everybody can express their point of view. Nobody comes away feeling like, 'oh, this person is against me,' or 'so-and-so is the decision maker, my hands are tied.'"

In the case of SK-II City and the Tokyo Olympics, we had a vision, but did not know the interim steps. This uncertainty bred fear, conflict and stress, all of which could be addressed in the Third Space. It was absolutely crucial, though, to eliminate all hierarchy from these discussions. Just because someone was senior did not mean that they knew more or were right.

Setting the right tone for the Third Space initially fell to our Human Capitalists, who helped propagate a culture of trust. I also made myself extremely available for these Third Space discussions, whenever anyone on the team asked for one. Before long, these "timeouts" became second nature to us, and we were able to move in and out of these discussions quickly.

OVER THE COURSE of more than a decade, Bill Cornwell explored why companies were spinning their wheels. Why was employee engagement so low? Why were teams constantly misaligned? Why did success evade leaders, even if they were asking the right questions? And why did most business literature ignore the vast majority of employees who were not officially in leadership positions?

As he reflected on these questions, Bill developed the Enterprise Leadership Model to transform how organizations communicate and operate. He continually searched for holes in his approach and ways to improve it. The outcome, which you will find in the pages that follow, written in collaboration with Michael Switow, is outstanding.

Embrace the Enterprise Leadership Model and you will find that your organization works more efficiently and effectively. Members of your team will proactively take responsibility for the success of the organization. If you are a leader, this will lighten your load and enable you to focus better. Human Capitalists will think strategically to ensure your team has the right people and resources, all the while helping people to advance their careers.

"Sometimes you need to slow down, in order to speed up," Bill taught me. He is absolutely on point.

Sandeep Seth
Global Chief Marketing Officer and
North American President, Coach (a Tapestry brand)
Former CEO, SK-II (2017-2021)

Introduction

BACK IN THE 2000s, I was coaching a top-ranking officer in the Singapore Police Force. He was smart, well-educated and a good leader. But his team was not responding. Whenever T. Raja Kumar asked his direct reports, who were aspiring leaders in their own right, for ideas and input on the department's strategy and how the police force could do its job better, he was met by the sound of crickets.

What struck me about Raja is that he is the type of leader whom you think should be easily approachable. He listens and is open to exploring new solutions. He would never reject another's input out of hand. Raja also bonded easily with his colleagues in the Police Intelligence Department over a shared passion for soccer and the English Premier League.

Still, without the active participation of his team, it felt like the weight of the division's success rested on his shoulders alone. So, Raja and I practiced the skills that executive coaches and their coachees often review — how to run a meeting, how to ask questions, how to challenge your team. He was doing everything right, but as much as he wanted to encourage participation and solicit suggestions, it wasn't working.

After some time, it dawned on me. Raja did not need to do anything differently. The problem was systemic. Officers in his department were scared to stick their heads up too high. Nothing Raja could say could ease their concerns; the problem was the hierarchical structure of the police force itself.

My interaction with Raja set me on the path of a 16-year journey to analyze when hierarchy is needed and when it should be jettisoned.

In today's hyper-competitive world — characterized by constant digital disruption, technological innovation, falling industry boundaries, an ongoing "battle for talent" and a highly-mobile workforce — it is more important than ever to reexamine the relationship between leaders and their team members as well as that between all employees and the organization itself.

THE LACK of a committed, engaged workforce is one of the gravest problems facing organizations today. Employee engagement rates worldwide are horrendously low. Four in five employees are disengaged or actively disengaged.[1] The advent of virtual and hybrid working environments, coupled with long-distance onboarding via platforms like Zoom, present additional hurdles to the growth of corporate culture, as employees are less likely to feel a sense of belonging.

The price of this disengagement is well-documented, with higher absentee rates and lower productivity costing the US economy more than $8 trillion annually. Break that down by employee and this is a 34 percent tax. For every $10,000 in salary paid to a disengaged team member, $3,400 is lost,[2] and this does not even include the cost of employee turnover, which typically adds another 33 percent.

We are facing a "disengagement pandemic" that not only affects productivity, but mental health as well. Told to "burn bright," leaders and their direct reports increasingly burn out instead.

The vast majority of business literature purports to solve these problems. Are you a humble "servant leader," a pacesetter who motivates, a hands-off or transactional leader? Do you "break all the rules" or "(make) numbers count?"[3] While these leadership theories and tips have their place, they ignore the 99 percent of employees who are relegated to the role of "follower." Bear in mind that even good leaders are told to be followers when interacting with their boss. It is no wonder that leaders are working too hard. Organizational systems do not enable leaders to effectively motivate and engage their teams.

In traditional hierarchical models, leaders are personally responsible for the success of the organization. Imagine if every team member accepted this same responsibility. A huge weight would be lifted from leaders' shoulders. Innovation and creativity would flourish as ideas surface from every level of an organization.

But you cannot simply will this shared responsibility into being.

Organizations must first commit to several key transformations. Among them, they must clearly communicate change. They need to articulate an authentic purpose, a "North Star" to be integrated throughout its strategies and operations. And they can no longer manage employees like resources; instead, they must provide opportunities for growth. More than ever, workforces are mobile and if organizations do not accept proper responsibility for their people and actions, employees, particularly younger ones, do not have any qualms about voting with their feet.

I AM A STRONG BELIEVER in tangible reminders — a phrase on the back of a name card, a handheld model, a photo or even a song lyric — any tool to reinforce an idea. Over time, I have been captivated by circles and pyramids;

they are among the basic building blocks of most mental models. So, as I explored how to tackle the disengagement pandemic and lack of alignment afflicting modern organizations, it is perhaps no surprise that I created a tetrahedron to represent the Enterprise Leadership Model.

Successful organizations listen and learn from people at every level; then, like water flowing over a pyramid, they cascade these new learnings throughout the organization.

The Enterprise Leadership Model provides a radical, new framework for management and systems — one that encompasses and supports existing leadership strategies, but also empowers every team member to proactively take personal responsibility for an organization's success.

Human resource departments are transformed into "human capital" that supports the growth of people and embodies organizational culture. Human Capitalists are not relegated to administrative processes; they are business partners, internal consultants and coaches.

Fundamental to the model's success is the creation of a "Third Space" where thought can be safely and easily challenged in the support of organizational growth.

Any organization — big or small, profit-driven or charity — needs to harness the creativity, intelligence and passion of all its members, then ensure that all parties are aligned for success. This cannot happen in a world where leaders always dominate. At key moments in an organization's life, rank and title must be set aside to achieve greatness. The cost of omnipresent hierarchy in a hyper-competitive world is failure.

THE STRUCTURE of this book is unconventional. The first half of *Activate the Third Space* alternates between the intellectual underpinnings of the Enterprise Leadership Model and the story of a fictional company, Cascade Trading, where the leadership team grapples with issues of engagement, misalignment and more.

While we hope you enjoy the story of Cascade Trading, we encourage you to read it with an active mind. Reflect on the similarities that may exist between Cascade and your organization. As you read, you may even recognize yourself and your colleagues.

The book's latter chapters present a field guide and examples to assist you with the implementation of the Enterprise Leadership Model in your own organization.

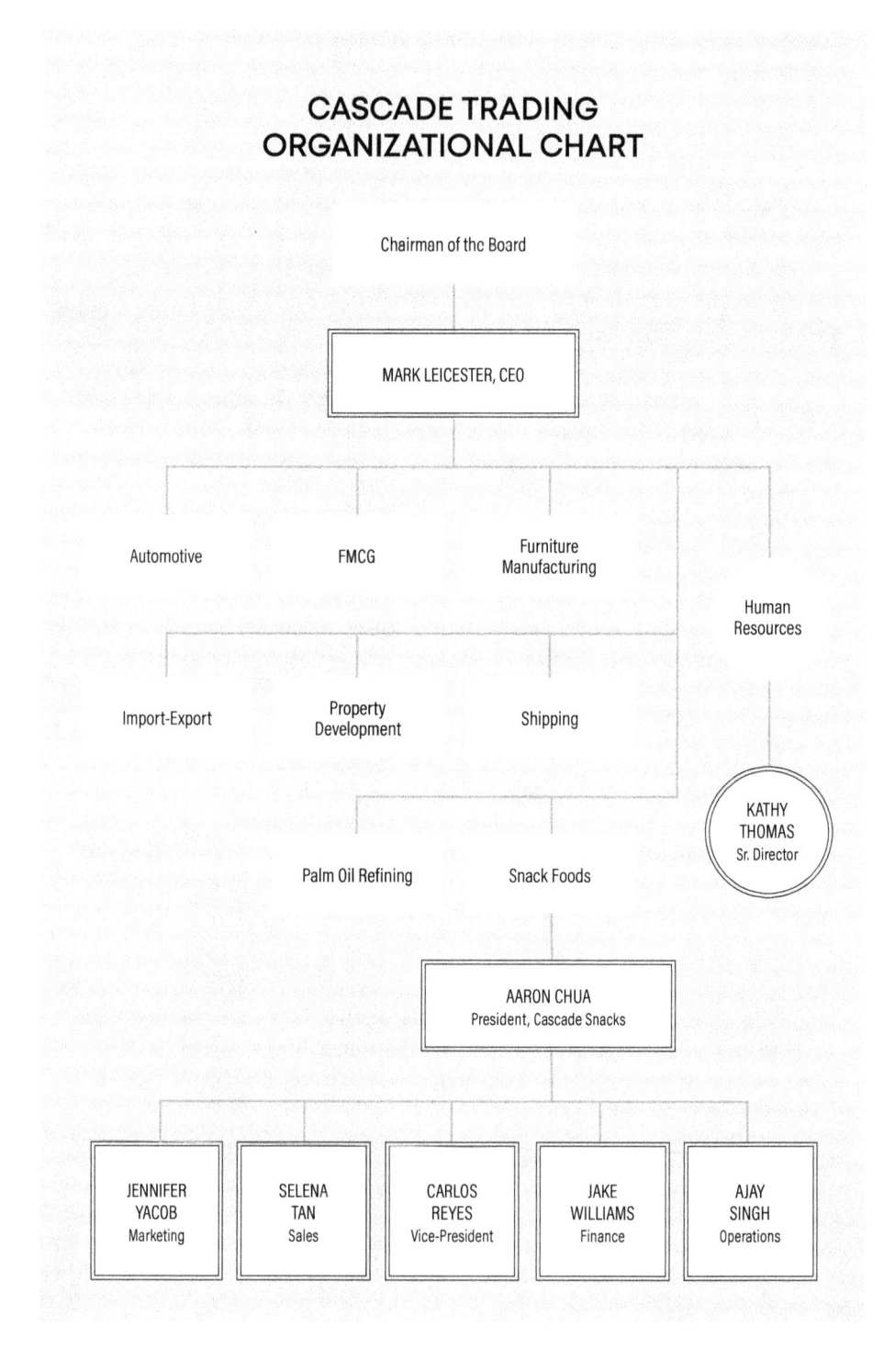

CASCADE TRADING ORGANIZATIONAL CHART

Chairman of the Board

MARK LEICESTER, CEO

- Automotive
- FMCG
- Furniture Manufacturing
- Human Resources
- Import-Export
- Property Development
- Shipping
- Palm Oil Refining
- Snack Foods

KATHY THOMAS — Sr. Director

AARON CHUA
President, Cascade Snacks

JENNIFER YACOB	SELENA TAN	CARLOS REYES	JAKE WILLIAMS	AJAY SINGH
Marketing	Sales	Vice-President	Finance	Operations

INTRODUCTION

Cast of Characters

AARON CHUA is the President of Cascade Snacks, a unit of Cascade Trading. Born in Singapore, Aaron spent the last 18 years in the United States before returning to his home country. Aaron moved to the US in his mid-20s to attend UCLA's Anderson School of Management. Upon graduation, he worked with several Silicon Valley firms, then joined Amazon, where he enjoyed success and rapid growth as a director of business development. Cascade Trading poached Aaron from Amazon to lead its struggling snack food division, which has global ambitions but currently operates exclusively in the Asia-Pacific region. Aaron has a hands-on leadership style. While some colleagues might consider this to be micro-managing, Aaron initially believes this is a key to success.

MARK LEICESTER is Cascade Trading's Chief Executive Officer. He oversees a multinational, Singapore-headquartered conglomerate that has automotive, FMCG (Fast-Moving Consumer Goods), furniture manufacturing, import & export trading, palm oil refining, property development, shipping and snack food divisions. A lifelong "Cascader," Mark has held roles in Cascade offices across four continents. He is the first Cascade CEO who is not a member of the Cascade family that founded the British colonial company in the 1840s.

CARLOS REYES is the Vice President of Cascade Snacks. A former commercial attaché with Mexico's foreign service, Carlos retired from the diplomatic corps at the age of 50 to embark on a second career in the private sector. As Aaron's deputy, Carlos oversees logistics and works to ensure the smooth implementation of strategic objectives. A father of three, Carlos is also part-owner of a small pub that has developed a reputation for its wide selection of imported tequila.

AJAY SINGH is Cascade Snacks' Head of Operations, responsible for production and distribution. Born in Hyderabad, India, where he studied industrial engineering, Ajay moved to Singapore with his family more than ten years ago. Ajay started his Cascade career in the company's furniture manufacturing division before applying to join the snacks division and subsequently being promoted to his current role.

SELENA TAN, Cascade Snacks' Head of Sales, has a proven track record of exceeding sales targets and expanding the company's customer base. She started her career in Cascade Trading's FMCG division, where she initially focused on cosmetics before switching to the snack food line. A self-proclaimed foodie, Selena is on the search for Singapore's best chicken biryani; at home, thanks to her daughter's environmental activism, she has learned to compost and use fewer plastic bags.

KATHY THOMAS is a Senior Director of Human Resources with more than two decades of HR experience. Before Cascade Trading, Kathy worked in-house at one of the world's largest oil companies, where she introduced new training platforms and was responsible for realizing synergies across multiple departments. Kathy first joined Cascade Trading at the director level, more than one decade ago, before subsequently being promoted to Senior Director. A certified professional coach with expertise in organizational development and people strategies, Kathy spends more time than she would like resolving administrative crises and debating headcount with department leaders.

JAKE WILLIAMS is Cascade Snacks' Chief Financial Officer. A London-born, King's College graduate, Jake first joined Cascade Trading in its London office, where he worked as an accountant. In the early 2000s, several years after Amazon began selling books, music and video games in the UK, Jake joined the online platform's finance team. He rejoined Cascade Trading's London finance team, where his keen attention to detail and ability to aptly navigate office politics caught the eye of his supervisors, who supported Jake's internal application for a move to the Singapore head office. Outside the office, Jake invests in currencies and enjoys playing tennis.

JENNIFER YACOB is Cascade Snacks' Head of Marketing. At 32 years old, she is the youngest member of Aaron's leadership team. Prior to working at Cascade, Jennifer spent several years in Japan, first as an exchange student and then in the marketing department of a Japanese F&B distributor. Jennifer remains in touch with her Japanese host family and former colleagues, who never fail to smile when they receive a short video of Jennifer and her two fast-growing toddlers.

THE FIRST SPACE

CHAPTER ONE

Rethinking Hierarchy

AS AARON CHUA reflected on the previous year, he felt a pit rise in his stomach. He reached for the Pepto-Bismol on his desk and took a swig. It was only 8:00 am, but the 50-year-old regional president sensed that time was not running in his favor.

He stepped to the doorway.

"May Ann," he said quietly to his assistant, "schedule a meeting with my direct reports in thirty minutes."

Nine months earlier, lured by the opportunity to turn around a struggling company in his hometown, Aaron had left his job at Amazon, where he routinely oversaw double-digit revenue growth in his role as a director of business development, to return to Singapore. There, he took up a position in a multinational firm called Cascade Trading, a company whose name belied its focus on fast-moving consumer goods.

Cascade had been founded as an import-export company, back in the days when Great Britain's Royal Navy ruled the seas. The 175-year-old company still ran a trading house, but the conglomerate made most of its money selling cosmetics, toilet paper and unhealthy snack foods in supermarkets across the globe.

At Cascade, Aaron was now responsible for transforming the Asia-Pacific division of that snack unit. Less sugar, more vitamins and a 15 percent jump in profits were the order of the day. Cascade's CEO, Mark Leicester, who had risen through Cascade's ranks, had given Aaron 15 months to turn the division around, and nine of those months were already past.

Back at his desk, Aaron reviewed the latest sales figures. Profits were up, but only by five percent, and margins had hardly budged. "Why are the figures so paltry," he wondered. "I told the team what to do. My strategy makes sense; these numbers don't."

In the 20 minutes remaining before the meeting, Aaron skimmed through his notes. He was a quick reader with a near-photographic memory, a skill that had helped put him on the fast track during his school years. In front of him was a plan to increase marketing and shake up the supply chain to get

CHAPTER ONE

Cascade's snack foods into stores quicker. If implemented correctly, Aaron told himself, the strategy would cut costs and increase sales simultaneously, enabling him to reach his target.

INSIDE THE DRAB conference room, ten members of Cascade's snack division prepared for the impromptu team meeting. Five were Aaron's direct reports: his vice-president plus the divisional heads of finance, sales, marketing and operations. They sat at the table. Forming a second row, behind the department's leadership team, were their deputies and personal assistants, notepads and pens in hand.

"Anyone know why Aaron called this meeting?" Jennifer Yacob, the head of marketing, asked her colleagues. "I had a Zoom call scheduled with the web team in Japan that I've had to postpone."

"I'm not sure," replied Ajay Singh, the head of operations. "An internet outage in the Philippines shut down our assembly line for a few hours last week, but our factories are still on schedule to meet production targets, so no issues there."

"We're gaining market share and profits are up five percent! Not only are we on target, but we're also doing better than Mondelez," added Jake Williams, with a smile. The finance whiz was another Amazon alum, though prior to working at Cascade, he had only known Aaron by reputation.

"Guess we'll find out soon enough!" exclaimed Selena Tan, the head of sales, before turning to Aaron. "Boss, how are you?"

As Aaron entered the room, the others fell silent.

Not really one for small talk, Aaron took his seat at the head of the table, in a chair with a higher back than the rest, then launched into business. "I just looked at the numbers. Our division's profits are up five percent, which means we are significantly behind target. Why? Tell me."

Aaron's team members glanced at each other, but no one said a word. As chatty as they had been a few minutes earlier, the atmosphere had changed. It felt like a school principal was on hand to scold anyone who gave a wrong answer or spoke out of turn. Jake's gaze ventured to the room's front wall, where a large mural of Cascade's 19th-century founders looked down upon them.

Aaron waited until the silence became awkward.

"Why are you waiting for me to give you the answers? You're nothing but a bunch of seat warmers," he grumbled, the frustration evident in his tightened shoulders and clenched fist. "Look, the problem is clear. We need to increase profits by another ten percentage points within six months or you can forget about your bonuses.

"Selena, Jennifer, we need to boost sales further. Increase the promotions campaign across the region and make sure the new Japan microsites are online within a fortnight. We need more buzz. Check out that list of social media influencers I sent you: Tokyofoodee is busting the charts.

"Ajay, Jake, our inventory is sitting in the warehouses for too long. We need to get those snack bars to market sooner. Nothing should sit in the warehouse for more than 30 days. See to it that production is more tightly linked to new sales. I want an updated Supply Chain Report on my desk by the end of the week.

"Any questions? OK, meeting adjourned."

Aaron gathered his papers and left as quickly as he had arrived. The second-tier assistants followed, returning to their desks, but the leadership team stayed behind.

"Who needs to follow up on food influencers?" Selena asked. "Aaron mentioned both me and Jennifer."

"What does he mean that we're significantly behind target? The annual plan called for a 5 percent increase in profits and we've delivered!" Jake exclaimed.

"Ajay, can you follow up on the supply chain report? I'm swamped this week," said Jake.

As they sorted out who would do what, the team also let the "seat warmer" comment sink in. They had heard it before, many times. It was one of Aaron's favorite refrains. In the year they had been working together, they realized no matter what their suggestions, Aaron already knew what he wanted to do, same as their previous bosses before him. Better to lay low than be the target of their boss' ire.

"Guys, I know everyone's busy, but let's take a moment to sort this out," interjected Carlos Reyes, who had been quiet up to this point. Aaron's number-two, Carlos was accustomed to straightening out the miscommunication that often seemed to flow from these meetings.

"Jake, I think Aaron's been expecting a 15 percent increase in profits, not five percent," he said calmly, but with a degree of authority. "I'll verify and get back to you. In the meantime, see what you can do to boost the numbers, OK? Ajay, I'll help you with the Supply Chain Report, but I need you to take the lead on it. Selena and Jennifer, divide up the work by market. I'll check in with Aaron, then get back to you again."

"Fifteen percent! Seriously, Carlos? That's not even *f-ing* reasonable. Aaron said five percent!" Jake shook his head, but he had known Aaron long enough to realize it wouldn't matter. He would wade his way through this crisis like he had so many before: implement Aaron's strategy to the letter and be sure to document every step along the way. If things went awry, they wouldn't come tumbling down on his head.

Ajay, on the other hand, took a different approach. He saw no reason to bust his butt for a project that was doomed to fail. How many bosses had he worked with at Cascade? The company had reorganized so many times, he had lost count. Aaron wanted a Supply Chain Report? Sure, his team could pull that together; just don't expect it to transform operations.

AARON'S MOOD remained sour in the days ahead. Time was short, and he was having trouble seeing a way out of this predicament. Carlos had recounted his post-meeting conversation with the team. How could there be so much misalignment? Five percent growth, my ass, he thought. The target had always been 15. But then again, he couldn't find the paper trail.

Aaron sighed. He needed to prepare for a meeting with his boss. Mark Leicester was summoning him; he must have seen the latest numbers by now as well.

Your Turn: Five Questions for Reflection

WE HOPE you've been enjoying the story of Aaron Chua's journey in Cascade Trading. Perhaps you recognize some of your own attributes, or those of your colleagues, in this telling. Don't be too harsh now. There's room for all of us to improve, indeed to transform, but we need a supporting structure and space.

Before we proceed to the next section, take a moment to reflect on Aaron's story and the following questions. Write down your answers in the space below or in a notebook.

1. How would you describe Aaron's leadership style?
2. What is the impact of Cascade's leadership structure on Aaron? How about on his teammates?
3. What is the impact on Cascade's business?
4. Do you recognize Aaron's leadership traits in yourself or members of your team? Please describe.
5. If you were in Aaron's situation, how might you handle the perceived shortfall differently?

CHAPTER ONE

About Hierarchy

IF WE ASKED you to draw a figure that represents the structure of your organization, what would it look like?

Odds are, you'd think about it for a moment, then go look for your company's organizational chart.

But if we asked you again, only this time to simplify the drawing, what do you think it would look like then?

You'd probably draw a circle at the top of the page for your boss; then, depending on where you sit in the company, you'd draw a straight line down to the head of your department, then to you, then to your direct reports, etc. You'd basically have a column of dots, connected by vertical segments.

This is classic chain-of-command, the same structure that Aaron's company, Cascade Trading, follows in the first part of this chapter, one that we refer to as the First Space. The boss is at the top; everyone else is below. It's probably not written anywhere in the Employee Handbook, and certainly not in the About Us section of your company's website, that your organization has a hierarchical structure, but everyone in the company knows it. It's a mental model. The CEO is responsible for the company's success. He tells the team what to do, and they do it (except when they don't, though that's a topic for another discussion).

There's one key element missing in this diagram, though, and that's the company itself, which sits at the very top. Many people forget about the Organization, focusing instead on their boss' demands. They conflate Elon Musk with Tesla, Jeff Bezos with Amazon and their own departmental head with the company.

Even Musk and Bezos are expected to act in their companies' best interests. They may be prominent, possibly even majority shareholders, yet they still report to an organization that has been created to serve a purpose that exists regardless of who is in the top seat. When Musk and Bezos go to work in the morning, they presumably ask themselves, "What do I need to do to make this company more successful?"

In traditional firms, this has created a mindset where employees look to leaders to solve every problem. No matter how intelligent, hard-working, experienced or dedicated a leader may be, the pace of 21st-century business is too fast for a single person or small group of leaders to manage alone.

Organizations that rely solely on leaders suffer because they cannot obtain and process information quickly enough. Imagine how tiring this can be for people at the top of the chain, and how discouraging for employees, many of whom are intimidated by the boss. Team members are told to implement, not innovate, and then, when a direct report does have a great idea, her boss often feels threatened or takes credit for it himself.

The drawbacks of hierarchical business models — including lower employee engagement, higher turnover, silo mentalities, confusion, wasted time, extra red tape, burnout and reduced innovation — are well understood by HR professionals, consultants and business leaders.[1]

We should also acknowledge, though, that traditional hierarchy worked well for businesses for more than 200 years. Since the Industrial Revolution, workers have been given repetitive tasks. We show you how to do it, then do it. Place this bottle here. Tighten that bolt there. Companies don't look to frontline workers for input. If improvements are needed, managers bring in consultants from outside the organization instead of looking inward.

In today's digital age, where competition can come from anywhere, and often from outside one person's or one company's area of expertise, hierarchical models move too slowly. One person simply doesn't have all the answers. But hierarchy does not encourage subordinates to share their opinions. For one thing, trust is fragile in a system where there is no safe space for discussion. Why share a viewpoint if it is not acknowledged and respectfully considered, or worse, possibly disparaged during a team meeting? Why offer potential solutions to a leader who does not listen?

When trust breaks down, mutual respect disintegrates as well. Team members will work overnight during a crisis for a leader who is respected for their integrity, commitment to the company and is willing to work alongside them. In the absence of that trust, productivity and innovation founders.

There are still times when the leader-follower model makes sense. We'll get to that soon, but first, let's take a step back to see how traditional business hierarchies emerged to become the dominant form of corporate organization and how they have evolved, often insufficiently, to meet current needs.

Evolution of Hierarchy

ANTHROPOLOGISTS generally agree that the earliest human societies were egalitarian.[2] I picture men and women sitting around a campfire after dinner, discussing plans for the next day. "The wind has shifted direction," one woman might say, "it's time for us to move."

"Yes, the bison are on edge," a hunter agrees. "Winter is coming. The herds will journey soon."

"But the grass in the plains is plentiful and the quail are abundant," another man proclaims. "There's no need to go anywhere yet."

"Do you recall the year that Crystal was born?" a woman asks. "The snow and cold were fierce. We stayed on these same plains too long. We should have left sooner."

The leaders of the group listen to each other and continue to discuss. Every voice is heard, which is not to say that agreement is immediate. By the end of the night, though, a consensus is reached. The group will stay another night but prepare to journey soon.

"Hunter-gatherers are not passively egalitarian; they are actively so," writes Peter Gray, who presents an interesting and insightful argument about how nomadic societies use humor to diffuse tensions.[3]

The elders sitting around the campfire also recognize that different people have different areas of expertise. Some hunters are best at picking up the signals of the bison; others know more about birds or the history of the group's own movements. The points are judged on their merits. Each viewpoint is weighed and contributes to the consensus decision.

Yet, these egalitarian groups are few and far between in today's world.

"Almost everywhere we look, human beings, especially men, organize themselves into hierarchical social structures," writes Gray.[4] These top-down structures are prevalent in governments, schools and businesses.

At some point in human history, communal decisions gave way to charismatic leadership. Instead of suppressing a community member who was stronger, faster or smarter, or whose lineage was perceived to be better, people gave that person's views more credence. The Heroic or Charismatic Leader was born.

"I know better than you because I've been here before," the Charismatic Leader says. "We need to plant corn this year and put aside enough to make it through a harsh winter."

"I built this company" or "I rescued this business" say the Charismatic Leader's more modern successors, individuals like General Electric Chairman Jack Welch, Chrysler CEO Lee Iacocca and Hong Kong property tycoon Li Ka Shing, who made his start manufacturing plastic flowers.

Modern-day companies led by charismatic leaders take a top-down approach. Change can be hard to accept and happens slowly, if at all.

While Welch and Iacocca streamlined processes, and Li became famous for his business acumen, the computer revolution of the 1980s and subsequent advent of new technologies led contemporary business heroes like Bill Gates, Steve Jobs, Jeff Bezos and Elon Musk to focus on products and change.

"I have a Big Idea!" they cried. "We will change the world!"

Over the past 35 years, though, corporate leaders have realized they need to take a different approach to move faster and bring out the best in their teams. Some companies have tried a flat organizational approach, eliminating middle-management positions and encouraging leaders to communicate across departments. Other companies promote "Universal Leadership Capabilities" that include people skills, coalition building, business acumen, the ability to drive change and a focus on metrics.[5]

With this approach, leaders begin to listen differently to team members. They encourage feedback and take a more active role in coaching direct reports. The primary focus, though, is still on the leader. How can the leader give better feedback? How can she create a resilient organization? What does he need to do to coach and retain talent? Everyone else is still secondary, except as a resource to be cultivated by the leader, while the leader is the final arbitrator and decision-maker, who is expected to understand and solve problems, big and small.

What we find is that despite efforts to modify how companies make decisions, the vast majority of firms still rely, in one way or another, on a hierarchy that is long since outdated.

A new model for organizing companies is needed, one that empowers individuals; fosters a sense of personal responsibility, at all levels, for a company's success; and fosters conversations about issues without the drama and dynamics of corporate politics and traditional mentalities.

First, though, let's acknowledge that hierarchy is not dead, nor should it be. There will always be times in the corporate environment when a traditional leader-follower relationship is appropriate. But these times are not nearly as frequent as most leaders seem to believe.

When Hierarchy Is Needed

AS WE SHIFT to a new model, some aspects of traditional hierarchy remain. Leaders can still hire and fire team members. Together with human resources, they are still responsible for setting KPIs, conducting performance reviews and determining salary levels and bonuses.

When actions need to be taken quickly, yet team members don't know what to do next — for example, during a crisis or when faced with an unexpected, impending deadline — it can be appropriate for a boss to say to a direct report, "I need you to do this now."

Consider the onset of COVID-19. No modern company had confronted a pandemic this severe, one which threatened the health and safety of workers, disrupted supply chains, shuttered offices, indefinitely postponed meetings and exhibitions and made remote work commonplace. Businesses that did not have contingency plans in place — and few would have had detailed plans for a pandemic of this magnitude — needed to develop them quickly.

During a crisis like this, it's entirely appropriate for a CEO to meet with his top leadership team, ask a few questions to gather information, then provide instructions.

"HR, you need to create new policies for safety on the factory floor and remote work for the office team. Operations, determine where we can plug holes in our supply chain and develop estimates for how the workflow will be affected by those gaps that can't be filled. Finance, I need to see the best- and worst-case scenarios."

When it comes to developing and implementing strategy and business plans, traditional corporate leadership systems work best during a crisis. However, this is only true if leaders have earned the trust and respect of their teams during non-crisis times, and the best way to do this is by fostering nonhierarchical communication.

The problem is that most leaders act as if their businesses are constantly under threat. Companies need to recognize that they are not living in a crisis 24-7. After facing an initial threat, such as introducing new COVID-era health and safety policies, companies have time to assess their next moves.

In today's hyperactive business world, sometimes you have to slow down to speed up.

Rushing ahead risks needlessly going off-course. One of my clients lost months and millions of dollars on a project because the team lead and others did not share a common understanding of the job at hand. They assumed they were working in the same direction, but in actuality, they had gone down different paths. If they had taken additional time at the beginning of the project to discuss it — in a manner that allowed first for a free exchange of ideas and then for clarifications to ensure that everyone was on the same page — they would have avoided a great deal of frustration and saved the company money.

Hierarchy in a New Millennium

IN MULTINATIONAL companies, you don't run into too many "I say, you do" leaders anymore, though this approach still seems to hold sway in many traditional Asian firms. Leaders are learning to get more out of the people who report to them.

At the same time, younger employees, particularly Millennials and Zoomers, are demanding greater opportunities for their voices to be heard. Having grown up in the internet era, when the answer to nearly any question can be found in an online search, workers in their 20s and 30s don't rely as greatly on their corporate elders for information. Instead, they demand opportunities to share their views and provide input on strategy. These younger workers want more than a paycheck. They expect their employers to serve a greater purpose.

"If anything, the pandemic has reinforced their desire to help drive positive change in their communities and around the world. And they continue to push for a world in which businesses and governments mirror that same commitment to society," writes Michele Parmelee, Deloitte's global chief purpose and people officer, in the introduction to the company's 2020 Global Millennial Survey.[6]

This places an onus on companies to improve communication, both internally and externally, and to articulate a vision for how they are improving people's lives. To this end, some leaders are becoming better at asking questions and encouraging team members to speak up. Even high-profile leaders with big personalities have recognized that they must always ask better questions.

But they continue to operate within the hierarchical model, and this can only get them so far. By its very nature, hierarchy's shortcomings do not support the deeper engagement that is needed in the 21st century. For this, we need a new mindset and a new model, one in which responsibility for the success of the organization is not the realm of a select few, but rather of every employee.

CHAPTER ONE

Be Aware

1. Most companies rely heavily on an outdated mode of governance: the vertical chain of command.

2. Hierarchical businesses suffer from a long list of ills, including lower employee engagement, higher turnover, silo mentalities, confusion, wasted time, extra red tape, burnout and reduced innovation.

3. In traditional organizations, employees look to leaders to solve every problem. What a waste of talent and ideas! And how tiresome for the leaders who feel every issue rests on their shoulders.

4. In today's hyperactive business world, sometimes you have to slow down to speed up.

5. Asking open-ended questions creates greater understanding.

6. Younger employees expect their voices to be heard.

7. Hierarchy is not dead. Traditional leadership models still make sense during times of crisis.

8. But leaders need to realize that businesses are not living crises 24/7.

9. Many companies are making modifications within the "I say, you do" model, but hierarchy's shortcomings are too great to meet the demands of the 21st century.

10. To paraphrase Albert Einstein, no problem can be solved from the same level of consciousness that created it. A transformation, a new mindset, is needed to overcome the deficiencies of hierarchical business models.

THE
SECOND
SPACE

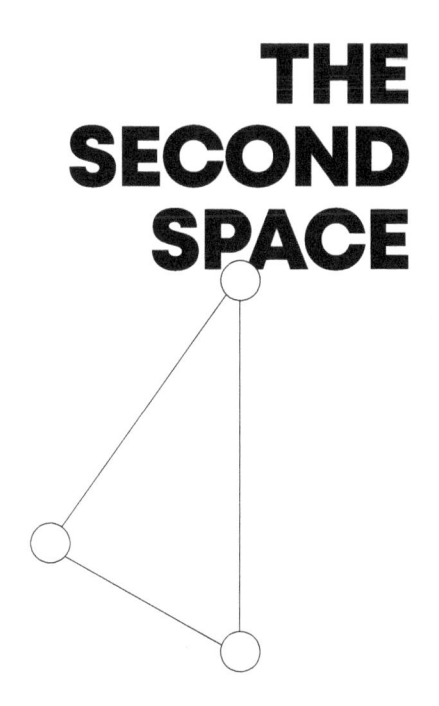

CHAPTER TWO

Proactive Self-Leaders

MARK LEICESTER was a company man, a lifetime Cascader. He enjoyed recounting how his first job had been in Cascade's London warehouse, where he had been a part-time clerk responsible for tracking inventory. He had a passion for business that only grew with time. After university, Mark landed a job in Cascade's Sydney office. From there, he moved to New York, Los Angeles and finally Singapore, where he served first as a deputy CEO before moving into the top slot two years ago.

Although he had spent his entire career inside Cascade, at every stop along the way, each boss had a different leadership style. In the warehouse, his supervisor was nice, but autocratic, a typical "I say, you do" boss who insisted on quick, accurate implementation. In Sydney, where he did a stint in the finance department, his boss was more hands-off, a laissez-faire leader who made sure his team had sufficient resources, then left them alone to do their jobs.

In the US, where he worked on teams that were responsible for opening new market segments and identifying acquisition targets, Mark reported to leaders who were either pace-setters, demanding long hours; inspirational, perhaps having attended too many Tony Robbins seminars; or transactional, using carrots and sticks to generate results.

Now occupying the top spot himself, Mark's leadership style was a potpourri of traits internalized over the past forty years. At times, he could be stern, even losing his temper. At the end of the day, though, he always wanted what was best for the company, and that meant a strong focus on consumer needs as well as the bottom line.

"Aaron, good morning. Come on inside. How are you today? I'll be with you in a moment."

As Mark closed one file on his computer and opened another, Aaron took a seat. He glanced at the family photos on Mark's desk. His two teenage boys were posing with scuba gear during a beach holiday. On the wall behind him were pictures of Mark shaking hands with other corporate leaders, and even a photo taken with former US President George Bush, most likely from one of the many leadership summits his boss had attended over the years.

"Aaron, I'll get right to the point. I'm looking at your latest report, and I have to say, it looks like you're coming up short. What are you going to do to turn things around?"

"Mark, I'm working with my team on this, and we're taking action on three fronts. One, we're reducing the time that merchandise sits in the warehouse. Two, we're increasing ad spend, particularly for targeted marketing in key markets, and three, we're launching new microsites for our best products. I realize we're behind schedule, but taken together, I expect these changes will boost sales and cut costs, allowing us to meet the 15 percent target by year's end."

Mark nodded for a moment as he thought about Aaron's proposal. It was clear Aaron was trying to move the goalposts. The end of the year was nine months away, but his target was to be met within the next six months. Of even more concern, Aaron was only addressing one aspect of the task that he had been assigned.

"Aaron, do you recall why I hired you?"

Aaron paused. He was not sure if Mark was expecting a reply or asking a rhetorical question. Before he could answer, Mark continued.

"You had a track record at Amazon of overseeing double-digit growth in your areas of responsibility. You assured me you could achieve the same with Cascade's snack division. But more than that, we were impressed with your quick grasp of the sector. I recall asking you about Cascade's energy bars. You didn't have one in front of you, but you knew the ingredients, the nutritional value and how it stacked up against our competitors."

Aaron looked at Mark. He did not know where his boss was headed.

"But you know, Aaron, your latest report focuses only on the numbers. If you recall, your mandate was two-fold: we tasked you with creating healthier snacks and boosting profits. Your three-part plan only addresses the profits side of the equation. I need you to tackle both. Cutting sugar and selling healthier snacks is important for our brand and our consumers. Of course, the products still need to be scrumptious, or they won't sell."

Silence fell over the room. Aaron was not sure if he should speak or not.

"Listen, Aaron, I like you. But I need you to hit both targets, and I need you to do so within six months. Understand?"

"Yes, I'll get on it right away."

"Oh, one more thing. I've been hearing talk that morale is not so good in your department. It seems some members of your team are disgruntled."

Aaron was stunned. He did not want to complain about his team members, even if he was not getting the support from them that he felt he needed, because he realized that grumbling would reflect poorly on his own leadership.

"Mark, this is the first that I'm hearing about this. I'll look into it."

"Aaron, a happy team is a productive team. Get your house in order."

IN THE AFTERNOONS, Aaron liked to swing by the desk of each of his direct reports to check on their progress. Today, though, he was fuming. He could not believe that one or more of his team members had complained to his boss or, just as bad, that they were disparaging him behind his back. He tried to suppress his anger.

"I have to present a poker face to the office," Aaron told himself as he took another swig of Pepto-Bismol. "There's just too much work to do."

Aaron took the elevator down to the 23rd floor, where his team's hot desks were located. As he arrived, Carlos, his number-two, caught his eye.

"Aaron, Ajay has uploaded a copy of the latest Supply Chain Report to the team folder. I've reviewed it and we have an idea about how we can hit the numbers."

"Thanks, Carlos, I'll read it later. I chatted with Mark and if we don't make 15 percent, we're all going to be royally *f@#%ed*. Mark also says we need to do more on the sugar front. Take a look at this, will you? Prepare a spreadsheet showing the sugar count for each of our products and any recent changes that have been made."

"Sure, Aaron. No problem. We'll get right on it."

"Thanks, Carlos. In the meantime, I'm going to get a report from Jennifer on the marketing campaign."

Jennifer Yacob was Aaron's youngest direct report. She had worked with an ad agency overseas before coming to Cascade three years ago. He had not been the one to hire her, so Aaron did not give much thought to her previous experience. He knew, though, that she was keen to be promoted.

As he approached her desk, Jennifer stood up. She did not waste any time with pleasantries. She knew Aaron's style. He would want an update right away.

"Hi Aaron, we've launched ten micro-sites across the region this week, including three in Japan for the products you wanted to promote: Sweet Apple Potato Chips, Honeyed Peach Energy Bars and Cherry Chocolates."

"Thank you, Jennifer. What's the latest on the influencer outreach? I have Tokyofoodee's Instagram feed right here," Aaron exclaimed, pointing to his phone, "but I don't see any mention yet of Cascade products."

"We followed up with Tokyofoodee, as you requested. His real name is John Peterson. We sent him product samples and even offered a factory tour.

CHAPTER TWO

So far, though, he's been slow to respond."

"Jennifer, I'm not interested in excuses. You know as well as I do that cracking the Influencer Code is the key to better sales."

"I understand, Aaron. We all do. The thing is there's a . . . "

"We need results, Jennifer, results. I'm sick and tired of excuses. Implement the plan!"

The strain of the day was beginning to wear on him. Aaron was becoming testy, despite any admonitions to himself to stay calm.

"Boss, if you'd just listen for a moment, I have a suggestion. Tokyofoodee is the account of an expatriate living in Japan. Yes, he has good reach among the English-speaking population, but he focuses on restaurants. Look at these numbers."

Jennifer handed Aaron a print-out that was sitting on her desk.

"What am I looking at, Jennifer?"

"Sorry, I haven't had a chance to translate it from the Japanese yet, but this is a list of social media influencers with lifestyle content. On the right, you can see their subscriber numbers, reach, engagement figures and engagement rates. I've filtered out accounts that focus on haute cuisine. The top five names on the list all have better impact numbers, among Japanese, than Tokyofoodee. If we work with the influencers on this list, we'll definitely create a buzz."

Aaron was taken aback. He was not used to Jennifer speaking out.

"Where are these numbers from?"

"A few of the stats are online," she replied, "but you have to search in Japanese. The rest are courtesy of contacts I made while working in my old job in Tokyo."

"Jennifer, what you're showing me here makes sense. Follow up on this and keep me posted. I want an update before the end of the week."

Aaron retreated to his office to think. Jennifer's idea was a good one, better than his own, in fact. Plus, Carlos mentioned that he and Ajay had an idea on how to boost sales. He had been too focused on speaking with Jennifer to give Carlos a chance to explain; he would have to take a closer look at their report.

BACK AT HIS DESK, with a piping-hot espresso, his third of the day, Aaron pulled up the file that Carlos mentioned. Sure enough, the bottom-line forecast was for 15 percent profit growth. But how were they getting there?

As Aaron reviewed the spreadsheet, Ajay's strategy popped out at him: Cascade's channel partners in each country were committing to buy significantly more products in each of the next three months. On paper, this could certainly help them reach their target. But if the distributors did not sell the merchandise, Cascade would face a sharp decline in Month 4. It was risky, but worth exploring.

AARON'S PHONE vibrated. It was a calendar reminder: Group Strategic Meeting in ten minutes. Mark had set aside a three-hour block of time for this session. Fortunately, it was on Zoom, so he might be able to make some more progress on his own work during the call. Carlos had sent him the "Sugar Report" and, clearly, his team would need to do more work to reduce the average sugar content of Cascade snacks, without sacrificing sales.

The participant list on the Strategic Meeting stretched to more than 30 people. There were country directors from the international offices, departmental leaders from finance and human resources, as well as people like himself with divisional responsibility. In terms of rank, he was one of the lowest on the totem pole in this meeting, which meant he could coast through on silent.

"Hi everyone, thanks for joining today's quarterly strategy meeting," Mark began. "I realize we all come from diverse departments and geographies, but it's important we set aside our silos to think about the company as a whole. Where are we today? Where are we headed? And what's our purpose?

"Cascade has reinvented itself many times over the course of our 175-year history, and as you know, we are committed to achieving sustainable growth and solid returns for our investors. More than that, though, what drives us?"

"Bonuses!" someone joked.

"Commissions!" added another.

Mark smiled. "Yes, of course, incentives are always a good motivator. But they're not enough. What if Jardines or Unilever or Bob's Retail down the street offers a slightly higher commission? Will you all jump ship? Will we be able to attract good talent? Without a clear purpose, we're sunk. At best, we'll just tread water."

As the discussion continued, Aaron's mind wandered. He thought about Jennifer's outreach plan and Ajay's distribution proposal. There might be some kinks to work out, but they were good ideas. It was nice to feel like he was getting some support from his team, but there was still so much more to do.

"Aaron, Aaron, are you there?"

He was brought to attention by Mark's voice emanating from his PC speakers.

"Aaron, what do you think of the strategic ideas that have been presented so far?"

"Stellar, Mark. Just stellar. We may have to work out the details, but overall, it sounds like the elements of a plan are coming together."

CHAPTER TWO

In truth, Aaron had no idea what the others had presented. He also did not think it would make much difference. These strategic meetings rarely impacted his department. He just wanted to get Mark off his back and it seemed to have worked.

After the meeting, though, Mark stopped by his office.

"Aaron, I was just on my way downstairs to have a cup of coffee. Join me."

The Starbucks at the base of their building did a brisk business, but visitors could almost always find a table.

"Aaron, Starbucks netted three and a half billion dollars last year. Why do you think it's so profitable?"

"Well, they do a great job franchising. They have more than 30,000 stores. Did you know that when they first went public, back in the early 90s, there were less than 200 outlets? Plus, Starbucks chooses good locations, and they've done a solid job of building up the brand name."

Once again, Aaron questioned where Mark was headed, but he felt comfortable with the topic. He had been tracking the Seattle-based company long before it was even listed on the NASDAQ.

"Yes, that's all true, but I don't think that's the secret to their success. Other coffee chains have come and gone. You could even argue that the coffee at the local place across the road tastes better. But we come here to talk. Why is that?"

Mark paused. When Aaron did not answer, he continued, "Starbucks has a purpose and a plan: they bring people together 'one person, one cup and one neighborhood at a time.' It says so right over there on the wall. They're committed to providing a gathering place for colleagues and friends. And they invest resources in their supply chains to create positive change.

"Aaron, what are you doing to improve Cascade's supply chain?"

"Mark, we're working on a plan right now to get products to market sooner and boost our distribution channels."

"Those are important steps, Aaron, and I imagine they will help you hit your KPIs. But that's not what I am asking. I want to know: where are you on the implementation of the strategic plan?

"You were awfully quiet during today's meeting, and I've yet to see any movement from your department towards sustainable sourcing. You do realize that was a key element of the plan that we discussed, and which the Board endorsed, last year."

"We'll definitely take action on sustainable sourcing, but it just hasn't been a priority yet. There have been too many fires to fight — internet outages at our production facilities, the recent jump in commodity prices, to name just a few."

"Aaron, the problem is that you're doing everyone else's job. You've taken the weight of the entire department on your shoulders instead of empowering your team. Some people might even say you're micro-managing. You're so busy trying to solve every issue, you don't have time to do your own job."

He had never been called a micro-manager before, and while the accusation stung, Aaron knew there was an element of truth to it.

"Mark, if you had asked me last week, I would have told you that my team was too quiet, too reactive. Any time we faced a stumbling block, they knocked on my door for solutions. It often became easier to take action directly — to pick up the phone and call a partner or log into the CRM system to make an update — instead of wasting time explaining what they needed to do."

"Maybe you're not giving them a chance, Aaron, to solve problems themselves. Next time one of your direct reports comes to you with an issue, ask them, 'What would you do to solve this?'"

"I hear you, Mark. Just this week, two of my team members have offered interesting solutions to boost sales. I'll give them more space to implement. And when I ask the rest of the team for ideas, I'll listen instead of rushing to tell them my own solutions. I realize the meeting might take longer, but I expect it will free up time for me to work on strategy."

"You're halfway there, Aaron."

CHAPTER TWO

Your Turn: Five Questions for Reflection

DID YOU KNOW that J. K. Rowling penned a 157-page book by hand? Her handwritten, leather-bound copy of *The Tales of Beedle the Bard* sold for nearly $4 million at auction. Your answers may not fetch such a high price immediately, but they will pay off over time. Writing by hand increases neural activity and sharpens the brain. Reflect on the questions below and write your answers on this page or in your notebook.

1. What motivates Mark Leicester? How would you describe his style of leadership?
2. Communication
    (a) How is Mark communicating his directives to Aaron's department? Is his message getting through?
    (b) If you think Mark's communication is effective, what aspects could you replicate in your own work? If you think his message is not being delivered properly, what could he do differently?
3. What is your company's purpose? How does it relate to your job and daily responsibilities?
4. What motivates Jennifer? Why do you think she proposed a marketing plan that differs from Aaron's?
5. In Aaron's conversation at Starbucks with Mark, what is he missing? Why is he only "halfway there"?

Tower of Babel

WHAT DOES CHANGE feel like when it happens in your organization? Whether it be a corporate restructuring, execution of a fresh strategy or simply a new project, the communication and implementation of change confounds many companies. In a seminal work published in the early 1990s, MIT Professor Michael Hammer and organizational theorist James Champy estimate that up to 70 percent of change programs fail to achieve their goals.[1] While that figure has been sharply debated ever since, anyone who has lived through corporate change will likely willingly testify to higher blood pressure, an onset of grey hair and unwelcome stress.

So why is it that change management fails?

Most analysts point to employee resistance and a lack of management support. One factor that is often overlooked is a failure to secure alignment at the beginning of the process. This, in turn, is due to the hierarchical way that companies are organized.

To illustrate this point in corporate workshops, I assemble a group of thirty volunteers in a straight line. At the front of the queue is the organization. Next up is the leadership team, followed by their direct reports, and then everyone else.

"A change is coming," I proclaim. "I'm going to share this change with the first person in line. She'll turn around and tell the person behind her, who will pass the message on to the next person, and so on and so on, until the change message reaches the back of the queue."

If you have ever played the game of "telephone" as a child, you might be able to guess where this story is going.

Before beginning this exercise, I take a step back and say, "There's a change coming! Tell me, there at the end of the line, how do you feel?"

Someone invariably leans out from the line so they can see me and shouts back, "I heard something's coming. I'm feeling uncomfortable, though, because I don't know what it is."

"I want to help," adds a colleague. "I want to do the right thing. I want to implement the change correctly, but I don't know what to do."

At this point, I turn to the first person in line to start the process. Quietly, I tell her, "We are changing our computer hardware and software as we migrate applications to the cloud." I recite the phrase two more times and ask her to repeat it back to me to ensure we are on the same page.

Then, let the games begin.

When the message reaches the halfway point, we pause.

You can feel the anxiety levels rising throughout the room.

I walk to the back of the line.

"How do you feel?" I ask.

"Not great," a man wearing a blue corporate polo shirt tells me. "I heard there are going to be layoffs. Is it true?"

Back at the front of the line, I ask the same question, "How do you feel?"

"Uneasy," she says. "I hope what I said is being translated down the line correctly."

The message chain resumes. When it reaches the end of the line, the man in the blue company polo steps out proudly to proclaim, "We are seeding clouds to make sure the crops will grow!"

The tension in the room is broken. People laugh. But then the boss asks, "Who didn't do it right?"

Quiet.

His first impulse was to look for someone to blame.

Bending the Line

THE BREAKDOWN in communication that typifies the Tower of Babel is more common in corporate environments than many leaders acknowledge and its impact is most severe when a business is launching a project or charting a new direction.

Consider the case of a fast-moving consumer goods company, one of my clients, that had embarked on a multimillion-dollar e-commerce initiative. The only problem, though, was that team members were not aligned around a common understanding of what needed to be done. Nearly half a year was lost — and countless meetings held with agency partners and among working groups — before the people involved could figure out what had gone wrong. Only after identifying this misalignment could they discuss the steps needed to right the course.

The core of the issue is that most of us see a linear, one-way relationship between the organization, leaders and followers. When an organization launches a new initiative, leaders are called upon to implement it through the ranks of followers, who in turn are expected to comply by cooperating and executing it, without providing undue input. Initiative, control and information flow one way, downward, while responsibility for success rests with the leader.[2]

Organizations look to leaders to solve every problem. Followers are not provided with the same information about a company's strategy or goals, and as we see with the Tower of Babel, the information that is communicated can be warped along the way.

When the manager in the Tower of Babel experiment asks, "Who didn't do it right?", he casts a chill over the room. No one wants to be at fault. The manager's question flows from the hierarchical model: identify a problem from above, fix it and avoid being at fault. This is a systemic issue that is more closely correlated to how a company is organized than to its personnel or leadership philosophy.

What happens, though, if you bend the line?

Back in the training hall, I examine this question. I walk to the center of the queue of volunteers. Some fifteen people are in front of me and fifteen behind. I ask the latter fifteen to rotate around me. Instead of a vertical line, we now have an L-shape.

"How do you feel?" I ask the participants again.

"Hey, I can see the front of the line now!" exclaims the man in the last position. "If there's a change coming, I can see who to ask about it!"

"I'm not as anxious as I was before," pipes in the woman next to him. "This time, it's easier to see where we are in the chain and how far the message has come down."

BUSINESS LITERATURE is littered with books on how to become a better leader. Amazon alone offers more than 60,000 tomes on the topic. *Start with Why, Find Your Leadership Voice, Leadership is Language* and *Leaders Eat Last*. There is probably a book called *Leaders Eat First!*

Given the hierarchical forms of organization that dominate modern corporations, is it any surprise that the vast majority of organizational development initiatives focus on leadership, while ignoring or negating the role of other team members?

Yet leaders constitute only a sliver of a company's human capital. Why is everyone else being neglected?

Like most coaches, I must admit that throughout most of my career, I have also focused on leaders. I have coached them on how to ask better questions, identify strengths, manage weaknesses and motivate teams. But even when leaders do everything right, they run into blockages. It is not their fault; they are operating within outdated hierarchical systems.

The system itself needs to be transformed. There is too much weight on the shoulders of too few people and too many workers whose full potential is not realized. How many times have you heard a company exclaim, "People are our best resource!" and then fail to incorporate their input?

Some management gurus have decried that "Everyone is a follower! Hooray for #2!" Yet even the term "follower" is commonly understood to be "lesser than." If you are a follower, you do not have what it takes to be a leader, at least not yet, even if you are on a leadership track. In traditional organizations, everyone not in a leadership role is inherently a "follower."

Fostering Self-Leadership

BENDING THE LINE — forming the "L" — is the beginning of the first transformation away from hierarchy and into what we call the "Second Space."

In the Second Space, leaders and their team members both have a good view of changes that are taking place in the organization. Team members have less anxiety because they have a better understanding of business strategy, corporate structures and new projects.

With this understanding comes responsibility. Every team member must now take personal responsibility for the success of the organization. They no longer act like followers, simply waiting for instructions to execute.

With this step, the hierarchy that has defined and hampered corporations for decades is replaced by a new structure, in which team members are empowered, indeed encouraged, to ask questions and provide feedback to achieve a shared goal: the organization's success, which is defined not solely by profitability, but also by realizing a company's mission, vision and statement of purpose.

When an organization enters the Second Space, followers become self-leaders. This is more than a semantic shift.

Followers are passive. They wait to be assigned to a project. They might do a good job once they are on a team, unlike an "anti-follower" who is disengaged and can drag others down, but followers are not likely to put their hand up to volunteer.

Self-Leaders, on the other hand, are more engaged; they have a growth mindset. As the hierarchical line shifts to an "L," providing a clear view of the organization and changes coming down the line, self-leaders think, "How might this new project or strategy affect my career?"

"What do I need to learn to be better at my job?" they ask. "How do I need to improve? What are the next steps I need to take to advance my career?"

When asked to join a team or take on new responsibilities, a self-leader is likely to say "yes." If they have too many projects already and feel overstretched, a self-leader will ask for additional resources to achieve the new goal. More than that, self-leaders do not wait to be asked. If they see an opportunity to expand their capabilities, they volunteer to be part of it.

A self-leader feels confident about providing feedback and may even be comfortable challenging leaders in order to advance a project. At the same time, a self-leader is willing to look to others for support and is not intimidated or scared to sit down with their boss, several times a year even, to discuss performance and career progression.

Some employees are naturally self-leaders. These are the high performers, with solid track records, whom leaders regularly choose to lead projects. If asked, "Why?," a boss will likely reply, "I went to her because she leads herself well." Self-Leaders might appear to be the busiest people in the department, but if you want something done, go to them. They are engaged and want to be supportive.

Now imagine that your team is filled with self-leaders. This is what happens when you enter the Second Space.

Leadership Qualities: The Importance of Being Proactive

WHILE A GOOD LEADER must have many qualities, proactivity is, without doubt, near the top of the list. Every leader I know is proactive, or they should be, because being proactive is the essence of leadership development.

Leaders are expected to look to the horizon, to "begin with the end in mind," as Stephen Covey famously writes in his *7 Habits of Highly Effective People*. Leaders must envision where they want a company to go, then work out how to get there. Each day, they ask themselves, "What do I need to do today to get to that horizon?"

Of course, there are fires to fight, but unless a leader looks forward, he will not know what his next step will be. Leaders are continually thinking proactively to develop solutions to issues that arise.

Strategic planning used to be static. If you go back to the 1960s, companies embraced Strategic Planning Units to develop step-by-step instructions for managers to implement strategic initiatives.[3] Rarely did the plans turn out as envisioned. By the mid-1980s, these planning units had fallen out of favor and responsibility for forward-thinking fell once again on leaders' shoulders.

Strategic workshops and off-site retreats for the leadership team to discuss strategies for the upcoming year, or longer, then came into vogue. Unfortunately, the outcomes of those meetings are often not shared with leaders' direct reports, nor widely distributed throughout the company.

In today's digital world, strategic thinking and planning need to be highly organic and malleable, not set in stone.

If you will excuse the sports analogy, old industrial organizations were comparable to American football teams. Coaches put together a game plan and the team stuck to it throughout the game. However, modern companies need to operate more like the NBA. Each time a team comes down the floor, the players need to read the defense, evaluate mismatches and look for gaps. Similarly, the defense needs to adapt to the changing offense. Management consultant Adrian J. Slywotzky takes the analogy a step further, arguing that companies need to think like chess masters, envisioning multiple future scenarios and taking steps to achieve the best one, adjusting along the way in the event an opponent makes an unexpected move.[4]

Corporations are getting better at shifting and adjusting to new trends and realities. Look no further than the COVID-19 pandemic, when firms had to quickly adapt to remote work. Yet, leaders still carry the brunt of the burden. They are expected to focus on the future, create alignment with their teams, celebrate group and individual successes, all the while developing new leaders and creating an environment for innovation and change.[5]

No leader, no matter how good they are, is capable of doing all this by themselves, which brings me back to their direct reports, the self-leaders.

Adding Proactivity to the Mix

IF PROACTIVITY is so vital to an organization's success, why do we confine it to the C-suites?

Imagine what happens when Self-Leaders take a further step into the Second Space and become proactive. Proactive Self-Leaders do not simply report to work in the morning, scroll through their inboxes and calendars to see what to do next, then proceed with the day's tasks. Instead, they frame each day with a question: "What can I do to support the organization to be successful today?"

IF YOU LEAD a team, when is the last time one of your direct reports came to you on a Monday morning and asked:

"What are you working on this week? How can I help?"

"That never happens!" you are probably thinking.

Yet most leaders report to someone as well. So, when is the last time you walked into your boss' office and said, "What are the big things you're working on? How can I support you this week?" When I pose this last question in seminars, the room becomes so quiet you can hear crickets.

IN THE SECOND SPACE, leaders and their team members both have a responsibility to work to ensure the success of the organization.

As this happens, workplace engagement soars, leaders receive much-needed support and companies prosper.

Proactive Self-Leaders do not wait to be told what to do by those higher up in the chain of command. Rather, they intentionally seek opportunities to engage with their bosses, peers and colleagues to successfully support the company. They ask how their current work fits in with what the organization is doing overall, and if it does not appear to support the company's mission, Proactive Self-Leaders ask questions and adjust.

Before they can take personal responsibility for the success of the organization, though, team members must first understand an organization's purpose, as well as its mission, vision and values, particularly as these core tenets relate back to the entity's raison d'être.

As Proactive Self-Leaders step up — posing questions and seeking responsibility — leaders become more attuned to their team members' growth potential. They coach and mentor Proactive Self-Leaders to play a greater role.

LET'S RETURN to the auditorium where we were conducting the "Tower of Babel" workshop. As you will recall, the message of change that came down the line was vastly distorted until we bent the line and formed an "L." With this action, followers were no longer below their bosses. Leaders and their team members found themselves on level ground. They could both see the change coming down the line at the same time. Followers became Self-Leaders and Leaders rejoiced at the weight being taken off their shoulders. Admittedly, I am taking some liberties with that last description; no one was dancing in the aisles, but they could have been.

To think about the change that is taking place, consider a marathon. Two athletes can be running at exactly the same pace, but with one several steps ahead of the other. Hierarchy can feel like this. Everyone is running hard, but the boss is always in the lead. Once a self-leader takes a few proactive steps, she finds herself shoulder-to-shoulder with her boss. The pace is the same, but now they can talk more easily, without shouting back and forth, and the leader no longer needs to turn around to explain what is going on.

Recall that the top of the "L" represents the Organization. Let's shift the Organization so that it sits above the middle of the segment formed by Leaders and Self-Leaders. From here, the Organization is equidistant from both parties. This is what happens when you add proactivity to the mix.

When Leaders and Self-Leaders are both proactive, they find themselves equidistant from the Organization. They both have a personal responsibility to ensure its success.

CHAPTER TWO

Proclamation or Purpose?

WHEN YOU MOVE outside the workshop and into the workplace, how does this further shift into the Second Space occur? How do you ensure that Leaders and Proactive Self-Leaders are equidistant from the organization and that both groups exercise personal responsibility to ensure its success?

There are two non-mutually exclusive routes to this destination. First, a company can simply proclaim it. Words have power. You can:

- Declare that your organization works within the Enterprise Leadership Model
- Assert that every individual in the company is expected expected to be proactive
- Explain what that means
- Enroll employees to look beyond their own roles, to support their colleagues and bosses, in order to excel
- Ensure new hires understand that this model is an integral part of your business culture

Second, the shift to proactivity and personal responsibility can happen organically as well. For this to occur, employees must be driven by purpose. Purpose-driven companies stand for more than profits, sales and services. These organizations continually strive to answer the question, "Why do we exist?"

"Purpose-driven businesses truly embed purpose in every action," writes Deloitte's global chief marketing officer Diana O'Brien, in collaboration with three of her colleagues. A clear purpose answers the existential question and articulates "what problems (an organization) is here to solve, and who it wants to be to each human it touches through its work."[6]

Deloitte, for example, defines its purpose as "making an impact that matters." This purpose "influences and fuels life in all parts of our organization, work, and talent," writes O'Brien. "Our purpose guides everything we do—from hiring and learning and development to who we want to be for our customers and the communities in which we work."

The vast majority of business leaders agree that purpose is a key to success,[7] yet less than half of employees surveyed by Gallup know what their company stands for.[8]

Authenticity is essential to corporate purpose. Leaders need to be transparent and accountable to ensure that a business' actions match its words.

When this happens — when purpose is clearly defined, communicated widely and embraced by people throughout the organization — a transformation takes place. Decisions are driven by purpose and employees become motivated to take action. In a word, they become proactive.

Be Aware

1. The first step to enter the Second Space is to foster the development of Proactive Self-Leaders.

2. Internal corporate communication regularly breaks down, particularly when change is afoot. These communication failures are not the fault of any one person; hierarchical systems are to blame.

3. Leaders constitute only a small part of any company's workforce. Do not neglect the role of your team members. Consider how every employee can be empowered for success.

4. "Anti-Followers" are a drain on your organization; they hurt morale and hamper progress.

5. Followers are passive. They might do good work, but only when assigned a project.

6. Self-Leaders actively want to improve. They are likely to accept new responsibilities in order to learn and advance their careers.

7. Clearly communicated, broadly disseminated change management reduces employee anxiety, increases engagement and fosters self-leadership.

8. Being proactive — looking to the horizon and actively working to achieve a vision — is an essential component of leadership. No one leader can do it all, though. When Self-Leaders become proactive, businesses flourish.

9. Proactive Self-Leaders recognize that they have a personal responsibility to ensure organizational success.

10. There are two ways to foster proactivity: through proclamation and purpose.

CHAPTER THREE

Human Capitalists

AT 8:15 AM, Kathy Thomas' phone rang. Fortunately, she was already at her desk. "Ms. Thomas," the receptionist said, "there's a gentleman at the front desk who says it's his first day here, but he doesn't have a pass. His name is Jimmy Lim and he says he was hired by Shane Oliveiro in automotive sales."

"Thanks, Betty. Give me a moment, please."

Kathy logged into the hiring system. There was no record of a James Lim. No Lims listed at all.

"Betty, I'll need to call you back."

"Shane, this is Kathy Thomas in HR. There's a James Lim at the front desk."

"Hi, Kathy. Yep, James is part of the channel partners team. He's late. He was supposed to be here half an hour ago."

"Well, we don't have a record of him in our system."

"We hired him through an agency. Didn't realize I had to inform you."

"Yep, you need to update us through the intranet portal. Otherwise, we can't onboard him. Don't worry; I'll sort it out. Appreciate, though, if you can take note of this going forward."

"OK, thanks. Guess I should also tell you that I hired three people for the Bangkok office this month: an Aussie guy and an American woman who live there, plus a Thai salesman we poached from another dealer."

"Do you know if the Aussie and American have permits to work in Thailand?"

"No, I don't know."

"Well, that could be an issue, but I'll look into it. Send me their details."

"Sure, thanks, Kathy. Sorry to cause you any problems. We're just running on all cylinders here to make the latest sales targets."

Kathy looked at the clock again: 8:20 am and she already had two fires to extinguish.

Bing! A calendar reminder popped up on Kathy's screen. She had a 9 o'clock budget meeting with Aaron Chua and Jake Williams, the regional head of snacks and his chief financial officer, and she was dreading it! Kathy had nothing against Aaron and Jake personally, but she could already see the conversation playing out in her head, and it was not fun.

KATHY JOINED CASCADE around 2010 at the director level and had since been promoted to a Senior Director spot. Like many of her colleagues, Kathy liked to think of herself as a "people person," which is why she had chosen to enter the HR field after university. Well, that, plus she wasn't very fond of accounting or sales. Before Cascade, Kathy had worked in-house at an oil giant. A merger there led to her redundancy, though not until after she had supervised 15 percent headcount reductions across three departments. "Realizing synergies" certainly wasn't pleasant, but she learned a lot in the process, not just about "increasing efficiencies" but also about how she could guide colleagues in other departments to make good, people decisions.

She walked into her meeting in the 22nd floor conference room, coffee in hand, a few minutes before nine. Aaron and Jake weren't there yet, so she had time to settle in and pull up the needed files.

The strategic plan envisioned Cascade's snack division growing personnel by ten percent in the year ahead, but only if the unit met this year's profit targets. Otherwise, the directors were ordering a ten percent cut.

Kathy's phone chimed. A Slack message. Aaron and Jake were working from home. They wanted to Zoom-in instead. She clicked the link, and after some small talk, shared a summary of next year's plan.

"So, first, I should ask, where are you on this year's profits? Are we going to be looking at growing the department next year?"

"We're making headway, Kathy. No worries on that front," Aaron replied. He wasn't keen to share his concerns. Better, he thought, to present a positive face.

"Well, if you have any issues, I'm happy to look at them with you. In the meantime, let's talk about personnel. If things go well, we can increase headcount in your department by ten percent; otherwise, we need to trim by the same amount. Either way, we're working from the same base." Kathy glanced again at her file. "Since your headcount is currently 115 across the region, that means you can plan to . . . "

"Kathy," Jake interrupted. "Our headcount is 142, not 115."

Kathy reached inside her purse for a bottle of paracetamol.

"Jake, are you looking at actual head count for your department or planned head count?"

"Planned."

"Full-time equivalents or 'butts-in-seats'?"

"Butts-in-seats."

"I'm looking at payroll and see actual headcount is currently 115. Looks like you have several members of your team in Manila leaving the company at the end of the month, so actual headcount will be lower then."

"Kathy, we budgeted for 142 this year," Aaron chimed in. "So next year, we should be allocated sufficient resources to employ 156 people."

Kathy popped two paracetamol to head off the headache she knew was coming. Cascade's Finance and HR departments were using different platforms to calculate personnel. They could barely agree on the same definitions, much less the same inputs.

Before she knew it, an hour had passed, the meeting was over, and the issue of headcount in the snack division remained unresolved, pending another tedious discussion. And they hadn't even had a chance to discuss the strategic questions of where and why new personnel would be deployed.

PERCHED OVER his desk, two days later, Aaron was reviewing a nutrition report that he had asked Carlos to prepare. The average sugar and salt content of Cascade's best-selling products had barely budged. True, they had launched new organic products that were sugar-free, and the packaging shouted, "Reduced Salt," but the snacks weren't selling. Clearly, consumers were not moved to buy products with names like Whitney's Whole Wheat Wafers or Stevia Banana Popsicles.

Not only are we failing on the profit numbers for the quarter, Aaron realized, but we're a long way from achieving our health targets as well. Mark is going to crucify me over this unless we turn it around.

Aaron's thoughts were interrupted by a knock on his office door. Carlos, Jake and Ajay had arrived for a snack food supply chain meeting.

"Ajay, last we talked about this, I told you we needed to reduce the time that inventory sits in the warehouse. I've been looking over your report and I see we're not there yet. But I understand you have an idea. Tell me about it."

"It all boils down to Channel Partners," Ajay explained. "We offer a small discount and, in exchange, our partners agree to increase purchases by an additional six to eight percent. If we do this for the next several months, we'll hit the 15 percent target before the deadline."

"And you think our distributors would agree?"

"We have great relationships with most of our channel partners. Getting them to accept the additional supply shouldn't be an issue."

"Jake, you looked over Ajay's numbers?"

"Yes, they add up. The increased sales volume will boost overall profits by 15 percent."

Distracted by a group text message from one of the web designers, Aaron

CHAPTER THREE

was looking at his phone and had started to reply.

"So, Aaron, what do you think?" Carlos asked.

Carlos, Ajay and Jake waited, impatiently. When Aaron looked up, Carlos asked again, "Aaron, do we have the green light to proceed?"

"One of my colleagues tried this when we were at Amazon," he responded. "Like you say, it will boost our sales numbers in the short-term. But it could easily backfire if we're forced to repurchase the products once the expiration date nears. This didn't work at Amazon; I'm not going to try it here at Cascade."

AT HOME that evening, working out on the treadmill, Kathy was scrolling through her YouTube feed when she stumbled on a video by Dave Ulrich. She clicked and watched on the television in front of her, accelerating her pace to a fast jog.

"What's the most important thing HR can give an employee?" Ulrich asked.[1]

Kathy thought about it. There were a lot of different ways she could answer the question: fair compensation, a safe environment, opportunities to learn and grow.

Ulrich was a legend in the field of human resources and no stranger to provoking debate. A business professor at the University of Michigan, he was best known for arguing that HR leaders should play a key role in shaping, not simply executing, people strategies.

Hearing him talk, Kathy recalled a book by Ulrich that she had read in university: *Human Resource Champions: The Next Agenda for Adding Value and Delivering Results*. She still kept a copy of it on her bookshelf at the office, though she hadn't picked it up in some time.

Ulrich's voice leapt back out to her from her TV on the wall.

"People can be champions," Ulrich declared, "but organizations win championships!"

"What wins in the marketplace is not individual talent, but organizational systems," he continued. "HR people need to be increasingly competent at building the systems, culture and capabilities. They need to focus not just on the workforce, but the workplace; not only on people, but also process."

The business professor continued by ticking off the elements that define a successful enterprise: access to capital, sound strategies and systems.

"But what's the differentiator?" he asked. "It's organization. It is people and talent. That's why HR is moving into a more prominent position!"

Ulrich then returned to his earlier question, the one that first caught Kathy's attention, and shared his own answer.

"The most important thing HR can give an employee," he exclaimed, "is a company that wins in the marketplace!"

As Kathy concluded her workout and drank a glass of water, she thought of all the HR conferences she had attended over the years. There was always at least one session in which participants decried the lack of respect shown to human resource departments. It seemed they were always the last in line for software upgrades or their needs were only an add-on to those of another business unit.

Ulrich consistently argued that human resource leaders need to be treated as business partners in order for companies to prosper and realize their full potential. A number of companies, including some high-fliers like Master-Card and Standard Chartered Bank, advertise positions for HR Business Partners. Even Cascade had given a nod to the idea, from time to time, though it never gathered steam.

Kathy switched from YouTube to Spotify as she headed upstairs for a shower. The first song in the Daily Mix that the app had created for her was by Dylan. A classic. She bobbed her head as a 23-year-old Bob Dylan strummed the guitar and joined him at the refrain.

"The Times Are A-Changin'."

Yes, that seemed about right.

Kathy sensed that times were changing. She knew she could contribute more, but first, she would have to find a solution for those tedious head count debates.

FROM CASCADE TRADING'S corporate break room on the 25th floor, Aaron looked out onto the marina below. A bevy of Laser sailboats was learning to jibe. Aaron could see the boats maneuvering into the wind, their booms quickly shifting from right to left, as the sailors worked to round a series of markers. Their coach observed from a speedboat. She didn't appear to interfere much, but she had a bullhorn, all the same, and Aaron could see her using it from time to time.

Aaron thought about his last conversation with Cascade's CEO, Mark Leicester. He had promised Mark he would give his team more space and that he would listen more. "You're *halfway* there," Mark had counseled him.

""What else do I need to change to get the most out of my team?" Aaron wondered.

One of the laser boats in the marina had drifted off-course. The novice sailor was struggling to tack into the wind. As he reflected further, Aaron realized he had shot down Ajay's suggestion to increase distribution too quickly. He still didn't think it was the right strategy, but there was some-

CHAPTER THREE

thing nagging him in the back of his head. Perhaps if he had given them more time to explain ...

Jake and Kathy were chatting in the doorway. Aaron could pick up snippets of the conversation: "Five new sales agents ... three brand managers ... an insights manager."

Aaron was counting on new personnel to grow sales revenue, but if he did not make this quarter's targets, the whole discussion would be mute.

"I'm going to leave one spot open for a dietician-nutritionist and another for a sustainable sourcing manager. Think about it," Aaron heard Kathy tell Aaron.

As they made their way into the room, Kathy picked out a few Cascade snacks from the pantry while Jake made a cup of matcha green tea. They joined Aaron at the table by the window.

"Good news, Aaron," Jake said. "Kathy and I have had several more discussions since our last meeting with you. It took some time, but we're on the same page now regarding the snack division's head count. We were just going over the summary. Here's a list of our current personnel, planned hires, departures, as well as new positions we'd like to add in the next fiscal year."

"Kathy, I couldn't help overhearing part of your discussion with Jake. I know I've put on a few pounds," Aaron said, patting his belly with a chuckle, "but do you think I need to lose weight?"

"Sorry, Aaron. I don't follow."

"You told Jake that we should hire a dietician. We didn't include that in our budget request. Why do you suggest we hire one?"

"Ah, that. Not only do I think you should add a professional dietician/nutritionist to your team," Kathy replied. "I would recommend using one of your current vacancies to hire one right away. Don't wait until next year. It will make a big difference to your division's performance."

Aaron bit his lip, along with an instinct to tell Kathy to stick to her own lane. The suggestion to hire a dietician was amusing, he thought, but he did not appreciate being told what to do, particularly by someone from another department.

"Before I explain why we should hire a dietician-nutritionist, let me ask you both a question," Kathy continued. "Which teams are the most productive?"

As he looked at the sailboats in the harbor, Aaron saw that the errant laser had rejoined the beginner's regatta. The coach's bullhorn was by her side. Recalling his pledge to actively listen, he considered Kathy's question and asked Jake to reply first.

"I don't know if there's a clear-cut answer," Jake responded, "but I'd say it's the teams that have the best resources — money, talent, good leadership

— not to mention the hardest workers."

"I won't argue with you about resources," Kathy replied. "But even a well-financed team can fail. How do we ensure that people are productive?"

"You have to motivate them."

"That's true, but how? What are the best motivators?"

"Certainly, money plays a role. Bonuses, commissions, the opportunity to get a raise or promotion."

"We talked about this last week in the Group Strategic Meeting," Aaron chimed in. "Sure, money is a motivator, but to attract and retain good talent, we need to offer more than a paycheck."

Thinking back to the example of Starbucks, he added, "Purpose and plan. We need to have a clear *purpose* and a *plan* to achieve it."

"Yes, that's absolutely right. So, what is the purpose of the snack division that you run for Cascade?"

Aaron looked at Jake and reflected for a moment. While Cascade was a smaller company than Amazon, its purpose seemed less clear. Amazon, he recalled, uses the internet and technology to "help consumers find, discover and buy anything." Jeff Bezos had declared that the business should be "the most customer-centric company on Earth." Before joining Cascade, Aaron's last role at the shopping giant had been as a director of business development, where he was responsible for pursuing partnerships that helped it do just that — provide better, faster and more engaging customer experiences.

Aaron thought then about Cascade. From the Mission Statement, he knew that Cascade was dedicated to "achieving sustainable growth and delivering solid returns for investors." But what was its purpose?

"Aaron, let me ask the question another way. What drives you and your team?"

"We're focused on meeting our KPIs."

When Kathy didn't respond, Aaron added, "We need to raise profits and sell healthier snacks. But, to be honest, we've concentrated mainly on the profit numbers."

"And you're currently having trouble meeting those targets, right? That's why you'd like to add more salespeople and marketing managers."

Aaron nodded.

"If you'll forgive me for saying so, a bigger Sales & Marcom team isn't going to do the job. You need to think back to the Purpose of the snack division, and I think that's linked to the other side of your KPIs, delivering healthy snacks. That is why I'm recommending you use at least one of your existing vacancies to hire a nutritionist, who can help you develop healthier snacks that are still tasty.

CHAPTER THREE

"Look at the snacks I picked up from our company pantry: they're filled with sugar and salt. My dentist and doctor would have a field day with me if I ate these every day!

"I also shared with Jake that I recommend hiring a sustainable sourcing manager. As you know, Cascade is moving in this direction. You can be at the forefront, and if your team rallies around a common purpose, you'll find it much easier to deliver on the profit numbers."

"AARON, THE FOOD HERE is delicious! But what made you suggest a vegetarian restaurant for lunch? That's not like you!"

"Carlos, what do you mean? Aaron rarely invites us out for lunch at all!" Ajay joked as he bit into a jalapeno-topped Impossible Burger.

"Selena, pass me some more of those spicy 'chicken' nuggets! It's amazing how much they taste like the real thing."

The snack division team was enjoying a group lunch, several days after Aaron's meeting with Kathy in the Cascade break room.

"This place is new and it's gotten great reviews," Aaron said in reply to Carlos' question. "I figured it would be good for us to meet outside the conference room for a change." Aaron looked at his team members around the circular table.

"I think I also owe you guys an apology. There have been a few times recently when I've been short-tempered, and I shouldn't have been. I apologize for losing my cool. It won't happen again. If it does, I promise to buy you all lunch at Shinji's." Shinji's at the St. Regis was one of the best, and most expensive, Japanese restaurants in town. "Even better, when we hit our targets, Shinji's is on me too!

"As you know, the clock is ticking. We have 11 weeks to increase profits and sell healthier snacks. I'm open to your ideas."

While they relished the idea of a Michelin-starred lunch on their boss' tab, no one responded to Aaron's opening. But instead of clamping down discussion, as he had done in the past, Aaron waited, then added, "No rush. Enjoy the lunch, everyone. We'll still have plenty of time to talk over coffee before heading back to the office."

"Aaron, thank you, um, while the team is taking in your introduction to today's meeting, let me say this," Carlos interjected, before pausing for a moment, "No doubt, we'd all enjoy some fantastic sushi and saké! My mouth is watering already. But I think what really has got us thinking is the memo you sent earlier this week about the types of snacks that Cascade sells, how we source ingredients, and the impact that our decisions — the decisions we make at this table about sugar content, additives and vitamins — have on the communities where our products are made and sold."

"Speak for yourself, Carlos; I'm moved by the idea of lunch at Shinji's," Ajay joked again, but this time, while his colleagues chuckled, they too considered anew the people buying and eating their products, not as numbers on a spreadsheet, but as individuals and families.

Selena set her cup of tea down on the table.

"Aaron, I have a suggestion, but it's related to manufacturing, not sales. I know manufacturing isn't my department, but is it OK if I share the idea?"

"Please, go ahead! We're going to need to fire on all cylinders. All ideas are welcome."

"Well, as you know, Cascade is initiating a new focus on sustainability. As my daughter likes to tell me, 'There's no Planet B.' So, I did some digging and I found a supplier whose manufacturing lines use 30 percent less energy than our current partners. They've installed oil-saving filters, they buy fuels made from animal waste and they've painted their warehouse roofs with a special coating to reflect sunlight. It reduces their air conditioning bills. They apparently started down this road to earn tax credits, but then it worked so well, they applied these solutions to their plants across the region."

"How is their pricing? Do they need to charge more in order to be green?"

"Just the opposite. They're saving on electricity bills and passing those savings on to their customers. They're actually less expensive than our current producers."

"How quickly could they take on new products?"

"Not long at all. They just expanded, so they could begin production right away."

"I'm impressed, Selena. Great idea. Please share the contact and background information with Ajay so he can follow up.

"Ajay, on a separate note, I took another look at your channel partner proposal, and perhaps I shot it down too quickly before. If we make a few adjustments, I think we could make it work. Come see me tomorrow in my office and we'll discuss the details."

Hearing that his proposal was back on the table again, Ajay smiled. He had to admit that Selena's idea was good too. He wouldn't stand in her way, he decided. He would help out. If the ideas worked, the whole team would benefit and they would have a good CSR story to boot; if the proposals went South, at least he would still get credit for being a team player.

"Alright, who else has an idea?"

"Aaron, I've been doing some research, not only into the Japanese market but across Southeast Asia, and I think there's space for a new line of fiery fusion snacks."

CHAPTER THREE

"Jennifer, you're making me hungry, even though I'm already stuffed from lunch!"

Jennifer smiled. "It's no secret that we Asians love our spicy food, but the spices are different in each region. So, let's leverage our presence across Asia-Pacific to cross-market products: We can sell spicy Chinese ginger treats in Japan, wasabi peas in Thailand, Sichuan mala potato chips in Indonesia. If we focus on spice instead of sugar, we'll have a healthier product, and if we market the products right, we'll have a hit."

"That's interesting. How long do you think it would take to roll out a new line?"

"I've talked to several suppliers already and I've prepared a list of a dozen existing products that we could rebrand and get to market in less than one month."

"I love the idea. What do you need from me to make this happen?"

"We have enough funds in our existing marketing budget to cover the launch. I've also discussed this with the rest of my team, and they're on board to fast-track the branding. I'd need some logistical help, though, to assist with distribution."

"Ajay, Carlos, what do you think? Are you in?"

"Jennifer, we'll see to it that you get all the support you need."

"It's a go then!" Aaron exclaimed, "Great initiatives. This was a really good session. I should take you all out to lunch more often!"

"**KATHY, THANKS** for stopping by today," Mark Leicester said as he stood up from his desk and walked towards the brown leather Chesterfield sofa set against the back wall of his office. He motioned for Kathy to take a seat, then positioned himself in the matching leather chair across from her. A silver tea set, embossed with Cascade Trading's logo, was atop a three-tiered side table, while a coffee-table book commemorating Cascade's 175th anniversary was on the table in front of her.

"Would you like a cup of tea? Sheryl, could you bring us a fresh pot of tea, please? Thank you!" While Mark and Kathy chatted, Mark's assistant carried in a tray with a brightly colored teapot, a small saucer of warm milk and biscuits.

"Cascade Trading has a long history. Did you know that our current Chairman traces his family line all the way back to the founder of the business? Cascade's heritage is all around us and the traditions have taken us a long way, but change is also a constant, don't you think? We need to modernize, to identify better ways of doing things without losing sight of who we are. That's the only sure way to grow. Small touches, even, like using a contemporary tea set instead of that beautiful relic over there, broadcast a message about who we are.

"OK, I can see, you're wondering, 'Why the history lesson?'"

"No, it's interesting."

"You're very polite, Kathy. Let me get to the point. I heard about your conversations with Aaron and Jake. You suggested they create several new positions in the snack division that they hadn't previously considered. It might not sound like much, but in fact, you did much more than that. You helped them regain focus on their dual mandates — profits and health. Before, they were only concentrating, somewhat unsuccessfully I might add, on the former. I'm impressed."

"Thank you, Mark! That's very kind of you. It's true; I encouraged Aaron and his team to think about why their division exists. It's no secret: when team members are inspired by a company's purpose, engagement levels jump."

"You demonstrated a great business mindset. The questions for me, now, are this: First, how do I support you so that you can continue assisting, not just the snack division, but other departments as well? And second, do you think there are other people in HR who can play this role too, or are you the exception?"

"You know, if you look at Cascade's strategic documents, there are sections that talk about the importance of human resources and how HR leaders should be full business partners. My job description even has a section about this. We're supposed to develop people strategies that are consistent with our corporate values and that help Cascade fulfill its mission.

"But the truth is we rarely have time for this. We are consumed on a daily basis fighting fires. When I log in each morning, there are hundreds of internal messages that need an urgent response. We are mired in myopic paperwork, payroll processing benefits, form filling, recruitment, interview guides — we spend our time there because the work needs to get done.

"And when we do schedule meetings with business leaders to discuss hiring and strategies, we find that the two sides lack a common point of reference. It can take hours, even days, before we even agree on existing headcount. It feels like we spend our lives in spreadsheets, reconciling core data, but it doesn't matter because Finance always wins in the end. The leadership team has more faith in their numbers than ours. No offense, Mark. It's not just here. The story is the same in most companies."

Mark took a deep breath. He understood Kathy's perspective, but then again...

"Kathy, you've clearly given a lot of thought to this. Tell me, what's the solution? Do you need greater headcount in HR? Do we have to outsource more functions?"

"Outsourcing isn't essential, though we could. The technology has advanced so much recently. Most of these processes can be automated and then managed in-house. Did you know there are more than 300 companies in Singapore alone building new HR technologies? They're using automation, artificial intelligence and virtual reality to more efficiently administer processes that span the whole spectrum of HR. If we invest in the right tech, that will definitely free up our time so we can concentrate more on strategic issues. Plus, it will be easier for different departments to agree on the key numbers. But, you know, even more than investing in technology, we need a cultural shift."

Mark took a sip of his tea.

"A cultural shift? How so?"

"My team doesn't want to manage 'resources.' Neither do I. That's not why we signed up for HR. And you've seen what we can offer when given the chance. Cascade needs to think about HR in a different way. Nobody, no department, understands Cascade's purpose, mission, vision and values better than HR. Empower us to help Cascaders flourish. In the same way that the finance team grows Cascade's accounts, let us grow Cascade's human capital."

Your Turn: Five Questions for Reflection

TIME FOR YOU to move from the spectator stands and onto the playing field! Before turning to the next section, reflect on the questions below and record your answers on this page or in your notebook.

1. Kathy is clearly frustrated. Why? Have you noticed similar signs in your company's human resource department?
2. What is the difference between Kathy's current job and the role that she envisions playing?
3. How do you think the shift that Kathy is proposing would be greeted in your company?
4. Proactive Self-Leaders
    (a) Which members of Aaron's team are acting like Proactive Self-Leaders? Describe how they are doing this.
    (b) Who is lagging behind? How would you describe their role?
5. Mark previously told Aaron that he was only "halfway there." Do you think Aaron has fully entered the Second Space? If so, how?

CHAPTER THREE

Human Resources' Fatal Flaws

HUMAN RESOURCE departments in most modern corporations are failing miserably, despite the hard work, long hours and best intentions of the many, very capable professionals who work in the sector. I'll explain more in a moment, but first, let me be clear: I am in no way laying blame at the feet of HR professionals. It is not their fault. The failure is systemic. There are, in fact, at least 7 Fatal Flaws in the realm of human resources.

1. "Resources"

THE FIRST FLAW can be found in the name of the profession itself: Human Resources. "Resources" are an input. They are something to be extracted or managed, not grown or cultivated. Be it in the world of business and commerce, mining or agriculture, industrialists and farmers alike generally wring as much value as possible from a resource.

What resources do you need to make steel? Mine some iron ore, smelt it into pig iron, remove impurities like phosphorous and sulfur, add alloying elements like nickel and manganese. Make sure you have enough workers on hand to run the mill.

How many welders do you need? Human Resources will hire them for you. What do the boilermakers require to come to work every day? Salaries, vacation days and insurance. HR will create procedures to set compensation, pay workers and administer benefits.

This management of workers stands in stark contrast to the philosophy that characterizes most finance departments, which are tasked not simply with managing money but rather growing a company's capital. Managing human resources does not help a modern company scale for growth or differentiate itself from its competitors. It does not create an environment that attracts new employees or encourages them to stay and tell their friends to work there too.

The term "resources" simply does not provide the respect to people that they deserve, nor does it create an optimal structure for developing what many leaders say is their company's most important asset, their people. But more about that in a moment.

2. Technocracy

HR PROFESSIONALS spend hours and hours in spreadsheets, reconciling core data, such as headcount and the number of vacation days that employees have remaining. They have become technocrats who are obliged to focus on myopic paperwork to process payroll, document performance reviews, identify new hires, produce interview guidelines, onboard successful candidates and much more, simply because "the work has to be done."

They are expected to produce statistics about engagement levels, diversity and inclusion, retention rates, corporate wellness and onboarding. No doubt that metrics are important, but this focus on administration has led many HR departments to develop a bad case of "technical-*itis.*" They become lost in the numbers and lose sight of the big picture.

On top of this, they can spend their days fighting fires, just like Kathy Thomas in the first part of this chapter. You might expect the HR department would be the first to know that new employees have been hired. After all, HR is responsible for ensuring that team members are legally employed. In the US, does a new hire have a valid social security number? In international offices, does the company need to apply for a green card for a new employee or does she already have the right to work there?

When a new hire joins the company, HR managers need to provide them with security clearance; they have to update the tax authorities and ensure that social security and other duties are paid, among other tasks. But in this age of matrix reporting and working with external agencies, the in-house HR team is often left out of the loop. Then, on an employee's first day, or even some time afterward, HR professionals are left scrambling to clean up the mess.

Human resources has become transactional and reactionary. Its leaders have little or no time to contemplate strategy and drive changes within the organization.

3. Overwhelmed!

GIVEN ALL this paperwork and near-daily attention on short-term, unexpected problems, is it any wonder that most HR professionals say they feel overwhelmed in their jobs?[2]

"Picture what it feels like to wake up in the morning and be inundated with emails and whatever platform you're on — Slack, Teams, Zoom, etc. — there may be thousands of things to respond to internally. It is a constant struggle to create capacity for yourself and your team to absorb, process and put out new information, when the demands of the day-to-day and internal stuff are sucking you in," reflects Stephanie Nash, the chief people officer and co-founder of an HR marketplace called Thrive HR Exchange.

Nash should know. She is an HR expert with more than 25 years' experience working with multinationals and startups across very different business environments. The COVID-19 pandemic has not made HR departments' work any easier, she notes. The pandemic introduced an additional, heightened level of expectations and responsibilities for human resource departments.

"Each time we think we're getting to a new milestone, we're thrown a new curve ball. It's like we all just figured out remote working, and then we're told everyone needs to return to the office. Wait, no, now we need to figure out hybrid workplaces," Nash explains.

Over the course of her career, Nash has pivoted a number of times, shifting focus from generalist to specialist and back again, from single-country to multi-country to Centre of Excellence projects that develop best practices for company-wide application. While working in-house for industrial and tech giants, as well as with smaller online startups, Nash's journey has so far spanned four continents.

Early on, she oversaw people policies for BHP in Chile, where the minerals marketplace was initially defined by high growth but also subject to commodity cycle booms and busts.

Later, in BHP's headquarters in Melbourne, she helped modernize the mining giant by introducing a global SAP system with business process re-engineering and shared services. Anyone who has worked with an extractions company knows that introducing new processes and technology can be an uphill battle.

In another role, with Microsoft in Seattle, she looked after HR for the tech giant's "rogue internet business," which at the time included Hotmail, MSN and Messenger. She has also experienced mergers and acquisitions, from both sides of the deal, including Alibaba's takeover of an online Singapore grocer called Red Mart, where she was the Chief People Officer.

All of this is to say that Nash has seen her fair share of economic and business place upheaval. None of it compares, though, to the speed of the 2020-21 COVID-19 pandemic, which forced HR departments to react faster than ever before and added to the overload that many in the industry were already feeling.

"There's so much happening at such a rapid pace. Expectation levels for looking after organizations, corporate teams and families have never been higher. There's no playbook and HR professionals are drowning. They're suffering from fatigue and stress."

4. Disengagement

EMPLOYEE ENGAGEMENT rates worldwide are atrociously low. Four in five employees are disengaged, or worse, actively disengaged.[3] The COVID-19 pandemic clearly did not help. New employees who are onboarded virtually and work remotely feel less affinity with their company and co-workers and, in some cases, can go months or longer without interacting face-to-face with colleagues.

Some readers may question why low employee engagement numbers are the fault of Human Resources. After all, the number one cause of employee disillusionment is having a boss who is unfair, unkind, overbearing or otherwise unpleasant. Practically no one says, "I'm unhappy at work and it's HR's fault."

But HR has an intrinsic responsibility to promote employee engagement, be it through hiring the right people, ensuring the right systems are in place to support them, offering opportunities for growth, and perhaps, most overlooked, working with business partners to foster a positive work environment.

Companies are notoriously bad at ferreting out bad apples, except in clear-cut cases when sales numbers are missed. Employees who are actively disengaged often attract more attention than high performers. There may be a natural inclination to help them improve, instead of cutting them loose. Many leaders would also rather have a poorly performing employee than a vacancy to be filled.

Instead of tolerating poor performance, neglecting high performers or interacting with colleagues in a way that hinders rather than promotes engagement, business leaders need to be trained to have talent conversations. And who better to conduct this training than certified human resource professionals who are also trained coaches?

AFTER A COUPLE OF YEARS in a job, professionals stagnate. They stop growing and improving.

In a great TEDx talk entitled "How to Get Better at the Things You Care About," Mindset Works co-founder and CEO Eduardo Briceño argues that most people spend too much time "performing" and not enough time learning.[4]

"Once we think we have become good enough, adequate, then we stop spending time in the learning zone. We focus all our time on just doing our job, performing, which turns out not to be a great way to improve," Briceño says.

From a young age, children fear that others will think less of them if they make a mistake. As a result, they spend too much time in the "Performance Zone," even at school. Once they enter the corporate world, this fear is magnified by "flawless execution cultures" that inadvertently encourage workers to "stay within what they know." As you can imagine, the result does not foster innovation, reflection or improvement.

Leaders need to slow down to speed up, and this means taking time to learn and practice. However, it's not enough to simply say, "Go learn!" Companies need to guide their employees.

"The way to high performance is to alternate between the Learning Zone and the Performance Zone, purposefully building our skills in the learning zone, then applying those skills in the performance zone," Briceño explains. "We must have an idea about how to improve, what we can do to improve. (It's) not how I used to practice the guitar as a teenager, performing songs over and over again, but doing deliberate practice."

And this leads us back to how HR professionals can effectively combat disengagement: by taking leaders to the Leadership Driving Range.

The Leadership Driving Range

ANY GOLFER KNOWS they need to spend time on the driving range if they wish to improve or even maintain their game. Some top-tier golf clubs do not even allow new players or guests onto the course until a pro has observed their swing on the driving range first.

Similarly, business leaders need coaching and training sessions to practice key elements of their jobs, such as how to talk with employees of differing performance and potential levels.[5] This is a key skill to develop future leaders, mentor team members and weed out workers who do not belong on the team.

A CORE COMPETENCY of modern HR professionals must be the ability to provide this coaching. Leaders should be required to clock at least two to three hours a month on the Leadership Driving Range (LDR), where HR coaches lead them in scenarios such as the best way to put a poor performer on a Personal Improvement Plan.

A golfer wishing to improve their game cannot simply go to the driving range and hit a lot of 7 irons. Rather, the practice must be deliberate. For example, a pro might advise them, "Drive the ball 130 yards, within ten feet of the pin, using a 7 iron. Repeat, successfully, 15 consecutive times." Likewise on the LDR, leaders should work on specific scenarios, such as how to talk to a poor performer who has high potential.

SOME LEADERS WILL no doubt balk at the idea of obligatory training. "I've got real work to do," they'll say. "I have to make money for the company. I don't have time for this." These leaders need to understand that disengaged workers pull down the entire team and hurt profits. The cost of filling a vacancy can easily run into the hundreds of thousands of dollars, after taking into account recruitment and onboarding, not to mention the soft costs of educating new hires and dealing with disengaged employees in their last months before quitting. Capture these numbers in a department's accounts and you can be sure that leaders will pay closer attention to them!

THERE IS NO SHORTAGE of apps to record the time spent training and competencies covered. HR leaders need to promote these systems and follow up with their business partners to ensure they spend the time required on the driving range. Top corporate leaders must also set the tone by telling their leadership team that training and practice is an integral part of their work.

5. Road Blocking

A BUSINESS LEADER in New Delhi reaches out to the regional headquarters in Singapore during the midst of the COVID-19 pandemic. A second wave was devastating India. More than 100,000 people would die from the coronavirus in less than six weeks, by official counts. With bodies washing up along the Ganges River, many observers believe the actual number of deaths was significantly higher. Life-saving oxygen and bed space in hospitals was in such short supply that even wealthy, connected families were being turned away, to fend for themselves.

"We're facing a national disaster," the Indian leader tells his HR colleague. "Let's put together an Asian-wide initiative to assist our employees' families and the greater Delhi community."

Instead of reacting quickly, the senior HR leader replies, "Why should we do this? Did our company send aid to Fukushima after the earthquake and nuclear disaster there in 2011? And, if not, would it be fair for us to spend resources now in India, if we didn't do so in Japan? What will be the implications for us going forward when the next crisis strikes somewhere else?"

Human Resources can be the engine for corporate success or it can be a roadblock. All too often the latter is the case. HR leaders become a force for inertia instead of action. "You can't do this," they say. "Company policy prohibits it" or "there's no precedent for us to do that."

"I'm trying to protect the company," the HR leader in the example above explains to me. By being a constant devil's advocate and deliberately placing obstacles in the paths of new initiatives, he fosters a stereotype in which business executives have grown to see Human Resources in the same vein as the legal and accounting departments ("If you want an innovative project to die, take it to legal. If you have an idea about developing your people, take it to HR; you'll never see it again.").

"Some of us may envision scenes from The Office and our own experiences with ineffective and dispassionate HR representatives who are out of touch with the realities of the modern workplace and its accompanying challenges," writes Geoff Hash, a California-based lawyer who specializes in employee matters. "These reactions are understandable when we look at how most businesses, managers, employees and even popular culture have approached human resources over the past two decades — an afterthought or necessary annoyance that is barely human and rarely resourceful."[6]

Contrast this approach with other sectors of a company. Can you imagine a marketing team that doesn't take client preferences and perceptions into account or a sales team that always tells customers "No"? Over the past two decades, most companies have become more customer-centric, striving to create positive experiences for their clients in a bid to build trust, loyalty and a stronger brand.

This client-centric culture has not filtered through to most HR departments. If HR is to be a force for growth, an engine instead of a roadblock, modern HR professionals need to treat their in-house colleagues as clients; some may even go a step further to ensure that internal policies and processes contribute to an external customer-centric business.

6. Subservience

DID YOU KNOW that the vast majority of mergers and acquisitions fail? Up to 90 percent of M&A deals would have been best left on the table, according to a commonly cited study by the Harvard Business Review.[7]

There are several theories as to why so many deals flop, from misguided strategies and poor execution to unanticipated, external factors; however, I would argue that a prime, oft-overlooked reason is the subservience and lack of respect given to human resource departments.

Prior to any major merger, lawyers comb through reams of documents, while CFOs and accountants study the finances and prepare spreadsheets for amortizing costs and models for how the proposed deal may produce synergies, which of course is often a codeword for retrenching employees. Instead of being viewed for their individual talents, people become line items: "We don't need two Chief Operating Officers. Let's save money and fire one. We only need one marketing department; we can retrench half the employees and save millions of dollars each year."

Yet "mergers and acquisitions fail more often than not because key people leave, teams don't get along or demotivation sets into the company being acquired," writes Forbes Councils member David Garrison.[8]

Human Resources is only brought in when it is time to implement the strategy, instead of during earlier discussions when they could highlight mismatches in corporate culture and other people-related challenges that might scuttle success. But if people professionals are not at the table from the beginning, how will change occur effectively once a deal takes place?

"PEOPLE ARE THE MOST important asset in our company."

I have lost count of how many times senior leaders have told me this.

"Where does the head of human resources sit in your company's organizational chart?" I always ask. "Does she report to the CEO?"

"No," they reply. "She reports to the CFO."

"So, they're not at the most senior table?"

"No, no."

"But if people really are your company's most important asset, shouldn't there be a strategic people thinker among the leadership team? Shouldn't managing and nurturing your employees be a portfolio that reports directly to the top person in your business?"

"Well, we've hired HR managers to administer internal policies and ensure compliance. We don't really have strategic HR thinkers."

ARE SENIOR LEADERS disrespecting HR or do the professionals in this arena lack the requisite training to provide strategic advice? The answer, while likely a combination of both, highlights a systemic issue related to educational systems. Every lawyer, regardless of where they went to school, has a legal underpinning. They have earned a law degree and, depending on their country of residence, passed a certification test like a bar examination. Similarly, Chief Financial Officers have been trained in finance; most have earned an MBA.

HR experts, though, do not share a common foundation. Some have studied "human capital management" or "strategic human resource management and analytics" in programs like the ones offered by the Singapore University of Social Sciences and the University of Kentucky's Gatton College of Business and Economics, but many have not, and those that have may have focused on process application instead of strategic thinking.

Moreover, as in many fields, there can be a reluctance to introduce change.

"I think we have varying degrees of curiosity and willingness to learn," reflects Thrive HR Exchange's Stephanie Nash. "We can risk finding ourselves in our own echo chamber, becoming comfortable in who we know and what we know, and pacing ourselves in an incremental way, instead of embracing things that are new and potentially risky. We value our relationships inside the organization so greatly that sometimes we don't want to rock the boat or be seen as challenging the status quo."

Business leaders are often complicit in fostering this mentality. "Don't worry about strategy," they say, "that's our domain. We just need you to fill vacancies."

7. Misalignment

THE LACK OF RESPECT provided to human resources can be seen as well in the technology choices made by companies. Over the past twenty-plus years, businesses have invested heavily in Enterprise Resource Planning (ERP) systems to manage day-to-day business activities and integrate diverse functions such as accounting, compliance, procurement and project management. These technology platforms are typically selected by the chief technology or information officer, or perhaps by the head of finance, and the systems are built primarily for supply chain management and financial reporting. Human Resources is an afterthought.

"What HR receives at the end of these selection processes is a tool they are expected to use, but no one has ever asked them about their requirements or how technology choice will impact the way they work," Nash explains. "So, they get this system, and don't forget a significant investment in the software, change management and training has gone into it, but the new tool doesn't actually do anything to help human resources be more efficient or more effective."

The new tools end up being unused or implemented differently by different departments, resulting in a misalignment of data. Whether it is the Human Resources or Finance system feeding payroll, the two sides quickly become out of sync, and in the absence of a single, accepted source of truth, tedious disputes develop.

"The SAP and Oracle ERPs were meant to provide a single source of truth," she adds, "but what ended up happening is that the quality of the HR part of these systems was so poor, HR would manage headcount on a spreadsheet instead. But if HR can't even be confident and accurate about headcount, why would we have the credibility to speak on other topics?"

THE ONSET OF CLOUD COMPUTING and application programming interfaces (APIs) provides a fresh opportunity to rectify this technology deficit and foster realignment.

First, there are many new technologies that can automate the more mundane aspects of human resources, from managing compensation to on- and off-boarding employees.

Second, the cost of integration between apps and systems is significantly lower, so companies can be less dependent on large ERP systems. As long as the databases and technologies are linked, so that they can communicate with each other, arguments over data can be relegated to the dustbin.

Which is not to say that all disagreements will disappear. The transition to new systems will still provoke debate between HR and other departments, particularly as different teams discuss whose system should store core segments of data. Adopting cloud computing and HR APIs will not be a panacea, but it is most certainly a step in the right direction.

CHAPTER THREE

Human Capital

ADOPTING NEW TECHNOLOGIES and effectively integrating them into a company's processes and workflow is an important step that will liberate human resource professionals to add strategic value. However, technology on its own is not enough. The world of work has changed dramatically since management guru Peter Drucker refined the concept of human resource management in the 1950s and even more so since the Welsh textile manufacturer Robert Owen and the English mathematician and engineer Charles Babbage first introduced the idea of managing workers as a resource during the Industrial Revolution. Yet most companies have not sufficiently evolved.

Human Resources developed as a concept and industry because managing people presents different issues than managing other inputs. But workers are still viewed as a resource, an input to be utilized to achieve a goal. HR is then centered, as we have seen, on allocating workers to fill vacancies, monitoring vacation days, implementing salary increments and other non-strategic tasks.

If Human Resources is fatally flawed, though, what should replace it?

We need to create a new role and function that is strategic and focused on creating value: Human Capital.

Human Capitalists are stewards of corporate culture responsible for employee growth. They are strategists who promote an organization's current and future needs. They understand what a business requires, from a human operations perspective, to be successful. A Human Capitalist asks, "How do you grow people? How do you make each individual stronger in the area that they have responsibility for?" Just as a Chief Financial Officer is responsible for growing money within an organization, the Chief Human Capitalist has a mandate to create value. They are expected to proactively engage the most senior people in an organization to ensure that the company has the right leaders and workforce in place to realize its purpose and vision for the future.

This transformation of Human Resources to Human Capital is the second step required for a company to enter the Second Space. This shift can be made in tandem with the transformation of followers into Proactive Self-Leaders.

With these transformations, every employee has a personal responsibility to ensure the success of the organization.

But who represents the Organization? You might say that the Chairman,

CEO or Founder best personifies a company. After all, they are at the top of the hierarchy, and if anyone in a business is in the public eye, it is likely to be a top leader. Chief executives are understandably focused, though, on profit and loss, which is not the same as an organization's essence. Chief executives also articulate strategic plans and provide directives, but when Proactive Self-Leaders ask, "What do I need to do today to ensure the success of the company?", they are not acting out of personal loyalty, but rather out of a desire for the company itself to succeed.

On the other end of the spectrum, you might reply that every employee represents a company. In a sense, this is also true. Each person's actions reflect on it. But not everyone equally understands a business' purpose.

Ask a room full of employees, "What is our company's purpose? What are its mission, vision and values?" and you are likely to receive more blank stares than replies. Ask the same questions to a group of human resource professionals — or even better, human capitalists — and hands will shoot up.

Human Capitalists are the custodians of a company's culture. Not only do they understand an organization's values, but they can also embed them into all people processes. From recruitment, hiring and onboarding through performance management and employee recognition and rewards, human capitalists can build programs that foster organizational values. They know what stellar employee performance looks like, what it doesn't look like and what is not acceptable. They can train people throughout the organization to embed these cultural values.

ORGANIZATIONS ARE LIVING ENTITIES. They can grow, stagnate or die. Yet no single individual represents a company in a traditional business model. There is no slot in the organizational chart for "Company." Even in the early days of the Enterprise Leadership Model, I realized there was a void. Identifying Leaders and Proactive Self-Leaders was self-evident but putting a human face to the Organization presented a challenge. Without this human face, it is more difficult for Leaders and Proactive Self-Leaders to process change or resolve conflicts.

At the same time, Human Capitalists are also Proactive Self-Leaders. What happens when they ask themselves, "What do I need to do to be personally responsible for the success of the Organization?" As someone who is responsible for growing human capital, the Human Capitalist answers, "I need to ensure that everyone in the Organization understands and lives its Purpose, Mission, Vision and Values."

No one, it turns out, is better placed in the Enterprise Leadership Model to represent the Organization than a Human Capitalist.

CHAPTER THREE

ORGANIZATIONS NEED to be conscious not to make Human Capital the sole domain of internal governance and responsibility.

All too often, human resource professionals are viewed as the "bad guy" in the room. They are required to have difficult conversations with poor performers. Human Capitalists, though, are neither police nor judges. They act with positive intent and the best interest of the organization in mind. Human Capitalists weave this spirit of positive intent into the fabric of a company as they develop Leaders and Proactive Self-Leaders and train them how to ask good questions, what it means to listen deeply and how to respond with a level of empathy.

Underpinnings of the Model

IN THE TRADITIONAL WORLD of corporate hierarchy, an employee can only be as creative as their boss allows. When they become personally responsible for the success of the organization, they are empowered to be as creative as necessary.

Human Capitalists provide the underpinnings that make this possible. In the Enterprise Leadership Model, they become more than just a keeper of Purpose, Mission, Vision and Values. They propagate organizational culture throughout a company and take a stand to support business teams.

From the moment talent is first recruited, through onboarding and other key moments, Human Capitalists introduce team members to a company's culture.

"If you're going to join Cascade Trading, here's what you need to know about us," a Human Capitalist says. "We are not a hierarchical company. We embrace the Enterprise Leadership Model. This means that you are personally responsible for the success of the organization in your area of work. From Day 1, we expect you to accept that responsibility."

The Human Capitalist's responsibilities do not stop at a welcome speech. They have a duty to teach new hires and existing staff how to operate within this corporate culture. Through processes, programs, systems, symbols, training and behaviors, a Human Capitalist embeds the Enterprise Leadership Model in an organization.

In exchange for accepting a nonhierarchical way of working, Proactive Self-Leaders have a right to expect an environment that nurtures and grows their careers. Leaders play an important role in this regard, but Human Capitalists set the tone and provide the necessary resources.

In the course of business, whenever a team member has concerns about strategy, processes, implementation or anything else that impacts the workplace or an organization's ability to realize its purpose, they can meet with their business partner in Human Capital to share, "I don't think we're doing this right." Similarly, if change is taking place in an organization, the Human Capitalist is available to meet with employees who do not understand the change or how it impacts them.

Responsibility is a key word and concept in the Enterprise Leadership Model, and Human Capitalists have a trio of responsibilities: to Leaders, Proactive Self-Leaders and, of course, the Organization itself.

When Human Capitalists learn about issues in a team, they have a responsibility to share them with Leaders. This needs to be done in a manner that promotes understanding and encourages resolution. As part of the process, the Human Capitalist might organize strategic planning and change management workshops or facilitate conversations that foster alignment.

To do this effectively, the Human Capitalist needs to be an internal executive coach. For many years, the ability to coach team members has increasingly been recognized as an important skill that human resource leaders need to master. The focus, though, has largely been on executive coaching and the uptake has not been huge. The COVID-19 pandemic — and the accompanying stresses associated with loss, uncertainty and remote work — have increased the pressure on HR departments to provide counseling.

A Human Capitalist takes this trend a step further. They should preferably be certified in more than one coaching discipline and capable of facilitating conversations with leaders and team members alike to address a broad range of challenges in the workplace. Their coaching expertise includes the ability to suggest different frameworks to approach these issues and then work through each stage of the chosen framework with their internal business partners and colleagues.

Ten Characteristics of a Human Capitalist

COACHING SKILLS are just one of many that a Human Capitalist needs to possess. Many human resource professionals will need to re-skill or undergo additional training to play this role. Here is a top-ten list of characteristics and capabilities that could form an integral part of a Human Capitalist's job description:

- Certified internal executive coach
- Ability to facilitate business workshops, particularly for strategic planning, transformation and change management

- Supports lifelong learning
- Aptitude for growing team members and crafting long-term Career Development Plans
- Promotes and ensures high levels of employee engagement; if engagement is low, ability to determine why and offer solutions
- Displays a business mindset and acumen; ability to produce an evidence-based, data-driven business case with insights and proposals
- Experience and sufficient corporate knowledge to be a Business Partner
- Confidence and ability to sit at the senior leadership table
- An eloquent communicator who is passionate about an organization's Mission, Vision and Values
- Champion and steward of an organization's Purpose

A Human Capitalist must demonstrate curiosity and a willingness to challenge the status quote. They demonstrate gravitas in terms of understanding the organization's business as well as the broader industry. Must follow trends outside the industry, with an eye to potential new competitors and innovation, as these may impact human capital issues within the company.

How a Human Capitalist Thinks

IN SEPTEMBER 2019, Amazon founder Jeff Bezos unveiled an ambitious plan to tackle the retail giant's carbon footprint and meet the goals of the Paris Climate Accord ten years ahead of schedule. He pledged that renewable sources would fuel 80 percent of Amazon's energy usage by 2024 and that the company would achieve zero emissions by 2030.

"It's a difficult challenge for us," Bezos told the National Press Club in Washington, D.C., "because we have deep, large physical infrastructure. So, if we can do this, anyone can do this."

As part of the "Climate Pledge," Bezos also committed Amazon to help companies in its supply chain decarbonize and to encourage other large corporations to endorse the pledge. Since then, more than 100 companies, employing five million people across 16 countries, have signed on.

How would a Human Capitalist inside one of these companies react to the news?

After all, the scale of the commitment will impact people throughout the business. Hopefully, Amazon's top HR leaders were not surprised by Bezos' pronouncement and were given a role to play in its preparation. However, this certainly was not the case for all firms involved.

"What are the policies, processes and systems we need to have in place across Amazon to ensure that every employee understands their role, individually and as a team and department, to achieve the Climate Pledge," a Human Capitalist would ask.

The Human Capitalist would look internally within the Human Capital department to determine how it could play a proactive role to assist the entire company achieve its goal. She would assess where different teams across the globe are on the path to meeting the pledge and explore ways to support them. And she would likely organize events and seminars across the company to foster support for the pledge and share guidelines on how to meet it.

An authentic commitment to sustainability likely contributes to a sense of purpose within a company, but it may not be enough. At Amazon, many employees have demanded an even faster transition from fossil fuels. A Human Capitalist needs to be cognizant and sensitive to all employee sentiments in this regard.

TRADITIONAL HUMAN RESOURCE departments are typically 100 percent focused internally, aside from the occasional HR summit with other industry professionals. As a result, they miss out on innovation taking place in other disciplines and companies.

"HR professionals have stumbled or become stagnant," says Nash. "We pay attention to our own business unit. If we have multiple business units or geographies, maybe we cover that remit. If we have a little extra time, we might read about something that's come from corporate or another business unit, but we rarely leave our organizational confines."

"A true Human Capitalist thinks as much about the external environment as the internal one," she adds. "To make that leap, we've got to become much more in tune with trends that are happening in the marketplace."

Consider, for example, the case of mobile payments.

DBS Bank, southeast Asia's largest financial company, would traditionally view other Asian banks and multinationals like Citi Group (prior to its withdrawal from the region) as its primary competitors, not just for business but also for talent. DBS' human resource professionals likely understood their company's value proposition as an employer vis-a-vis other banks.

But then in 2016, a gig-economy startup called Grab, which is Asia's Uber,[9] branched out beyond ride-hailing and began offering consumers the opportunity to use its mobile app to pay for a wide variety of services beyond transport. Restaurants, small hawker stalls, pharmacies and even 7-11 quickly adopted GrabPay, which has become the top mobile wallet in Malaysia and Singapore.[10]

Grab strengthened its fintech capabilities by acquiring an online payment startup called Kudo and investing in the e-payments platform Ovo, both of which are in Indonesia. It also launched Grab Finance, which offers loans, credit lines and cash advances to merchants.

Within a short period of time, a competitor emerged from out of nowhere, from a non-financial space, to compete with Asia's biggest banks. Not only does Grab offer financial services to consumers and small businesses, it also competes with banks for talent. Payments experts, treasury specialists and professionals with regulatory expertise, among others, might all be enticed to leave the banks for new opportunities. Grab's entry into the fintech space changed DBS' human risk levels, particularly around employee attraction and retention.

A Human Capitalist needs to have time and space to stay abreast of trends outside their own company in order to think about the unexpected and prepare for disruption.

IN ONE OF THE COMPANIES where I coach, the recruitment department is continually refilling the same position.

It is a familiar story.

The boss is demanding; some might call him mean.

The average time a new hire spends in the role is less than six months, because the work environment is so unpleasant.

The company does not take any action because the boss is a "top performer." He always hits or exceeds his numbers.

Performance has many aspects, though. Do you think the recruitment department would consider him to be a star? Probably not. After all, he is killing their employee retention numbers. Don't forget to factor in the costs of continually searching for someone who is willing to take on the role and the onboarding expenses, not to mention the impact of disgruntled workers on the company. Then, add in the potential hit to brand reputation. In an era of social media, employees anonymously review employers on sites like Glassdoor. Poor reviews further increase the cost of hiring.

It turns out the "top performer" is not such a star after all.

A Human Capitalist in this situation needs to proactively have conversations with key personnel in the company, starting with the leader in question, to address the problem.

"What do you think this turnover costs us?" she asks.

Ideally, the leader in question will have an a-ha moment and change his behavior, but if not, the Human Capitalist will need to discuss the issue with other leaders higher up the chain. Importantly, these conversations come from a place of positive intent. The Human Capitalist is not playing the role of bad cop, enforcing a corporate policy, but rather from a position of asking good questions, listening deeply and responding with empathy. More about that, though, and how you can lead conversations like these, in the Field Guide.

Proclamation from Above or Below?

THE TRANSFORMATION from Human Resources to Human Capital underpins the shift into the Second Space and the success of the Enterprise Leadership Model. But how does it happen? Where does the drive to create Human Capitalists originate? And how can a company ensure that Human Capitalists are adequately trained and empowered to represent the Organization in interactions with Leaders and Proactive Self-Leaders?

Like the shift from Follower to Proactive Self-Leader, there are two non-mutually exclusive routes to this destination.

First, a company can simply proclaim it:

- Declare or reassert that your organization works within the Enterprise Leadership Model
- Define the Human Capitalist's role
- Recruit, promote and empower individuals who are qualified to be Human Capitalists
- Abolish Human Resources and create a Human Capital department, led by a Chief Human Capital Officer (CHCO)
- Ensure that the CHCO reports directly to the CEO and/or has a seat on the Board
- Clearly articulate and explain the differences between Human Resources and Human Capital so that Leaders and Proactive Self-Leaders throughout the company have a strong understanding of their role

Second, the shift to Human Capital can be driven from below by HR professionals who say, "I want to do more. I can do more. I am qualified to have a seat at the table."

There are plenty of experienced human resource leaders who are qualified to make this transition; some already have. But in many cases, companies may need to recruit from outside the traditional HR space to hire capable strategists to play this role.

Be Aware

1. Human Resources treats labor as an input; Human Capital grows people to make your company a success.

2. The transition from Human Resources to Human Capital underpins the Enterprise Leadership Model and is a second, parallel step that is required to enter the Second Space.

3. Human Capitalists are stewards of corporate culture who thoroughly understand an organization's Purpose, Mission, Vision and Values. They embed these values throughout all people processes.

4. No one is better placed in the Enterprise Leadership Model to represent the Organization than a Human Capitalist.

5. Adopting new technologies will liberate HR professionals to spend more time on strategy. But technology is not enough. A cultural shift is needed as well.

6. Leaders need to clock time every month on the LDR, the Leadership Driving Range, to hone their communication and strategic leadership skills. Human Capitalists should be certified internal coaches who can work with Leaders on the LDR, as well as with employees at every level of an organization.

7. Client-centric cultures are not for sales teams alone. If Human Capitalists are to be engines of corporate success, not roadblocks, they need to treat their business partners as clients.

8. Don't make Human Capitalists the "bad guy in the room." They are neither police nor judges. Ferreting out poor performers and providing them with a path to transform or leave is the responsibility of all leaders, including human capitalists.

9. Human Capitalists must demonstrate an understanding of an organization's business and follow external trends, with an eye to how these might impact a company's business and its people.

10. Human Capitalists must have a seat at the senior leadership table in any company that believes or wishes to proclaim that "people are their most important asset."

THE THIRD SPACE

CHAPTER FOUR

The Third Space

AS AJAY ENTERED the cookie factory in Jababeka, to the east of Jakarta, he was tired. He had taken an early morning flight from Singapore, then got caught in a traffic jam on the way to the industrial park. A one-hour drive had turned into three.

The long ride, though, had given him more time to research the energy-saving initiatives that Selena mentioned during their team lunch. The Jababeka cookie factory had apparently embarked on a sustainability drive and painted their roof with a white coating to reflect sunlight and draw heat out of the building.

There were a few companies in the market providing this service. If he could find out which one the Jababeka factory had employed, assuming the results were good, he could engage them to coat the rooftops of Cascade's factories and warehouses. Similarly, he wanted to learn more about their alternative fuel programs and whether they were able to improve the efficiency of the factory's boilers.

Home to more than 2000 companies from 30 countries, the Jababeka Industrial Estate is a buzz of activity. Three-quarters of a million people report to work there each morning to manufacture cars, cosmetics, toys and much more for both the Indonesian domestic market and export. Several of Cascade's competitors have factories there, like Mondelez, Lotte and Unilever. Cascade Trading's snack division once had a presence in this industrial heartland as well, but that was long before Ajay's tenure with the company.

Viewed from overhead, on Google Earth, the two-story cookie factory looked as big as an airport terminal. Inside, it seemed just as cavernous to Ajay as well. A middle-aged director named Abyasa greeted him. After an instant coffee in the lobby, the two men proceeded on a tour of the facilities. Like many Indonesians, Abyasa had only one name, and in this case, it was a popular one, a Javanese word meaning "clever." As the factory had recently upgraded its capacity, he was keen to bring Cascade Trading on board as a client.

CHAPTER FOUR

Inside the factory, a massive vat churned a double chocolate chip cookie mix. Ajay enjoyed the smell of fresh batter as an injection machine dropped dabs of batter onto a conveyor belt headed to the oven. Unlike many factories he had visited, the temperature inside this one was not uncomfortable, even though the oven ahead was heated to 350° Fahrenheit.

"Three thousand cookies a minute. We can produce more than 4 million cookies a day," Abyasa told Ajay. "You were asking about our energy efficiency. ESG is part of our DNA here. Environmental, social and governance principles factor into most decisions.

"Last week, the outside temperature topped 100° Fahrenheit. Add that to the oven over there and this area used to get pretty toasty, even with the air conditioners running at full blast.

"Now, though, we only need to run the A/C at 60 percent and we can still maintain a temperature of 75 degrees here in the factory. That cool roof coating has really made a difference. Between that and other measures, we've cut our utility bills by 30 percent, and that's a savings we can pass on to our customers."[1]

"Impressive. Did it take long to implement?"

"The biggest hurdle was getting clearance from Finance. But as soon as the results from a test that we ran with the vendor at a smaller site came in, Finance approved the expense. After that, applying the coating was quick, and as it took place outside, it didn't affect our operations at all."

On the far side of the oven, dark baked cookies emerged on their sides, ready for packaging, lined up vertically, one next to the other on fast-moving conveyor belts sized specifically to fit the cookies. Two employees, each wearing transparent hairnets and blue rubber gloves, watched closely to prevent clogging and identify any potential quality issues. Mechanical grippers picked up the cookies in batches of 11, then dropped them neatly into biodegradable packaging made from mushrooms.

"Over here, you can see we're cutting back on plastic usage. Depending on the client, we've experimented with packaging made from seaweed, hemp, cornstarch and mushrooms. The seaweed packaging is quite popular for teas and cereals, as it's edible and dissolves in water."

"What about the impact on costs?"

"Seaweed is usually more expensive than plastic because it takes more manpower to produce. We've been working with farmers and fisherfolk to set up a network of cost-effective growers. So far, we've been able to keep the costs in line. We'd like to bring the pricing down further. For the moment, though, gains elsewhere are more than making up for any difference in cost."

"Abyasa, once again, this is all very impressive. Like your company, Cascade Trading has new ESG requirements. We need to ascertain that these goals are embraced throughout our supply chain while, of course, keeping costs in line as well. Could I take a closer look at that testing data you mentioned for the reflective paint? I'll also need to see the specs and pricing for the packaging material, so we can choose which one is right for our products."

"Not a problem, Ajay. Happy to email it to you. Anything else you need, don't hesitate to ask."

Ajay smiled. Applying a new packaging solution to Cascade's factories in the Philippines might take some time to implement, but the other innovations looked sufficiently straightforward that he should be able to copy them quickly.

KATHY SETTLED INTO the meeting room a few minutes early. Fortunately, no one else had booked it. As she sipped a coffee and opened her laptop, she thought about her new assignment.

"I want you to play a more strategic role," the company CEO, Mark Leicester, had told her during their last meeting. "Become a full business partner for the snack division. There's no question you have the acumen to do this, Kathy. Feel free to try new processes, and if they work, we just might apply them across the entire company."

Mark had given her the green light to review any document within Cascade Trading's snack division and to attend any meeting, so she could observe the team's interactions and work with them to achieve the department's twin goals of raising profits and selling healthier snacks.

It would take time for the company to buy and implement the new technology platforms that could liberate Human Resources from the tedious processes that had dominated her days, but for the moment, at least, she had the authority to delegate more of these tasks to others on the team.

As Kathy reflected on the job ahead, Aaron's head of marketing, Jennifer Yacob, walked into the room. She was scrolling through messages on her phone, but when she looked up, Jennifer appeared startled to see Kathy.

"I'm sorry, we've booked this room. I think you may be in the wrong place."

"Hi Jennifer, pleasure to meet you," Kathy said as she stood up and introduced herself. "I'm Kathy Thomas from HR. Don't think we've met before. I'm going to sit in on this meeting if that's okay with you. I'm trying to learn more about the marketing side of the business, so we can assist you with manpower, training and other needs better. Don't worry. I won't interrupt or slow things down."

Kathy seemed nice enough, Jennifer thought, and while she wasn't fond of surprises in the workplace, there didn't seem to be any harm in letting her

CHAPTER FOUR

join the meeting. Before long, her team members had filed in, taken their places around the table, and they were knee-deep in images and copy for a campaign to launch spicy Chinese ginger candies in Japan. Fortunately, they had a few samples to fuel their imaginations.

"These are really good," Jennifer said, as she licked her fingers. "They remind me of sweets that I bought in a marketplace in Mutianyu, near the Great Wall. There's nothing quite like this in Japan. They're going to be a hit."

"Where are we on the ad buy?" Jennifer asked two of her colleagues who had Zoomed into the meeting from the Osaka office.

"We're ready whenever you are. We've booked space for a series of outdoor ads in the train stations and have purchased ad space across three social media platforms. We've also lined up influencers for taste tests and reviews; one is even keen to talk about it on her syndicated radio show."

"How about the design for the packaging? What do you have?"

Several images flashed onto the screen.

"Could we see what that version would look like in yellow?" asked Lina, one of the junior members of Jennifer's team. "Our research shows that candies in yellow packaging sell 15 percent better than those in other colors."

"Sure, we can share that with you in a moment. We just need to adjust the mock-up. OK, this is a rough image, but it gives you an idea of what it would look like."

"Which do you prefer?" Jennifer asked, as she looked around the room. "Should we go with the yellow?"

Heads nodded.

"Good idea, Lina, let's go with that."

AS THE MARKETING TEAM was finalizing next steps for the product launch, Aaron's deputy, Carlos Reyez, knocked on the door and walked into the room.

"Hello, everyone!" Carlos generally always appeared to be in a good mood. "I saw on the calendar that you're meeting today to discuss the spicy ginger candy launch, and I wanted to let you know that the logistics are on track. Despite some bottlenecks, we've secured the first shipment from China and it should arrive in Bangkok by the end of the week."

Jennifer looked up from the drawings scattered over the conference table, a look of confusion on her face.

"What do you mean Bangkok?"

"As we discussed, we're going to sell Cascade's spicy ginger treats in Thailand, and the shipment is on its way."

"No, Japan."

"What?"

"We said we're launching the candy in Japan. Look around, look at the image on the screen or over here on the table. We've been preparing to launch the product in Japan."

"Well, that's going to be an issue because the product's not headed there. It's on its way to Bangkok."

"The wasabi peas are to be sold in Thailand. The ginger treats are for Japan," Jennifer countered.

"Ajay and I discussed this with the logistics and sales teams. The consensus was ginger goes to Bangkok, mala chips are for Tokyo and wasabi peas are to be sold in Indonesia. Didn't you see the email thread?"

"This is a disaster. This won't work. Sichuan mala isn't popular in Japan. How could this happen? We don't have the time; we don't have the budget to start again!"

"Carlos, Jennifer, I don't mean to interrupt, but could I speak with the two of you privately?"

Exhausted and in disbelief that weeks of hard work and late nights appeared to be for naught, Jennifer sighed and said, "Sure, let's talk."

JENNIFER'S TEAM cleared the room. The Zoom call was shut down and Carlos took a seat at the table.

"I realize I'm coming at this as an outsider, and mid-stream on the project to boot, but help me understand what's going on. How did we get here?"

"Mid-stream?" Jennifer blurted out. "We're almost at the finish line, or at least we were supposed to be, but now the product is headed to the wrong place."

"Now, wait just a minute. It wasn't easy for the logistics team to produce and secure these snacks on such short notice," Carlos countered. "Whatever the source of this misunderstanding, you're just going to have to produce a new launch campaign for Thailand."

"Produce a new launch campaign? Are you serious? Do you know how much work my team and I have already put into this? Not to mention the budget. We don't have funds to start over."

"Carlos, Jennifer, let's take a step back for a moment. How did this project originate?"

"Aaron took us out for a team lunch a few weeks back, and he asked for ideas. I suggested that we introduce a new line of fiery snacks and that we cross market products by selling spicy Chinese ginger treats in Japan, Sichuan mala potato chips in Indonesia, etc."

"What happened then?"

"Aaron liked the idea and he gave us the green light to proceed. I had already sourced the suppliers, so all the logistics team had to do was sign the contracts and deliver the product."

"Now, there was a lot more to it than that, Jennifer. While we appreciate the contacts you provided, not all of them panned out. Two or three companies didn't reply to the RFP in time, while others couldn't meet the legal team's requirements."

"No one said anything to me about the Requests for Proposal."

"Well, that's because we were able to source other suppliers."

While her colleagues were still at odds, it was clear to Kathy that both Carlos and Jennifer thought they were acting in the best interests of the company. Neither had an ulterior motive. At the same time, it was understandable that neither wanted to see their efforts to date be for naught.

"Let's try to get to the root of the problem. Carlos, where do you think your team went wrong?"

"My team didn't do anything wrong! We had to sort out supply issues, and we did."

Even before Carlos answered, Kathy could sense that she had taken the discussion into the wrong direction. It felt like the air was being sucked out of the room, so she tried a different tack.

"Jennifer, why didn't you get together with Carlos and talk about this sooner?"

"We've been busting our butts to get the launch in place, and we've been following the plan to a 'T.' No one ever said anything to me about a change in sales locations. If they had, we would have sorted the issue out before we got to this stage!"

"You know what?" Kathy replied. "I don't think I'm asking the right questions here. If it's okay with you guys, let me think about this overnight, and we'll reconvene tomorrow. In the meantime, I'll stop by Aaron's office to give him a heads up, so he can be better prepared for your team meeting in the morning."

"Oh, great," Jennifer sighed. She feared Aaron would side with Carlos because he was more senior and the two men worked closely together. Keeping this to herself, she shared an additional concern: "You better hope he's in a good mood."

"Sorry?"

"You better hope Aaron is in a good mood when you stop by his office."

"Why is that?"

"Well, to be honest," replied Jennifer, "and I hope you don't mind me saying this, Carlos, but some days Aaron is supportive and easy to talk to, but then there are other times, when … well, I guess he's just under a lot of stress."

"It's true. There are days when Aaron can seem a bit abrupt or when he lets his temper get the better of him," Carlos replied. "But he's ambitious. He wants to succeed and, I can assure you, he wants all of us to move up the ladder with him."

AS SHE WALKED through the hallway, glancing at photos from a Corporate Volunteer Day, Kathy saw some familiar faces. There was Jennifer picking up trash off a beach on the north side of the island. In another photo, Carlos, Aaron and other members of the snack team were painting a bright mural in the home of a low-income family. She thought about the complexities of a new product launch, all of the pieces that had to fit together, and how if team members weren't on the same page, even if they were working toward a common goal, everything could fall apart.

Outside Aaron's office, his executive assistant, May Ann, was reviewing a stack of reimbursement forms. Her desk was situated like a sentry, guarding the entries and exits of those who wished to visit the boss.

"Hi May Ann, I think Aaron's expecting me. We have a meeting scheduled. How's his mood today?"

"It's OK. You can take your chances," she smiled.

Kathy opened the door and walked through the entrance of Aaron's office. Seeing her, Aaron motioned Kathy to take a seat in one of two leather chairs across from his desk. "I'll be right with you. I just need to send off this document first." Several minutes later, he looked up. "Sorry for the delay, Kathy. How can I assist you today?"

"Aaron, as you know, Mark has asked me to sit in on some meetings in the snack division to better understand the needs of marketing, logistics, sales and your other departments. The goal is to more effectively discern Cascade's human capital needs, so we can grow people and also so that HR can be a true business partner to other units."

"Yes, Mark sent me a memo about this. Kathy, I'm grateful for our conversation last month when you suggested we hire a nutritionist and sustainable sourcing manager. Much more than hiring for a couple of positions, you challenged us to refocus on Cascade's purpose. When I shared this with the team, then opened the floor for suggestions on how we could meet the division's targets, the ideas really flowed. I have to say, it was a stark contrast from our previous discussions."

"That's great, Aaron. Thanks for the positive feedback. I've sat in on a few meetings within the snack division already, including a marketing meeting with Jennifer and her team today. You can really see her dedication and passion for the job. An issue came up, though, which I think you should be

CHAPTER FOUR

aware of before the team meeting tomorrow.

"There is a misalignment between the logistics and marketing teams. New products are being shipped to one place, but launch materials are being prepared for another."

"I don't follow." A stunned look crossed Aaron's face.

Kathy glanced down at her notes. "The spicy ginger snacks are on their way to Bangkok, but the launch is planned for Japan."

"That can't be . . . how the hell could this happen? We're a half million dollars into this project already!"

While Kathy understood Aaron's frustration, she didn't address it directly.

"Aaron, you pose a good question. From what I see, the members of your team are proactive, which is good. They're taking personal responsibility for the success of the launch, which is also good. They want it to succeed. But when I talked to Jennifer and Carlos, they were clearly at loggerheads and we couldn't immediately find a solution."

"We have to make this work. There's too much riding on it."

"I have an idea how we can solve this issue and bring all the members of your team back into alignment. I need to think through the details tonight, but with your permission, I'd like to have another offline conversation with Jennifer and Carlos after tomorrow's meeting."

"Okay, you've helped our team before. I'm willing to give this a shot. But it's got to be fast. We don't have time to lose."

"Thanks, Aaron. Before I go, there is one more thing I'd like to discuss with you."

Kathy paused, thinking about how to proceed, before deciding it was best to be direct.

"Aaron, members of your team say you're moody and have a temper. In fact, they even avoid coming to see you if you're in a bad mood."

"That's ridiculous. I never allow my moods to interfere with work."

"When I first heard about this issue, I probed further and discovered that people will turn around and head right back out the door if they hear you're in a funk. They'd rather put an issue or idea on hold, because they figure they'll get a better outcome if they wait.

"Aaron, did you know that your team members regularly take a temperature check with your assistant before deciding whether to talk to you? They ask May Ann, 'How's Aaron feeling today?' and if she replies, 'It's one of those days,' they say, 'Okay, let me know when he's in a good mood because I have an important issue to discuss with him.'"

"Well, everyone has bad days. You can't expect me to be cheery every day of the year. That's just the way I am. My team will just have to deal with it."

"Aaron, think about it for a moment. I realize no one likes to hear negative feedback, but what impact do you think this has on your team?"

Aaron took a sip of tea, and then another, as he paused to reflect on Kathy's question. It didn't come naturally, but he made a conscious effort to put his ego aside for a moment.

"Well, I guess, everyone kind of waits on me and we don't move as quickly as we need to. Some good ideas might get lost along the way if my team becomes preoccupied with other projects or if they simply decide not to bring it up again."

"That's exactly right. If you're unapproachable, it negates your team's momentum. They spend too much time waiting for the right moment to talk to you. Even worse, you risk killing their initiative, and the great work you've done to increase engagement could be for naught. So, tell me, what do you think you can do about this?"

"I don't know. I'll try to always be in a good mood."

"Aaron, a moment ago, you were right when you said that we all have our bad days. As a leader, you need to be able to deal with this and put your best face forward. It's all about perception — how others perceive you. What is something concrete that you could do to address this?"

Aaron looked past Kathy towards the door of his office. She allowed the silence to hang in the air, rather than making an effort to fill it. A minute passed, then two, before Aaron replied. "I could ask May Ann to let me know when I'm in a bad mood rather than telling other people. If I'm aware of it, I can adjust."

"That's a great idea. Remember, it's about perception. You need your team members to feel that you are always approachable. Let me tell you a story that one of my colleagues at a consulting firm told me. There was a senior partner at the firm and he had an 'open door policy.' In theory, any staff member could drop in, at any time, to talk about issues that were pertinent to the company or its clients.

"Do you know how many people actually stopped in? None! Why do you think that was? That's right. He wasn't approachable. Even though he supposedly had an open-door policy, no one felt they could just walk in and speak with him. If they did, the vibe and attitude that they picked up was, 'Why are you here? I'm busy.'

"So, much like I'm asking you today, my colleague asked the partner, 'What can you do to be more approachable?'

"They came up with a plan where the partner would stand in the office pantry every Monday morning with a quart of orange juice. When a colleague would walk in, he'd offer them some OJ and then ask about their weekend. It took more than a month to really change people's perceptions, but before long, staff members were approaching him to chit chat, to ask if he'd like a coffee from the shop downstairs, and to talk about work issues."

"I guess I could do that, but do you think it would really work in today's corporate environment?"

"Well, standing in the pantry may not always be an option in today's hybrid world. But when you're having Zoom calls, take a few minutes to talk to people and find out how they're doing. If you're chairing the meeting, don't start with 'Alright, folks, I got a lot going on today. Let's just get straight into it.' Take time to really check in with people. Aaron, remember, you're not only responsible for the success of the division. You're also responsible for the well-being and success of your team members, and you can't do that well, if they think you're unapproachable."

"Kathy, thank you. I'll take this on board. Let me ask you, though, where did you learn all this? We never had conversations like this before."

"Well, Aaron, there was never an opening, and there was never any time, for either of us. Mark has taken some of the day-to-day tasks off my plate, for now, and we're looking for the right software to permanently automate many of these processes going forward.

"To answer your question, where did I learn about leadership and organizational development? Well, I read a lot. I attend the occasional HR seminar and networking session to compare notes with industry colleagues, and perhaps most importantly, a few years ago, I became certified as an internal executive coach. It's just that, until now, I rarely had the opportunity to apply these skills."

"Well, you're definitely going to have an opportunity tomorrow. Let's hope this idea of yours can sort out the misalignment between marketing and logistics, so we can get the product launch back on track."

BACK AT HOME that evening, Kathy poured herself a glass of white wine and thought about the day's meetings.

Why had her discussion with Jennifer and Carlos gone off the rails? Yes, they were both invested in the project. They had put a lot of time into it, and neither wanted to appear wrong. But more than that, each thought they had done the right thing.

When she challenged them to think about where they may have erred, their defenses went up. It was like watching a porcupine raise its spines.

Kathy sat down on her sofa and turned on Netflix. She was midway through *The Crown* and fascinated by the relationship between Queen Elizabeth and her sister, Princess Margaret. Margaret seemed to court controversy, intentional or not, while Elizabeth largely stuck to her role, except on rare occasions when she thought painting outside the lines would benefit the United Kingdom and the Commonwealth.

One such occasion was when Queen Elizabeth asked Ghanaian president Kwame Nkrumah to fox trot. Historians may debate the implications of the 1961 dance, but in the show, it's clear: the Queen conducted "dancing diplomacy" during the height of the Cold War. She went out on a limb, motivated by personal responsibility to the Commonwealth and the Crown, to convince a potential adversary, a revolutionary and the first post-independence leader of a former British African colony, to dance with her in public.

Princess Margaret often lived in her sister's shadow. She reportedly once told the writer Gore Vidal that "when there are two sisters and one is the Queen who must be the source of honor and all that is good, the other must be the focus of the most creative malice, the evil sister." While it's not certain Margaret actually uttered those words, it is true that her behavior could make Queen Elizabeth shine in comparison.

When the two sisters converse in the series, there are times when Elizabeth clearly pulls rank, such as when she forbids her sister from marrying an Air Force officer assigned to the royal family. There are other moments, though, when title doesn't matter; the two women are simply sisters who can talk freely with each other.

As Kathy sipped her wine, she thought again of Jennifer. Like Princess Margaret, she had the sense that Jennifer felt at a disadvantage. She was younger and lower on the totem pole than Carlos. Kathy wasn't sure, but if she could level the playing field, then perhaps they could each look at the issues objectively and share more openly. To do this, she thought, she would need to begin the conversation with some broader questions and set a few ground rules to ensure success.

Kathy quickly picked up a notepad and pen and began to sketch a diagram, jotting down notes and bullet points to the side of it. "This could work!" she thought. She reworked the plan in her mind and considered presenting it to her colleagues the next day.

AARON ARRIVED EARLY for his team meeting. May Ann had booked a conference room with a view of the harbor. At least half his team would be dialing in, due to Cascade's latest hybrid work rules. As he settled in, a technician tested the video conference equipment and projector.

Ten months had passed since he joined the company, and several weeks since the team lunch that laid the foundations for an updated strategy to increase profits and sell a new line of healthier snacks. If successful, the snack

CHAPTER FOUR

division would be at the forefront of Cascade Trading's push to promote sustainability. It was this last point that was the first item on today's agenda.

After everyone had settled in, Aaron turned to Ajay, who had zoomed in from his home office. His image, as well as that of at least a dozen other team members, appeared in a flat-screen monitor affixed to a side wall to the right of Aaron.

"Ajay, I understand you traveled to Jababeka this past week to check out the supplier that Selena mentioned. What did you think of their sustainability initiatives?"

"Aaron, they've done an impressive job. There's quite a lot that we can learn from their approach. They're draining their used cooking oil and re-selling it to a local cooperative that transforms the oil into a biodiesel fuel. The cooperative sells some of the fuel back to the cookie factory at a subsidized rate.

"The rooftop coating Selena told us about also helps keep the factory's utility bills under control. I've contacted the vendor and am discussing a test with them at one of our own facilities."

While Ajay's camera filter was set to blur the background, Aaron could see a Rajasthani carpet hanging on the wall behind him. One of Ajay's sons was quietly studying in the background as well.

"That sounds very encouraging, Ajay. Does the Jababeka factory have the capacity to produce our new snack lines? And if so, how quickly can we get them onboard?"

"Aaron, I'm not sure I get you. I went to Indonesia on a fact-finding mission, so we could explore how to upgrade our facilities in the Philippines."

"Ajay, we said that if the facilities in Indonesia are good, we want to work with that vendor. We only have two more quarters to meet our targets, and even less 'til the launch."

"Aaron, you asked me to check out the Indonesian factory's sustainability initiatives. You didn't say anything about linking that to the launch of our new products."

"Are you serious?!" Aaron thought. "We clearly talked about outsourcing. Is he an idiot? He's too senior to make this sort of mistake! How could Ajay not link the sustainability initiative to our launch and KPIs? Everything we do is linked to these goals." Aaron could feel the blood rushing to his face. "How could this be happening? How could we have two major misalignments so soon after our last meeting and so close to the launch?"

As much as he wanted to throttle Ajay, and in his mind, he could see himself doing so, Aaron caught himself. He couldn't simply tell Ajay what to do. He needed Ajay's full support — his expertise and insights — to make this work. He needed to think instead about the best ways to resolve this crisis.

"Ajay, how long do you estimate it will take to implement these measures in our facilities?"

"We have all the information we need. I know the vendors and the costs and have put together a timeline and budget. We can make most of the changes within nine months. It may take a bit longer to identify community partners and create pilot projects for a few of the elements, such as creating alternative forms of packaging and processing biofuel from used cooking oil."

"Ajay, we don't have nine months. The information you've gathered is great. We should definitely move to retrofit our existing factories along the lines that you're suggesting. At the same time, we need to expand our capacity and ensure that at least a portion of our new products is produced as sustainably as possible, as soon as possible."

"I could probably tweak the timeline and speed things up by a month, maybe six weeks. Let me review this and get back to you tomorrow?"

"Ajay, how long would it take the Jababeka factory to roll out several of our products?"

"I can't say for sure, but when I asked them about another white label product that they're producing, they told me it took a couple of weeks."

"That's great. It sounds to me like we could work with them now and get moving on upgrading our own facilities at the same time. Let's take a two-pronged approach. We work with the Indonesian factory to roll out products now, while upgrading our Philippine facilities at the same time. It's a win-win, but I need your support to make this work. What do you say?"

"Aaron, I can tell you for sure: problems are going to arise if we outsource. They always do. We should really keep this in-house."

"Ajay, I hear what you're saying. Let's take this offline."

AARON TURNED FROM the video screen to Jennifer and Carlos, who were in the room. "OK, let's talk about the new product launch. Let's hear from Marketing first, then Logistics."

After both departments had presented, it was clear that the misalignment between the two sides had yet to be resolved.

"Jennifer, I like the launch visuals. The ad spend plan looks good too. Carlos, you've moved quickly to procure the products. But it's clear we have a problem. Kathy highlighted this to me yesterday. She also has an idea about how we can work through this."

Aaron glanced at Kathy, and she nodded that she was ready to proceed.

"So, I'm going to ask the three of you to remain behind after this morning's meeting, so we can find a solution.

"Listen, everyone. You've all shared some great ideas and we're starting to gather momentum. But I can see we're also stuck in our own silos. We need to break out of that and work together as a team. We succeed together, or we don't. There's no middle ground. And I intend to ensure that we succeed."

Your Turn: Three Questions for Reflection

"THE FAINTEST INK is better than the strongest memory." No one knows for sure the origin of this saying, but it is generally considered to be an ancient Chinese proverb. Writing contributes to analytical skills, comprehension and learning. So, take a moment to reflect on the following questions and be sure to write down your answers.

1. Character Development
   (a) In this chapter, the main characters are operating in the Second Space. They have become Proactive Self-Leaders. How are they taking personal responsibility for the success of the organization?
   (b) How is Kathy acting like a Human Capitalist? What is she doing differently and what perhaps could she do better?

2. Misalignment
   (a) There are at least 2 cases of misalignment in the preceding chapter. What are they and why do you think they occurred?
   (b) When an issue of misalignment occurs in the workplace, is one party necessarily right and the other(s) wrong? If so, is it important to identify the errant party? Why?
   (c) Can you name one or more examples of misalignment in your own corporate experience? Why do you think it occurs?

3. What do you think Kathy is doing to ensure that Aaron's team members are aligned?

CHAPTER FOUR

Alignment

THE BITCOIN EXCHANGE[2] is a cryptocurrency and payments platform headquartered in Singapore with offices in multiple countries. It is a relatively young company, but it's scaling up fast. Ahead of an important board meeting, I coached their leadership team and challenged them to explore the company's direction, alignment and commitment, using a framework developed by the Center for Creative Leadership.[3]

The team members answer a series of questions about what the company is trying to achieve (its direction), if there is effective coordination and integration between teams (alignment) and whether organizational success is a priority (commitment).

The leaders give their company high marks on its direction. They hold a shared vision for what the platform could achieve and they say that group goals guide their decisions and priorities. Similarly, they believe that their team is committed to success, even in the face of setbacks.

But like most companies I survey, the Bitcoin Exchange's lowest scores are inevitably around alignment. On a scale of 1-5, with five being the highest, the leaders roundly give their company marks of 1 and 2. Is the work of each individual well-coordinated with the work of others? No. Are people clear about how their tasks fit into the work of the group? Not really. Does the combined work across task groups fit together? Get real.

"Competition and the marketplace are forcing us to look in too many directions," one director notes.

"We're trying to win on too many fronts," another adds.

"There are too many silos," says a third division head. "We don't have a good sense of what each group is doing and how it's impacting the organization's direction."

A MULTINATIONAL COMPANY selling beauty products is planning a multimillion-dollar marketing campaign tied to an international sporting event. The project is nearly half a year behind schedule and I am sitting around a table with the leadership team to explore why.

"Tell me, what is your understanding of the project?" I ask.

Midway through the first response by a member of the team, the leader cannot contain himself.

"That's not what I said!" he exclaims. "That's not what we're supposed to be doing!"

This was a classic case of the Tower of Babel. Every member of the group had a different understanding of the marketing campaign. There was no agreement about what the initiative was meant to achieve, what it would look like once completed or how it would be implemented.

What you said is not what they heard; what they heard is not what you said.

A CORPORATE DIRECTOR, who earns upwards of half a million dollars a year, has been given responsibility to work on a project. But he isn't clear about the details. What does he do? Does he go to the boss to seek clarification? Unlikely.

I work with leaders like this all the time.

"I'll figure this out on my own," they think. "I don't want to go to the boss and look like I don't know what I'm doing."

The director might try a back channel to ask someone else about the project, or perhaps he simply takes an approach that makes sense to him.

When the project comes due, his boss is aghast.

"What's this?" he exclaims. "This isn't what I asked for!"

The director didn't want to appear "stupid," but in the end, he wasted his time and the company's money.

ALIGNMENT issues exist in nearly every company and they are not fully resolved in the Second Space.

Most companies do not stop to check that team members are aligned. Leaders assume that team members know what needs to be done. They only notice problems when something goes wrong, such as price overruns, project delays or unintended outcomes. If they do stop to check for alignment, the result may not be much better. The leader is likely to interrupt, or even criticize, when he hears comments that do not correspond to his recollection and understanding. If a project has gone off-course, he may blame team members because he believes they have made mistakes.

You cannot foster alignment through hierarchy.

A leader cannot simply say, "Get on board! I need you to be aligned!" Such a directive overlooks the causes of misalignment. An employee who is not scared of his boss might reply, "I'm having difficulty aligning around this because three of my colleagues on this project are hearing different things from you." More likely, the employee wouldn't say a word, due to the unequal nature of the relationship between leader and follower.

Even in the Second Space, where Proactive Self-Leaders and Human Capitalists take personal responsibility for the success of the organization, hierarchy still exists, at times, in their relationships with leaders.

To overcome issues of misalignment, organizations need a safe space. We need to create a space where Leaders, Proactive Self-Leaders and Human

Capitalists are empowered to conduct issue-focused conversations in an atmosphere that is neither judgmental nor hierarchical.

Welcome to the Third Space!

THE THIRD SPACE can be a physical room, a virtual platform or a psychological space. A Third Space conversation can take place anywhere, as long as participants signal that it is a Third Space dialogue and agree to follow a few simple ground rules:

Rule #1 The Third Space is not your space. It's not my space. It's the Third Space, a place that fosters alignment and understanding.

Rule #2 Hierarchy does not exist in the Third Space. Rank does not matter. The Third Space is an issues space.

Rule #3 Anyone can call a Third Space meeting and every participant has the opportunity in the meeting to lead the discussion.

Rule #4 Third Space discussions are advanced through issues-based questioning. Critical thinking promotes understanding, not deadlines or assignments. Questions are multi-directional; any question that a leader asks a team member, a team member can also ask of the leader.

The Third Space promotes hyper-alignment. It is a peer-to-peer environment where team members collectively take personal responsibility for the success of the organization.

Slowing down for a Third Space conversation enables companies to speed up and achieve their objectives more quickly. It is also a space for fostering agreement and understanding around Big Picture issues such as an organization's purpose.

After establishing the ground rules, the Third Space is built with five interconnected tools: Dialogue, Reflective Questioning, Critical Thinking, Challenging Questions and Active Listening. These techniques are all used in contemporary organizational environments, to varying degrees, but hierarchy limits their effectiveness. A nonhierarchical, psychologically safe space is needed to unleash their full potential.

Let's take a closer look at each of these tools, one by one.

Dialogue: A Transfer of Understanding
The Cornerstone of the Third Space

IN A TYPICAL conversation, one person speaks, while the other listens. I tell you what I think. You wait for me to finish, then you reply. The listener's brain and inner monologue never stop. It is usually thinking, "What am I going to say once this other guy stops talking?"

Philosophers, academics and teachers have debated the essence of conversation and dialogue, and how best to have one, for millennia. In the 5th century BC, Socrates and Plato formalized a method of asserting truth that was based on confrontation and debate. The Chinese philosopher Mo Di articulated several rules for dialogue around the same time as his Greek counterparts; his students, the *bianshi* philosophers, were reputed for how well they argued.[4] Jewish rabbis in Babylonia and Palestine engaged in seemingly endless back-and-forth questioning over issues big and small in discussions that would become the Talmud.

In each of these cases, participants strive for truth. However, they could also be competing, just as we do in modern debates, to be right.

A contemporary dialogue, particularly one that is fruitful in an organizational setting, needs to be a transfer of understanding. This definition actually links back to the word's origins. "Dialogue" has Greek roots. It is derived from *diálogos; logos* literally translates as "word," while *diá* means "through." Dialogue is "through words."

"In essence, a dialogue is a flow of meaning," explains William Isaacs in *Dialogue and the Art of Thinking Together*. "In the most ancient meaning of the word, *logos* meant 'to gather together'."

Isaacs argues that *diálogos* may best be translated in English as a "relationship" and that dialogues are conversational relationships in which people think together. This "implies that you no longer take your own position as final," he writes. "You relax your grip on certainty and listen to possibilities that result simply from being in relationship with others' possibilities that might not otherwise have occurred."[5]

"The object of a dialogue is not to analyze things, or to win an argument, or to exchange opinions," agrees the renowned American physicist David Bohm in a classic essay entitled *On Dialogue*. "Rather, it is to suspend your opinions and to look at the opinions—to listen to everybody's opinions, to suspend them, and to see what all that means... out of this whole thing, truth emerges unannounced."[6]

But try achieving a genuine dialogue in a hierarchical environment.

It's not easy.

To arrive at a truth through dialogue, direct reports are often required to challenge their boss, be it on details of a plan or different understandings of what was assigned.

"You told me to focus on the youth market, but not specifically on Zoomers," or "I did what you told me, but the cost savings were not as large as you predicted," an employee might have to tell an unhappy boss.

A Proactive Self-Leader, who is taking personal responsibility for the success of the organization, may even feel a responsibility to challenge a leader if she thinks a project has gone awry or a strategy is misguided. But the power relationship between the two parties is unequal, leaving many direct reports reluctant to speak out.

Even in cases where a leader appears open to dialogue, his definition of it may be different than ours. His goal, consciously or not, is typically for the rest of the room to walk away, at the end of the conversation, with his understanding of the issue, not their own. He wants his team to be on board with his notion of what's right, without necessarily truly hearing other perceptions and viewpoints.

Yet "in true dialogue, both sides are willing to change," explains the Vietnamese monk and peace activist Thich Nhat Hanh.[7]

THE AMERICAN PSYCHOLOGIST David Kantor developed a model for communication that has been a building block for hundreds of prominent thinkers, including Peter Senge, Michael Jensen and Werner Erhard.

There are four, and only four, types of roles that people can play in a conversation, according to Kantor's four-player model. A "Mover" puts forward an idea. A "Follower" agrees. An "Opposer" disagrees. And a "Bystander" observes and adds perspective.

"Let's launch a new wasabi line of snacks," a Mover says.

"Great idea. Wasabi is really popular now," agrees the Follower.

"Too many of our competitors are selling wasabi products. The market is already saturated. Let's do something else," counters the Opposer.

"Let's take a closer look at the numbers. We could have sufficient budget to try both approaches," says the Bystander.

In *Dialogue and the Art of Thinking Together,* William Isaacs builds on Kantor's idea and suggests that business leaders should actively play each of these four roles, in turn.

The leaders rotate until they agree that an issue is well-defined. I first encountered this at the Singapore Police Force, which has adopted a method of Collective Leadership. As many as twenty division and deputy division heads would be in the same room as the Commissioner to discuss policing issues. One person would put forward an idea; others would actively challenge, agree and serve as bystanders. Then they switch roles and start again.

The model encourages Opposers to play the role of devil's advocate, even if they support an idea, while Bystanders interpret participants' underlying intent, not solely their ideas.

The foundation of Isaacs' work — a belief that conversations must take place in a safe space where people can speak freely without fear of adverse consequences — is solid. Participants are liberated from their job titles and day-to-day roles for the sake of discussion. Silos can be broken down more easily. Individuals from Logistics, for example, are free to share ideas about Marketing, and vice-versa. Leaders become temporarily divorced from their responsibilities to individual departments.

There is no shortage of research to support Isaacs' work, but the application of his model is complicated.

The process encourages strong opinions without necessarily providing participants the space to take a step back to understand what they are trying to accomplish.

Participants forget whose turn it is to play which role or exactly what that role entails. "Wait, let's take a look at that handout again to see what I'm supposed to be doing now." In theory, it should not be hard to remember the difference between an "Opposer" and a "Bystander," but in practice, it is all too easy to forget the intricacies of the role or allow personal opinions to intervene. The most senior person in the room then inevitably takes on the responsibility of facilitating the discussion, which despite the best of intentions, invites hierarchy, and all of its constraints, back into the room.

THE THIRD SPACE is built on dialogue. We take a simpler, more straightforward approach than Kantor and Isaacs, though. Hearkening back to the word's Greek roots, the primary objective is simply to arrive at a common understanding of a question or issue. Do we understand what we're doing together?

To arrive at this understanding, we rely on four further tools: Reflective Questioning, Critical Thinking, Challenging Questions and Active Listening.

Reflective Questioning

POLL an organization's leaders, or your own team members, about the direction of a company or its initiatives, and you're likely to find significant agreement. However, the consensus breaks down when you probe deeper and ask about specifics. Alignment is almost always low.

The first tool in the Third Space to bring people into alignment is Reflective Questioning.

Consider the following question that a leader may ask a direct report when a project is behind schedule:

"Aaron, what can you do differently to advance this project?"

The question is open-ended. It provides an employee with the opportunity to think critically about the project, and it's generally viewed as a good "coaching" question that a leader can employ to obtain better results.

By directing this question at Aaron, though, and employing the 2nd-person pronoun "you," it also limits the scope of his replies. Aaron will focus on his portion of the project and actions that he can take, most likely without considering the roles of other actors and stakeholders. After replying, it's unlikely Aaron will pose a follow-up question to his boss. The most evident follow-up questions — "What do you think I should be doing differently?" or "What do you think?" — face the same constrictions as the initial query.

Let's now consider a different version of this conversation:

"Aaron, what do you think we should do to advance this project?"

This formulation is more than a semantic change; it widens the realm of replies. As the question is not directed solely at the direct report, the resulting discussion will be more expansive and free-flowing.

Welcome to the world of Reflective Questioning.

Reflective Questions are designed to allow possibilities to emerge. They encourage each discussion participant to interpret an issue in their own way, from their own perspective. There is no single right or wrong answer. The focus is on an issue, not the person. Reflective Questions are intended to elicit thoughtful replies. The broader the question, the more reflective it is. This, in turn, enables people to pause and reflect on their depth of understanding.

CONSIDER THE QUESTION, "Why is the sky blue?" To some, this may be an academic question with a single, scientific answer. However, it is also a reflective question that can be "correctly" answered in different ways by different people.

One parent may tell their child, "Honey, the sky is blue because God made it this way."

When the child is in secondary school, she may reply, "we learned in class today that the sky is blue as a result of the angle at which sunlight enters the atmosphere and how its particles are scattered."

An artist or photographer might note, "the sky isn't always blue; sometimes, it appears grey or is filled with the beautiful hues of a sunrise or sunset."

Another respondent might have an entirely different viewpoint: "The sky doesn't look blue to me. I'm color-blind."

Having an open mind and posing a broad question allows different perspectives to emerge and deepens our collective understanding.

IN THE THIRD SPACE, reflective questions can be answered by anyone and everyone in the room. In many cases, every participant shares their thoughts before another question is posed. Each new question probes deeper or adds a new dimension to the discussion.

- What is your understanding of the current project?
- What are the benefits of this project?
- What factors are causing the project to be behind schedule?
- How do we bring the project back on track?
- How has the market changed?
- What are the benefits of acquiring a vendor (or competitor)?
- What factors should we consider when evaluating a potential acquisition in this space?
- What pitfalls will we need to avoid?
- What are your thoughts about ... *[insert any issue or business trend]*?

Discussions that begin with reflective questions may initially feel like a traditional brainstorming session. However, there is a big difference. In the Third Space, dialogues are freed from the constraints of hierarchy. Leaders actively listen as equals. Outside this space, bosses still listen as bosses. They judge every suggestion and are prone to quickly dismiss ideas that they do not think will succeed.

The Third Space, on the other hand, becomes remarkably powerful because even the smallest voice has the potential to impact the biggest change.

DIALOGUE in the Enterprise Leadership Model can be pictured as a funnel. At the top of the funnel, you pour in big, broad, reflective questions that serve to foster alignment and enable participants to examine issues from a wide variety of angles.

Questions become sharper and more targeted as Third Space participants apply critical thinking to the issue.

At the end of this process, Leaders and Proactive Self-Leaders exit the

Third Space to engage in a discussion of actionable items.

While a Third Space discussion does not have to be lengthy — and some can be completed within minutes, particularly if only two people are involved — a common pitfall is that participants move through the process of dialogue too quickly.

Don't progress out of reflective questioning until you've exhausted the reflective process:

Dialogue One

LEADER #1 *(asking a reflective question):* The launch of our new product appears to be two months behind schedule. Why do you think that is?

PROACTIVE SELF-LEADER: Our team has had difficulty prioritizing.

LEADER #1: I see! Let's talk about priorities. How could you prioritize better? What could you do differently over the next two weeks?

Dialogue Two

LEADER #2 *(asking a reflective question):* The launch of our new product appears to be two months behind schedule. Why do you think that is?

PROACTIVE SELF-LEADER: Our team has had difficulty prioritizing.

LEADER #2 *(asking a second reflexive question):* What issues have made it difficult for your team to prioritize?

PROACTIVE SELF-LEADER: We've had a lot of people out on medical leave recently. Plus, several parents on our team have had to take personal days, because the schools have gone back to home-based education and they need to be at home with their children. On top of that, our team is responsible for two other launches, both of which have larger budgets and are scheduled before this one.

In the first dialogue above, the leader thinks he has identified the problem — and he is ready to solve it! In fact, though, he has no idea what is really happening. He exited the realm of Reflective Questioning too soon.

If you don't continue to explore — asking broad, reflective questions in a space that permits honesty and vulnerability — you will not understand the full scope of an issue or its potential ramifications.

Just as the might of a tornado starts from the spinning at the top, the power of a dialogue begins with reflection.

Stay at the top of the funnel!

REFLECTIVE QUESTIONING in the Third Space facilitates employee participation in decision-making, which in turn fosters alignment and improves employee engagement.

The process of reflective questioning demonstrates that I am interested in your thoughts, observations, reasoning and any background that has helped shape your views. Posing reflective questions is a key trait of successful leadership. By their very nature, reflective questions prompt engagement, when they are raised in a safe space. Not only that, in the Third Space, every employee is free to pose the same questions to every member of the team, regardless of rank.

Millennials and younger employees, in particular, demand to be consulted and heard. If you do not ask for their views, they think, "Why would I care? You're just telling me what to do."

In contrast, ask employees in firms with high rates of engagement why they like working there. One reply that will be high on their lists is: "My bosses don't just tell me what to do. They ask what I think. My opinion matters."

Critical Thinking

WHILE REFLECTIVE QUESTIONS enable participants to explore possibilities and fully examine and create alignment around an issue, there are no actionable items that result from the discussion.

To advance a dialogue in this direction, and move further down the funnel, the second tool to apply in the Third Space is Critical Thinking.

Critical thinking starts the path of clarification and promotes "objective analysis and evaluation."[8]

Most research on critical thinking focuses on individual, rather than collective, applications. How can a person apply logical reasoning, for example, to arrive at a rational conclusion? When additional people are brought into the picture, traditional critical thinking tools include debate and argumentation.

In organizations, though, we are interested in arriving at decisions and aligning around them in a collective space, and while logical, rational reasoning is important in any environment, debate is just as likely to foster lingering acrimony as agreement.

So, what is the best way for leaders and their direct reports to critically think together?

Like reflective thought, critical thinking in the Third Space is based on open-ended questions; however, these questions are sharper and more targeted.

Reflective Question: What are the benefits of changing our approach?
Possible Answer: Improvements to the user interface and back-end of the website should shorten the time required for payment processing. In turn, this will increase sales because we will lose fewer people along the way.

Critical Thinking Question: Who will benefit from this change?
Possible Answer: The majority of consumers using this website are women between the ages of 18 to 35. Most of the people who drop off midway are on the upper end of that band, generally women over 30. In addition, we find that men over the age of 30 become discouraged on the site more quickly than women. So the primary beneficiaries will be women between the ages of 30 to 35, as well as men over the age of 30.

Critical thinking questions start with one of the six basic journalistic keywords — Who, What, Where, When, Why and How — and are designed to sharpen participants' thinking on specific next directions, while maintaining focus on the issue, not the team members involved.

- Who benefits from this project?
- What are the best- and worst-case scenarios?
- Where will this idea take us, in practical terms?
- When will we know that we have succeeded?
- Why is there a need for this solution?
- How does this benefit (or harm) us?

The Global Digital Citizen Foundation has developed a handy *Cheatsheet for Critical Thinking* with nearly 50 questions that can foster better understanding. Examples include:

Who	is most directly affected?
	would be the best person to consult?
	is this harmful to?
What	can we do to impart positive change?
	is another perspective?
	is getting in the way of our action?

Where	is there the most need for this? are areas for improvement? can we find similar ideas implemented?
When	is this acceptable? would this cause a problem? is the best time to take action?
Why	is this a problem? is change needed? is there a need for this today?
How	does this cause disruption? will we approach this safely? can we change this for the better?

Critical thinking places a team on the path to action. While it is a valuable tool in any environment, it can be difficult to have candid, productive, critical thinking conversations between a leader and direct reports outside of the Third Space. Part of the beauty of the Third Space is that any participant can ask a critical thinking question of others; leaders are not simply soliciting information from team members.

Collective critical thinking works best in a nonhierarchical, non-judgmental environment.

And once you have defined an issue, it is time to refine it further.

From Alignment to Action: The Role of Challenging Questions

THIRD SPACE DIALOGUES begin with Reflective Questioning. The key question, which every participant can ask and answer, is: "What is our understanding of the issue?"

Participants then apply Critical Thinking to analyze the issue and look at it from different angles. The key question here is usually: "What should we do differently?"

Once the answers to these questions have emerged, more challenging questions are needed to refine, align and create actionable items: "Now that we're aligned, what are our next steps?"

The purpose of Challenging Questions is three-fold: they encourage team members to coalesce around solutions, work more effectively together and align around responsibility. Within the Third Space, some examples of Challenging Questions include:

- Where can we find the data needed to advance this project?
- How could we complete the project more quickly?
- What could we do differently in the next two weeks to move this along?
- How can we lower costs or come in under budget?
- How do we connect with these customers?
- What is the best way for our team to work together on this?
- How should we update each other about the project's progress and any challenges encountered?
- Who is going to be responsible for driving this?

Challenging Questions enable team members to recognize their individual roles and responsibilities within the context of the group. They also shape interactions as employees work with each other to fulfill their responsibilities according to agreed timelines.

IN TRADITIONAL corporate environments, leaders hand out assignments. "Chris, you're in charge of layout and design. Julie, you're responsible for the focus group research."

At times, they hope team members will volunteer to work on a project. These leaders often find their presentations followed by silence. They are then obliged to follow up to influence or coerce their team members to take responsibility. "Jessica, what's your schedule like this week? Could you fit this in?"

In companies that adopt the Enterprise Leadership Model, Third Space dialogues provide greater clarity about what's needed. In the process, it becomes less risky for team members to embrace new responsibilities because they understand exactly what needs to be done. As a result, Proactive Self-Leaders are more likely to put up their hands to volunteer and take ownership of a project.

"I've led a few similar focus groups before. I'm happy to take on this one as well," a Proactive Self-Leader says.

"My team already has some good ideas on the layout, and they're consistent with what we've discussed here today. I can get you the mock-ups before the end of the week," another Proactive Self-Leader might add, further removing one of the burdens of leadership from their boss.

In situations like these, if a leader notices that a team member is not stepping forward, it can be the basis for a post-Third Space coaching conversation: "Jessica, I know you've done this kind of research before. In fact, you're one of the best researchers in the company. Why didn't you raise your hand? What kept you from stepping forward?"

This is when a leader becomes a coach.

"Companies are moving away from traditional command-and-control practices and toward something very different: a model in which managers give support and guidance rather than instructions, and employees learn how to adapt to constantly changing environments in ways that unleash fresh energy, innovation, and commitment," write London Business School professor Herminia Ibarra and Oxford University Saïd Business School scholar Anne Scoular in the *Harvard Business Review*.[9]

There's no shortage of literature on the importance of the Leader-Coach in today's corporate world; this evolution in how effective leaders manage people aligns well with the Enterprise Leadership Model.

CHALLENGING QUESTIONS are unique within the Enterprise Leadership Model since they can be posed both inside and outside the Third Space. Within the Third Space, Challenging Questions are collective questions; they are generally framed as "What can we do?" and like any other questions raised in the Third Space, they can be posed and answered by any participant, regardless of rank or position.

Once alignment is achieved around these Challenging Questions, it's time for action ... and to emerge from the Third Space. But this doesn't mean the discussion is over.

Leaders and their teams still need to identify next steps and clarify responsibility. To accomplish this, Leaders conduct Action Conversations with their direct reports by posing another set of challenging questions: "Now that we're aligned on this approach, what are you going to do?"

Some further examples include:

- What are your next steps?
- What are you going to do this week?
- How are you going to accomplish this?

- What is your overall timeline to complete the project?
- When can you send me an updated project timeline outlining these next steps?
- When will you update me on your progress?

As we exit the funnel, the Leader goes around the table to ask each participant to confirm their responsibilities, deliverables and timeline.

Active Listening

QUESTIONING, whether it's part of a dialogue, reflective discussion, critical thinking or bottom-of-the-funnel wrap-up, is an active process on the part of the person speaking. But it is 100 percent effective only if the Listener also plays their role fully.

For most people, listening is a passive exercise. We listen for what we want to hear. We concentrate more on what we will say next than on what is currently being said.

Active Listening is a valuable practice worth pursuing in all aspects of life, at home and in the office. Active Listening is particularly important in the Third Space, where it supports curiosity, appreciation and facilitates understanding.

The term was first coined by the psychologist Carl Rogers, who is a pioneer of modern psychotherapy. Rogers authored a groundbreaking essay in 1957, in collaboration with his student Richard Farson, entitled "Active Therapy." Rogers and Farson argue that active listening in the workplace leads to greater cooperation and clearer communication.[10]

To actively listen, you need to quiet the inner voice in your head. Listeners need to be fully present, suspend judgment and focus on the content of a person's speech as well as non-verbal cues. As a Listener, you also need to acknowledge the speaker: look directly at them and demonstrate that you're listening by occasionally nodding your head or even saying "uh-huh."

IN MY WORK with the Center for Creative Leadership, we expose participants to Active Listening with a short drill. Try this exercise at work with a group of at least five people.

THE SPEAKER reads a two-minute story, any story that is of interest to them.
LISTENER #1 takes note of the facts of the story.
LISTENER #2 pays attention to values.

LISTENER #3 is attuned to the speaker's feelings.
LISTENER #4 focuses on the speaker's worldview.

Consider an example in which the story being recounted is about the speaker's enthusiasm for a new community project that the company is undertaking.

- LISTENER #1 rapidly jots down everything:
  "In December last year," "the board issued a directive," "my team met," "we developed a plan," "for every meal purchased, the company will donate one meal to charity," etc.
- LISTENER #2 notes that the story is about being a good corporate citizen, contribution and charity.
- LISTENER #3 observes that the speaker is excited and happy.
- LISTENER #4 considers that the speaker is passionate about community service and the role companies can play in ending hunger.

In most conversations, though, we do not have the luxury of sharing listening responsibilities with others. Rather, we must listen for all four aspects: facts, values, feelings and worldview. On top of this, in the Third Space, participants should also listen from a perspective of curiosity to ensure that they fully understand the content being shared by a speaker.

"**OEL NGATI KAMEIE**," members of the Na'vi people say to greet each other in James Cameron's 2009 animated masterpiece *Avatar*. "I *see* you," they are saying in the fictional Na'vi language.[11]

What a beautiful phrase. It goes beyond physical sight ("I *see* you standing in front of me") to infer a deeper meaning: "I *understand* you. I *hear* you. I *respect* you." Just as on the lush jungle moon of Pandora inhabited by the Na'vi, someone who authentically practices active listening can essentially say to a speaker, "I see you." Their listening manifests itself as an active ac-know- ledgment of hearing and understanding a speaker's message.

Unlike the Na'vi, Active Listening does not come naturally to most people. The good news, though, is that it is a technique that you can learn and apply. Take note of these five listening keys to "thoroughly absorb, understand, respond, and retain" what is being shared by a speaker.[12]

1. Pay Attention

Be present. Listen respectfully. Don't interrupt. If you find yourself formulating a response, remind your inner voice to wait until later so you can focus on the speaker. If you have trouble focusing, try taking notes or repeating their words in your head. This will help reinforce their message.

2. Withhold Judgment

Our inner voices are constantly assessing whether we agree or disagree with others. In a business setting, judgment is amplified further by preconceived notions and our own experience working on a project or initiative. To truly hear someone, you need to quiet this inner voice and tell it to stop judging. When it's your turn to speak, do not argue and be sure to withhold your critiques until everyone has had an opportunity to fully share.

3. Reflect

Repeating or paraphrasing a speaker's comments is a great way to verify comprehension. "If I understand properly, you're saying that supply chain issues are cutting into profits, but you believe that we should be able to identify new suppliers in South Carolina and Mexico. Is that correct?"

4. Clarify

If you're not sure, ask. "I'm not sure I understand correctly. What do you suspect is at the root of our supply chain issues?"

5. Summarize

Before wrapping up a discussion or progressing to the next topic, restating key points and themes ensures alignment. "Our vendor contracts offered some protection against rising semiconductor prices, but higher costs are still hitting our margins. Moving forward, we're going to identify new suppliers in several jurisdictions, including southern California and Singapore. We expect this will ease constraints, but we will still have to raise prices by 5 percent."

After providing a summary, every participant in the conversation can indicate whether they share the same understanding. If not, it's time to discuss and actively listen again.

ACTIVE LISTENING is a back-and-forth process. It shows up in dialogue as an acknowledgment that I hear what you are sharing. To do this, I need to listen consciously to you and be fully present with your answers to my questions.

"Audrey, what's your understanding of this project?"

"I see. Could you expand on that for me?"

"Thanks for explaining that. How can we support you in this initiative?"

The speaker, Audrey in this case, will have a sense of "Wow, my colleague (or boss) is really listening to me. They understand what I'm saying and the pressures we're facing."

At the same time, you will know you are a good listener when you are not worried about what you are going to say next. When you listen actively, your next question is inside the speaker's answer.

Active Listening Outside the Third Space

LEADERS HAVE a responsibility to practice Active Listening in all their communications with colleagues, whether they are inside the Third Space or having a more traditional discussion. In a growing number of companies, the ability to actively listen and coach team members is now a performance criterion for assessing leaders.

At the base of the Enterprise Leadership Model, where Leaders interact with Proactive Self-Leaders in a more hierarchical fashion, Active Listening manifests itself differently. In these conversations, the goal is no longer hyper-alignment, which is achieved in the Third Space. Instead, it is to maintain this alignment and offer support.

Leaders are responsible for the growth of their team, as well as the success of the organization. They may pose challenging questions to their direct reports at the base of the funnel, such as "How are you going to approach the project over the next 30 days?" or "When will you complete this?" However, when team members reply, an Active Listening Leader is attuned to how she can support them in the project and their careers.

"Let's Have a Third Space Discussion"

THE THIRD SPACE is a win-win environment where Leaders, Proactive Self-Leaders and Human Capitalists align around solutions that enable them to collectively take personal responsibility for the success of the organization.

While we have identified a series of techniques to use to work your way through the Third Space Funnel — starting with broad reflections and critical thinking, then filtering down to action items — Third Space dialogues do not need to be lengthy. Once your organization is familiar with the model, alignment can often be found within minutes. Of course, some team discussions do require more time.

If you want to win, at someone else's expense, the Third Space is not for you. However, if you are looking for solutions, here are some simple clues that you need to head to the Third Space.

CHAPTER FOUR

Have a Third Space discussion when:

A PROJECT   is behind schedule
                                is not proceeding as planned

TEAM MEMBERS   do not work well together
                                do not seem to be working on the same thing

Any one of these clues indicates that there is a lack of understanding and alignment that can be addressed and rectified in the Third Space.

Another clue is hesitation. The moment you hesitate, the moment you are not sure what to do next to advance a project, particularly if a number of people or different departments are working on the same initiative, ask for a Third Space dialogue. Odds are, your hesitation is linked to a lack of clarity and alignment around the project, and there is no better place to address this than the Third Space.

IN ANY BUSINESS ENVIRONMENT, Third Space dialogues will surface new ideas and provide a forum to solve problems, from issues of execution to personnel issues. Here is a short list of topics that you and your team should discuss in the Third Space:

- Purpose, Strategy and other Big Picture issues
- Organizational Change
- New Projects and Initiatives
- Corporate Silos
- Stalled or Wayward Projects
- Mergers & Acquisitions
- Personal Conflicts

Holding Third Space discussions at the beginning of a project will avoid delays down the line. Similarly, whenever change is being considered, dialogue inside the Third Space enables companies to gauge what needs to be done to garner the support required to foster success.

Consider the case of a merger and acquisition. Third Space dialogues should be held before the deal goes through — to assess the merits and potential pitfalls — and again upon implementation.

In the high-profile 2020 attempted merger of two Real Estate Investment

Trusts in Singapore — the acquisition of Sabana REIT by its larger competitor, ESR-REIT — the two management teams were aligned, but a vocal group of minority shareholders scuttled the $3 billion deal.[13] Quarz Capital Management and Black Crane Capital contended that their investment in Sabana was being undervalued by ESR-REIT and that greater profits could be unlocked by simply following a different strategy.

There's no guarantee that a Third Space dialogue would have brought the opposing sides together, but an open discussion prior to setting the acquisition price would have stood a greater chance of reaching an agreement. If it became apparent during the dialogue that there really was no common ground, the ESR and Sabana managers might have decided to focus their energies elsewhere, rather than risk losing a lengthy, costly public fight, which is what happened in the end.

Let's imagine for a moment that the acquisition did go through. What then?

The vast majority of acquisitions go south because of poor implementation, misguided visions and cultural conflicts. All of these can be resolved in the Third Space. Marketing and operations officials from both sides of the merged entity can discuss questions such as "how do we ensure the continued quality of your product?" and "what's the best way for us to promote your business?" In traditional, hierarchical companies, these conversations go south because of a lack of trust between the parties and an "I win, you lose" mentality by the acquiring side. Within the Enterprise Leadership Model, these dialogues should take place as early as possible to ensure a smooth and successful transition.

Similarly, consider a debate over budgeting. Typically, business units feel like they are competing for resources, instead of looking at the numbers holistically to see what's required for overall success. If your next budget discussion turns contentious, call for a Third Space discussion. You can hold it right there on the spot. Start by exploring the question, "What does your division need for the company to be successful?" Recall that everyone in the room will have an opportunity to pose and respond to this question, as they contemplate it from a pure business perspective.

I'VE BEEN COACHING a senior human resource leader who has been fighting me every step of the way as I encourage him to take on the role of a Human Capitalist. (Let's call him *Elliot.*) He is stuck in his ways. Elliot sees himself as a protector of the company and enjoys playing the role of a devil's advocate, whose job it is to slow down the cogs of progress rather than smooth the way forward.

Elliot is coming around, though. He recognizes the need to obtain the support of his peers, if he is to accomplish anything big. HR initiatives, by their very nature, cut across multiple departments. Consider, for example, a new Performance Management System that is intended to provide clearer links between compensation and performance, furnish feedback to team members and identify training needs and opportunities for career growth.

While Elliot *knows* the system will be good for his company — he's seen it work in other firms and is convinced it will make an impact where he works as well — he can't simply ram it through. If he does, people are likely to ignore, or worse, actively undermine it.

Recognizing this, Elliot has decided instead to have Third Space dialogues with his peers, to learn more about their needs and how a new PMS system will, or will not, support them.

IN THE 1990s, when Larry Bossidy was the chairman and chief executive of the aerospace giant AlliedSignal, he had two direct reports who were constantly at each other's throats. Maybe they didn't like each other or perhaps they were each trying to position themselves to be Bossidy's successor. Either way, their attempts to undermine each other were disrupting leadership meetings and interfering with AlliedSignal's business.

One day, fed up with the running disputes, Bossidy calls the two men into his office.

"There's two things I want to tell you," Bossidy says. "The first is you guys have to figure out how you're going to work together, because we're not going to do this anymore. And second, if you can't work it out, one of you is going to have to tell me who I'm going to fire."[14]

Without knowing it, Bossidy was essentially sending his colleagues to a rough version of the Third Space, where they would have to address their behavior head-on.

"What's the problem here? How are we going to work together?" he was asking them.

Knowing that their jobs were on the line, the two men had an opportunity to work it out, and if they couldn't, one of them would have to leave.

Not everyone will thrive in a company that adopts the Enterprise Leadership Model. Not everyone will agree to accept personal responsibility for the success of the organization. But those that don't, particularly those who are given ample opportunity to adapt to the new system, should be shown the door, just as Bossidy was willing to do with his direct reports.

Be Aware

1. Misunderstandings and misalignment routinely occur in almost every entity. Hierarchy makes it difficult, if not impossible, to avoid or quickly rectify areas of misalignment.

2. Fostering an environment with Proactive Self-Leaders and Human Capitalists — where every employee takes personal responsibility for the success of the organization and corporate values are embedded throughout people processes — are essential building blocks of the Enterprise Leadership Model. But they are not sufficient to avoid misalignment. To do this, companies must take a further step, into the Third Space.

3. The Third Space is a psychologically safe space for resolving issues and achieving hyper-alignment.

4. Hierarchy does not exist in the Third Space. It is not my space, nor is it your space. Anyone, regardless of job title or rank, can ask a question of anyone else in the Third Space.

5. The Third Space can be a physical room or a virtual platform. Third Space discussions can take place anywhere, at any time. They can last minutes or hours. The duration is not important, as long as every participant respects a few simple ground rules.

6. Do not confuse conversation with dialogue. Dialogue — the active pursuit of a common understanding — lies at the heart of the Third Space.

7. Discussions in the Third Space are like a funnel: begin with broad, reflective questions, followed by critical thinking and challenging questions, until every participant is aligned on the issue and the next steps needed to address it.

8. Active Listening is essential to the Third Space, though it is also a practice that can be applied to any communication. Active Listening requires being present, withholding judgment and reflection. Seeking clarification and restating a speaker's key points ensure alignment.

9. If a project is behind schedule or not proceeding as planned, if team members do not work well together or do not appear to be on the same page, hold a Third Space discussion.

10. Having a Third Space discussion at the beginning of a project will avoid delays down the line.

CHAPTER FIVE

Cascade Trading

AFTER THEIR COLLEAGUES filed out and the Zoom projection was shut off, Kathy, Aaron, Jennifer and Carlos remained in the conference room. Jennifer and Carlos scrolled messages on their phones, avoiding eye contact, while Kathy turned to a page in her notepad where she had sketched two images, a pyramid and a funnel, had annotated both of them and drawn arrows along the sides.

The team meeting had run 90 minutes. At Aaron's request, Jennifer and Carlos stayed behind to sort out the snafus plaguing the launch. Kathy was prepared to lead this second discussion, but she decided it would be good to have a clean break between the two meetings.

"Hey everyone, thank you for staying behind. Why don't we pause for five minutes? Stretch, get some water, maybe a couple of snacks, then we can start refreshed."

Kathy looked out the window to her left. Beyond the iconic Marina Bay Sands towers, she saw what appeared to be a flotilla of container ships waiting to enter the port. In the distance, an Airbus flew east toward the airport. While visitor arrivals were on the rise again, she knew that air cargo also constituted an increasing share of carrier revenues.

After the interval, Kathy set the tone and laid down some ground rules.

"Jennifer, Carlos, Aaron, as you know, I've been observing the snack division for some time, and it's clear you've all been working hard to ensure that this latest launch is a success. I want to be clear: no one doubts your passion or professionalism. We're not here to look for fault or establish who's right or who's wrong."

"Think of this as an issues space," she added, making a sweeping motion with her hand across the room. "I've been working on a framework that will help us sort out misalignments and break out of our silos. I'm convinced that if we follow a few simple rules, we can resolve differences and promote alignment.

"OK, the first rule is this: this is a safe space. You can say anything you want. You can ask anything you want, as long as it comes from a place of truth and mutual respect. Do you understand?"

Kathy's colleagues nodded.

"The second rule is that there is no rank in this room. There are no bosses," she continued. "Aaron, Carlos, Jennifer, we are all on the same level here. We are all leaders and we're all responsible for the success of the company, not just of the launch but also for the snack division and Cascade Trading as a whole.

"Alright, so, our goal is to promote understanding and to do this, we're going to use a series of questions. I have one last ground rule and it's about how we ask these questions. Questioning can go in any direction. Any question I ask of you, you can ask of me, and vice-versa. The same goes for the dialogue. Jennifer, you're free to pose questions about the project to Aaron and Carlos, just as they may ask you. OK?"

Jennifer wondered how this discussion would unfold. She still feared that Aaron and Carlos would side with each other, but she nodded her agreement to Kathy and made a mental note that she was encouraged to ask questions of the others.

"We're going to start with some broad questions and then work our way down to the specifics."

Kathy glanced at her notebook.

"You can picture this process as a funnel, a Funnel of Understanding."

"Are you ready to begin?"

While there was still some unease in the room, Aaron answered first. "Kathy, thank you for that introduction. Thanks, as well, for putting together a framework for us to sort this out. Let's proceed!"

"Jennifer, what's your understanding of the project?"

"My understanding of the project? We're launching a range of spicy snacks across the region. We're taking a spice that is popular in one market and launching it in another.

"Carlos, what about you? What's your understanding of the project?"

"Like Jennifer said, Cascade is launching a new range of pan-Asian snacks across the region. The focus is on spice, instead of sugar. We expect this will resonate with consumers. Plus, the snacks are healthier, so that's in line with our overall objectives."

"Aaron, your turn."

"It's important to keep the big picture in mind. Cascade Snacks has a mandate to sell healthier snacks, which is in line with the company's ESG goals. We also need to increase profits by 15 percent. The launch of this new spicy Asian snack line is an integral part of that campaign."

"I see, that's good. Thank you all for sharing your perspectives. Now, let me ask you this," Kathy followed up, **"What are the benefits of this project?"**

"If it goes well, we should enjoy larger bonuses at the end of the year," answered Carlos, reflexively.

"I think it goes beyond that," interjected Jennifer. "I really think we have an opportunity to expand Cascade's market share and create a new line of signature snacks. If we get this right, who knows, our snacks could be the M&Ms for a healthier generation."

"Jennifer and Carlos are both right. We want to transform the way that consumers snack. Healthier snacks mean healthier communities. But no one will eat a healthy snack if it isn't delicious. So, that's where the spice comes in. This new product line should also help Cascade Snacks meet our KPIs, and that's good for the entire team," Aaron replied, when it was his turn.

"Alright, it looks like we are pretty much aligned around the importance of this project and why we are undertaking it," Kathy observed. "Tell me, **where are we now?** "

"We're kind of screwed," replied Jennifer. She paused, then looked up at Kathy, "Sorry to be so blunt, but the products are not going to the right places."

"That's not fair, Jennifer. You could just as easily say that the launch materials are wrong," Carlos responded.

"Everyone, let's take a step back. **Why do you think you weren't aligned in the first place?** Remember, we're not looking to assess blame."

"Clearly, our communication broke down."

"We were under a tight time frame. I don't think we cut any corners, but maybe our processes need updating."

"You both knew that this is a very important project. So, **what kept you from having closer conversations about it?** "

"The marketing team was just so focused on the launch that we had no idea there was any misalignment or miscommunication to begin with."

"I guess I just assumed Jennifer had read the messages on the Trello board."

"Kathy, you've been observing the team. Tell us, what do you think? Why weren't we aligned earlier?"

"From what I can see, this is a classic case of teams working in silos. There are also some communication issues. Some messages are not clear. That's not to say there's anything wrong with them. Even the best-written message can be misinterpreted."

"If that's the case, **what can be done?** "

"I think a two-pronged approach is needed. First, I suggest reviewing the

CHAPTER FIVE

ways in which the snack division communicates internally. Perhaps, there are too many different platforms, or maybe there needs to be more clearly defined processes for signing off at each stage. I'm happy to take a closer look at this with your team.

"I have a second idea as well, but I'd like to save that for the end of the meeting. First, let's take a closer look at the misalignment and **establish the facts.** Carlos, which snacks are being shipped where?"

Carlos pulled out a printout from his file, and as he shared his list of products, their origins, destinations and arrival dates, Kathy filled out a table with colored markers on a whiteboard at the side of the room.

"Jennifer, how about you? Which products are currently being prepared to launch in which countries, and what are the key dates?"

After adding Jennifer's answers, Kathy took a step back, regarded the table, then turned to her colleagues. "Tell me," she asked, "**what does being on track look like** to you guys?"

"For us to be on track, the ginger snaps need to arrive in Osaka next week and the Sichuan potato chips in Jakarta the week after," replied Jennifer. "We've staggered the launch dates, so we have one more week after that for the other products on the board."

"To be on track, I think we need to revisit the marketing strategy so that it matches the product locations," countered Carlos.

"I would say that being on track requires 4 R's," reflected Aaron. "It means having the *right* product, in the *right* place, in the *right* packaging, at the *right* time. For this launch to be successful, we need to get these four things right."

"So, **how do we determine what product should launch where?**" asked Kathy.

"We have market research."

"We need to look at the logistics on the ground."

"It looks like the Japan launch — the one that you and your team were working on this week — is the most imminent," said Kathy. "Why don't we zoom in on that first. The marketing team is preparing to launch ginger snaps, but they are currently en route to Bangkok, while spicy mala potato chips should arrive in Tokyo today.

"Jennifer, **what does the market research show** for ginger snacks and mala chips in Japan?"

"Fresh ginger is an indispensable ingredient in Japanese cuisine. I'm sure you've noticed the sides of crunchy pink pickled ginger when you order sushi or sashimi. More than that, Japanese use ginger when grilling chicken, frying fish and even when cooking rice.

"Japanese are also strong believers in the medicinal value of ginger. It can help with stomach aches and joint pain. It's supposed to boost your immunity against colds and flus, and it's even an important ingredient in hair tonics and cellulite treatments."

Jennifer glanced at her colleagues' hair, wondering if either of the men had tried a ginger hair tonic. Even in Singapore, you could see ads for these products in the trains and newspapers.

"I can tell you from my time in Japan, ginger drinks are very popular for this reason," she continued. "The numbers back this up too.

"Japan and China have a lot in common when it comes to ginger. The Chinese love to eat dumplings with ginger; traditional Chinese medicine also makes use of the root, as do modern aesthetic treatments.

"However, one area where they differ is when it comes to candies and snacks. Ginger snacks haven't taken off yet, the way they have in China. Our focus groups indicate there's a market for it, though, and that's where Cascade's Japan launch comes in. With the right branding and support, our research indicates that ginger treats could prove to be very popular."

"Thank you, Jennifer. Carlos, **what are the logistical factors** that we need to consider when preparing for the launch?"

Carlos connected his laptop to the projector, then pulled up a slide. "In the left column, you can see the production dates and the addresses of the factories. To the right of that are columns with our shipping partners, their availability and freight costs. As you can see, in addition to price, there were some bottlenecks that we had to consider."

"How would the mala chips be received in Japan?" asked Aaron.

"I chatted with a member of the sales team in Tokyo. He didn't think there would be any problem. In fact, he told me about a Sichuan restaurant that his friends like," replied Carlos.

"Sure, you can find just about any type of restaurant in Tokyo," acknowledged Jennifer. "When this problem first surfaced, I said that Sichuan mala isn't popular in Japan. The marketing team has done some more research since then, and I have to say there are signs that mala cuisine is more available now than when I lived there. But I think it's still a niche market. For most Japanese, the mala spice is too hot and they don't like the numbing sensation. That's why I think the mala chips won't be as well-received as ginger snacks."

"Have we, or has anyone else, done a focus group study?" asked Aaron. "Our first shipment of mala-flavored potato chips arrives in Tokyo today. Do you think they could sell?"

"I'm not aware of any focus studies looking into this. We could do one," replied Jennifer. "As to whether the chips could sell, if we had the budget and time to prepare a new launch, yes, I think we could sell them."

SO FAR, THE DIALOGUE was going pretty well, Kathy thought. While Jennifer and Carlos still seemed defensive, and perhaps even a bit ill-at-ease, she sensed they were trying to move past this to find a resolution to the issues at hand.

"We can look at the budget again," said Aaron, "but I don't know if spending more money is the right solution here. It seems to me that what we need to do is — "

Kathy placed a hand on Aaron's arm to stop him. She was glad he was actively participating and asking questions, but it was too soon to jump to a conclusion. She also thought it would be better if, in future discussions, everyone posed questions of their teammates. But since this was their first time using a new format, it was natural that she would need to guide the dialogue.

"Aaron, if you could hold off on that thought for a moment, we're not quite ready yet to leave the Funnel of Understanding. We're still in the middle of the funnel. Tell me, and this is a question for everyone, **what do you think is the best-case scenario** for how this launch plays out?"

At first, no one answered. Carlos broke the silence. "Best case: we find a way to quickly bring the launch products and launch materials into alignment."

"I agree with Carlos. On top of that, in a best-case scenario, the launch really takes off. It lights a fire that sparks consumption and each new product captures a 1 to 2 percent market share of the overall snack market, in the country where it's launched, within six months."

"What are the worst-case scenarios?" Kathy asked.

"Worst case? We need to delay the launches by two months or more to bring the products and marketing campaigns into alignment," replied Carlos.

"That's not going to work," interjected Aaron. "We can't afford a delay like that. We need to find a solution that ensures a smooth launch that is on time, or at least close to it."

"Do you have ideas on how we could do this?"

"We could air freight the ginger snacks to Osaka from Bangkok, where the current shipment is headed," Carlos suggested. "Alternatively, we have a second batch coming out of the factory this week. We could fly it in from there."

"How much more would this cost, do you think?"

"I can get you some exact figures this afternoon, but basically, I think air freight might eliminate our profits from the initial launch, but we could make that back over time."

"Perhaps we could fly in a smaller quantity than originally envisioned," Jennifer suggested, "If we bill it as a limited release and sell out, that could help build an even greater buzz."

"I like that. That's a good idea."

"And what about the mala chips that are already in Japan?"

"Let's store them in a warehouse while we focus-group this. If the numbers look good, we launch them there too; if not, we ship them to Indonesia."

"Are we agreed on this approach?" Kathy asked.

Her three colleagues nodded in agreement, looked at each other and back at Kathy.

"Could you summarize for me: what have we agreed? What's your understanding of how we're going to address this issue?"

After ascertaining that everyone was indeed on the same page, Kathy guided the discussion in another direction: "Aaron, I'm going to hand the discussion over to you in a moment, so you can establish the action points and next steps with the team, but first, before we exit the Funnel of Understanding, I'd like to return to something you asked me earlier. You asked how we could prevent misalignments like this in future."

"That's right. You said you had two ideas. The first was a review of our communication platforms and processes. What's the second?"

"I believe the type of meeting that we're having right now needs to take place at the beginning of every new project, and perhaps periodically after that. In fact, whenever someone on the team feels uncertain or is hesitant about the next step, they should feel free to call a meeting like this."

"I like that idea," replied Aaron. "Jennifer and Carlos, what do you think?"

"We've made good progress today," Carlos agreed. "But I'm not sure about institutionalizing this process. Time pressure and deadlines are a constant in our industry. I'm concerned about adding another layer of meetings and the time that this requires."

"Sometimes, you need to slow down to speed up," Kathy replied. "Ensuring that we're aligned at the beginning of a project will help avoid snafus down the line."

"Well, I certainly wish we had avoided the snafus around *this* launch earlier."

"If we're going to encourage the rest of the department to make use of this methodology, we need a name for it. Any suggestions?"

"I've been thinking about this," Kathy replied. "You know, since one of the core tenets of this discussion is that this is a psychologically safe space, where rank and title don't matter ... this isn't your space, it's not my space.

CHAPTER FIVE

Why don't we call it the 'The Third Space'?"

"I like that. Let's give it a try. We could even put a sign up on the door of this room. We'll designate it as 'The Third Space,' a place for Third Space discussions.

"Alright, if that's settled, let's get down to the nitty-gritty. Jennifer, when can we start that focus group in Japan?"

Kathy gently placed a hand on Aaron's arm to intervene. "Aaron, I know where you're headed with this, but let's wait a bit longer before you put your 'leader hat' back on. If we want to ensure alignment, it's important we ask Jennifer and Carlos for their input first. May I? OK, thanks. Jennifer, Carlos, **what do you think are the next steps?** "

"Top of the list are confirming the cost and timing to air freight the product to Japan. After we settle that, my team will arrange for a second shipment of the ginger snaps via the normal sea routes."

"From my side, my team will work with our Japanese partners to let them know that we're starting with a limited release. We'll need to tweak the marketing campaign so that we can generate further buzz when the initial product sells out. Carlos, we'll need to liaise with you regarding the sea shipment so that we can plan the next wave of publicity accordingly.

"At the same time, we'll put together focus groups to research the viability of mala chips. We'll form three groups — one in Tokyo, one in Osaka and another in Sapporo — to see if there are any noticeable regional differences."

"As for me, I'll prepare a brief document and a video outlining this new methodology, with guidelines for how and when our division should use the Third Space."

"Alright, that sounds good all around. Before we leave the room, though, I'd like to go around the table one last time to **confirm each person's responsibilities, deliverables and the timeline to complete them.**

"Carlos, let's start with you."

RAIN CLOUDS were gathering on the horizon. Aaron watched, from the 25th floor corporate lounge, as the sun tried to break through. Scattered thunderstorms were the norm this time of year, but it seemed the rain could just as easily dissipate as it could come pouring down.

As his gaze returned to the room, he noticed that Ajay had arrived, carrying an umbrella and wearing a sharp, white collarless shirt.

"Ajay, thanks for meeting me here. I always appreciate the view from this level. You can see the horizon, but when you look closely, it's not difficult to zoom in on the details, like the kite flyers over there on the barrage or the Maersk container ships farther out, waiting to come into port. Grab a cup of coffee and join me over here by the window."

After Ajay settled in and they had chatted for a bit, Aaron shifted the conversation.

"Ajay, as you know, I wanted to follow up with you about our sustainability initiatives and your trip to Indonesia. First, though, let me share with you that I had a great meeting with Carlos, Jennifer and Kathy. We managed to sort out the snafus around the product launches, talk about the source of the misunderstanding and, by the end of the discussion, bring everyone onto the same page."

"That's great, Aaron."

"We also used a new methodology that Kathy has developed. She calls it 'The Third Space.' It worked so well I thought we could try the same approach this morning." After explaining the ground rules, Aaron continued, "Alright, I'm taking off my leader hat. Remember, you can ask me anything in this conversation as well. To kick this off, let me start by acknowledging that I know you do great work, and you've also been with Cascade Snacks a lot longer than me, so I appreciate your perspective. Given that, **what is your take on our sustainability initiative and how it fits into the business strategy?**"

"At first, I thought sustainability was an area for the marketing department. I've seen a number of initiatives come and go here at Cascade, pretty much the same as anywhere else, I imagine, and I figured sustainability would be a fad or something, quite frankly, we would provide lip service to. However, it's become clear that ESG goals are becoming a required checklist not just for regulators, but for investors and the public as well. **What do you think?**"

"I agree that sustainability is becoming a requirement. Consumers are increasingly making decisions based on whether they feel an affinity for a brand, and that sentiment links back to the brand's values. I'm also not sure if you know this, but Cascade Trading is planning to publish an annual Sustainability Report, starting next year. Every division, including ours, is expected to contribute to it. Ajay, **what changed your mind about our division's sustainability plans?**"

"I've been keeping my eye on the market and on our competitors. But I think I have to say that my recent trip to Indonesia was really an eye-opener. There are so many new innovations and they're not that expensive. In fact, they should make us more efficient."

"When we discussed this in the team meeting, I asked how much time would be needed to implement the required changes in our existing facilities. You said it would take seven to nine months. The Indonesian facility, on the other hand, could start manufacturing our products within a matter of weeks. I suggested that we could take a dual-track approach and initially

CHAPTER FIVE

outsource production to Indonesia until the Philippines' plants are ready. You indicated, though, that you're hesitant to do this.

"Ajay, tell me, **what issues do you foresee** if we outsource some of the new products first — until the upgrading in the Philippines is completed?"

"From my experience, outsourcing always presents pitfalls and unnecessary challenges."

"Could you elaborate on that?"

"There are hidden costs and things can be lost in translation. I'd have to assign several people to be in the plant to supervise the work."

"OK, we can do that. **What else?**"

"Quality control can be an issue."

"But you've visited the plant and were impressed by their work, weren't you?"

"Yes, that's true, but we don't know how long it took them to get there with each client."

"Ajay, I understand the issues you raise, but it seems they could be managed. **Is there anything else standing in the way that you haven't shared yet?**"

"We're speaking frankly here, right?"

"Yes, of course."

"I've worked too hard and too long at Cascade to be sidelined by outsourcing!"

"Sorry, what do you mean?"

"It's a slippery slope, Aaron. Once we start outsourcing a couple products, even temporarily, it may not be long before Cascade decides to outsource altogether. Then what happens to my role? It's either redundant or not nearly as important."

"Ajay, let me assure you: in no way is your job in danger. Regardless of where or how our products are made, you have a key role to play. I want you to oversee the upgrade and transition of our in-house facilities. We don't have two or three quarters, though, to wait while these initiatives come online. Perhaps if we had started earlier, but I was late in coming to the table on this. I was too focused on the other aspects of our plan. I neglected the sustainability component, and now we have to play catch-up."

While they were speaking, it had started to rain outside. Thunder boomed in the distance as the storm washed away the dirt on the streets below. Aaron had never spoken so frankly with one of his direct reports, let alone admit a vulnerability as he had just done. It needed to be said, though. Ajay had taken a chance by opening up. It was only fair that he did the same.

"Ajay, please, work with me. Let's make Cascade Snacks the benchmark, within our company and beyond, for sustainable *and* cost-efficient production. You're not being sidelined. We need your expertise to ensure that production in all our facilities, both in-house and out, runs smoothly."

"Alright, Aaron. I'm on board. **Let's work through the details.** My first question is, where should we set our carbon footprint goal? And will we permit carbon offsetting or should all the reductions be accounted for within the production facilities?"

A SERVER IN A WHITE FLORAL *cheongsam* lifted the ceramic teapot from the burner and poured fresh imperial *pu'er* into matching pomegranate cups, first for Mark, then for other members of the team. As she made her way around the wooden, Japanese *chabudai* tables, which rose less than a foot off the ground, Mark savored the tea's vibrant, healthy scent.

Mark had invited Aaron and his leadership team to Tea Chapter, a tea house located in a traditional three-story shophouse, for a workshop and ceremony. They learned about the rituals of brewing tea leaves, as well as the characteristics of white, red, yellow, green, black, Oolong and floral teas. Who knew that the size of the cup could influence the taste? The amount of porcelain in contact with hot water, they learned, affects the strength of the beverage.

After the workshop, they retreated to the quiet of the tea house for savory snacks and a six-course tea tasting menu. Aaron, Kathy and Selena sat at the same table as Mark.

"Did you know that Queen Elizabeth herself enjoyed a cup of tea right here at this very table?" Mark asked. "Okay, maybe not at this low table. I can't see her sitting on the ground like us, but here in this room." He pointed to a photo of the British monarch, who had visited here in 1989. "The monarchy has undergone colossal changes during Queen Elizabeth's reign, but there she is, still at the top, smiling all the same."

Servers brought the next course of snacks — chilli crab buns, a distinctly Singaporean dish (though Malaysians might beg to differ).

"Everyone, may I have your attention for a moment," Mark said, after standing up and surveying the room. "I want to thank you for joining me here today. I hope you've enjoyed the workshop. I'm struck by the mix of cultures in this room, not just among our team, but on today's menu as well. It seems an apt metaphor considering the success of your division's new product lines and the way you cross-marketed snacks from one country in the region to another.

"I would like to acknowledge each and every one of you. Cascade Snacks did not have an easy task in front of it, and there were times when it looked like you would not be able to meet the challenges. You have more than risen to the occasion, though. You have proved yourselves to be leaders.

"Our brands are flourishing. Profits are up. Our snacks are healthier than ever, which is so important because we are helping to stem the rise of diabetes and obesity in the region. We know, though, that while nutrition may encourage consumers to try our products, they wouldn't keep coming back if the snacks didn't taste so damn good!

"I'm also impressed by the sustainability initiatives this division has undertaken. Our plants are top of the line, and I see we are becoming more involved in the communities where they are located as well. So, here's to Cascade Snacks!"

"Hear, hear! *Hear, hear!*"

After Mark sat back down again, he turned to Aaron and Kathy. "Congratulations, again. I'm proud of you. Since you began working together, Cascade Snacks has really turned the corner. Tell me, what do you think has been the key to your success?"

"Mark, I don't have a single answer to that question, but I've been thinking about it and I'd say there have been four keys to our performance," replied Aaron. "The first is *Purpose*. We placed Purpose back at the center of our projects. This reminds everyone of why we come to work every day and what we are here to achieve.

"Purpose encourages *Proactivity*. This is the second key. Proactive team members are engaged team members; they become leaders in their own right. I've learned to respect and encourage this, to see how I can support, not micro-manage. I have to admit, this doesn't always come easily to me, so that leads to my third point: *Practice*. I've been practicing my leadership and management skills, nearly as much as my chip shot. I couldn't do this without the support of Kathy and the HR team, which brings me to my fourth point: the importance of *Partnership*."

"That's an awful lot of P's, Aaron!" Mark joked. "Purpose, Proactivity, Practice and Partnership. You may be on to something there! Seriously, though, Aaron, looking at you and listening to you, it's like night and day compared with our conversations a year ago. You've not only risen to the task, you also strike me as being happier and significantly less harried than before."

"Ha, overall, you're right! Don't get me wrong. There are still challenging days and times when I feel my blood pressure rise. But when this happens, I take a moment. I pause and reflect. I know my team and I are all working toward the same goals, so if something unexpected does arise, we just need to address and discuss it together."

"Kathy, what about you? What do you think has been the key to Cascade Snacks' success?"

"Mark, you empowered me to play a greater role. Like Aaron said, I've been a true HR business partner for the snacks division. HR may not even be the right term anymore. I feel like we are growing people and growing the business, rather than managing people like resources.

"The key to this growth, I think, is that we set up a model for organizational success in which everyone on the team feels empowered and responsible for success. On top of that, we created a process for dialogue, so that anyone in the division can meet with anyone else, regardless of rank, to hash out issues in a psychologically safe, nonhierarchical space.

"Personally, I also discovered the importance of asking the right questions … and posing them in a way that does not put people on the defensive."

"Our team culture has changed over the past year," chimed in Selena. "I know my opinion is valued. Even if I have an idea that's outside my area of expertise, I can still share it. These different perspectives make us stronger.

"Plus, Kathy hasn't kept her methodologies to herself. She's trained all of us on how to use the 'Funnel of Understanding' and call 'Third Space' meetings."

"Do you believe this methodology, and Cascade Snacks' success, can be replicated in other divisions?"

"I think it can be, Mark," Aaron replied.

"Yes, I don't see why not," Selena added.

"Kathy, what about you? Is there anything about this approach that is specific to the F&B industry or to the people involved?"

"No. Like anything else, the people involved should be open-minded, but aside from that, I have no doubt we could apply this approach throughout Cascade Trading, and after some time, the results will speak for themselves."

"I believe you're right, Kathy. Aaron, I hope you can spare Kathy some time. She's going to be mighty busy in the days ahead, helping us roll out this new model throughout the company.

"Kathy, how does the new job title, Human Capitalist, sound to you?"

KATHY SMILED, and with that, the initial tale of Cascade Trading comes to a close. Aaron and his team successfully met and exceeded the targets set by Mark when Aaron first joined the company. Collectively, they've agreed upon a new set of stretch goals.

Spicy Ginger Snaps have taken Japan by storm. They are not yet the M&Ms of a new generation, but if Jennifer Yacob has anything to do with it, they will be before long.

Ajay Singh has expanded Cascade Snacks' production network. He's taking a course to get an ESG certificate, which he expects should boost his earnings potential over the long run. In the meantime, he has invested his entire bonus in a European startup that reduces container ships' fuel consumption.

Selena Tan's daughter, whose concerns about the environment prompted her mother to research sustainable manufacturers, has started volunteering with a cooperative in the Philippines that sells seaweed-based packaging to Cascade Snacks. She can occasionally be a thorn in Ajay's side, but despite appearances to the contrary, he doesn't really mind.

Aaron Chua no longer keeps a bottle of Pepto-Bismol by his desk. He has taken up yoga, continues to spend time on the Leadership Driving Range and meets regularly with Mark. During these meetings, he always offers to help.

Your Turn: Four Questions for Reflection

"READING is not just turning printed signs into sounds. Reading is something deeper. True reading means hearing what the book has to say and pondering it — perhaps even having a conversation in your mind with the author."

— *Simón, a character in* The Death of Jesus, *a novel by Nobel laureate and two-time Booker Prize winner, J.M. Coetzee*

AS OUR TALE of Cascade Trading comes to an end, we invite you to have a conversation with the characters in the story and with us, the authors, as well. Don't keep your reflections in your head; write them down!

1. What ground rules did Kathy set during her first Third Space meeting?

2. Review the conversation between Kathy, Jennifer, Carlos and Aaron, and draw a Funnel of Understanding.

    (a) Which questions in this discussion are Reflective Questions? Where do they go in the funnel?

    (b) Identify the Critical Thinking and Challenging Questions from this discussion and place them in the funnel as well.

    (c) Which questions appear outside the funnel?

3. Identify an issue in your current workplace that would benefit from a Third Space discussion.

    (a) Draw a Funnel of Understanding.

    (a) List the issue at the top of the funnel.

    (b) What questions could participants ask each other to foster a mutual understanding of the issue and arrive at a consensus solution? (For a list of sample questions, refer to Chapter 4.)

4. Did Aaron practice Active Listening in his discussion with Ajay? If so, how? If not, how might he have conducted the conversation differently? Be the author: write a dialogue in which both Aaron and Ajay actively listen.

CHAPTER FIVE

Be Aware

1. When you first hold Third Space discussions in your company, it may be useful to have a neutral facilitator to explain the ground rules and start the questioning.

2. Once you and your colleagues are familiar with the methodology — and it shouldn't take long to learn — you can hold a Third Space discussion at any time, in any place, without a moderator.

3. Any member of the team can request a Third Space discussion.

4. The Funnel of Understanding begins with broad, reflective questions. As the dialogue progresses, questions become more specific until alignment is reached and the details of implementation are understood and agreed upon by all parties.

5. Issues-based discussions in the Third Space may become tense when participants maintain a vested interest in the outcome. When this happens, take a step back to list the facts of the matter and examine them from different perspectives.

6. Third Space dialogues may be derailed by underlying issues. If two or more participants are at loggerheads and unyielding in their views, ask them to explain why they feel so strongly.

7. Decisions are often framed as "either-or," one direction or another, when the solution may actually be "either-and," with both approaches being pursued, at least initially, toward an agreed-upon outcome.

8. Don't forget to build the foundations of the model prior to entering the Third Space. Employees should be Proactive Self-Leaders who take personal responsibility for the success of the organization, while Human Capitalists are committed to growing people and recognized as the stewards of corporate culture.

9. Celebrate your successes. Team outings, bonus payments and authentic praise are important tools to boost engagement and morale.

10. Large companies may want to see a proof of concept before implementing the Enterprise Leadership Model. While adopting the model throughout the organization may save time in the long run, a pilot project can be done first within a single division.

THE ELM FIELD GUIDE

How to Implement the Enterprise Leadership Model

THE FIELD GUIDE

THE MODEL

THE ENTERPRISE LEADERSHIP MODEL provides a process to ensure that team members are hyper-aligned and working together for organizational success. It is based on an understanding that traditional forms of hierarchical leadership inhibit innovation, suppress engagement and are counterproductive when applied at the wrong times.

The vast majority of business and organizational thought focuses solely on the top — how can leaders lead better? But in so doing, organizations ignore the people who are essential to their success, the team members and working groups who are relegated to the status of "followers."

Leadership theories still have their place. Regardless of which model your organization prefers, it can never be fully realized until the entire team is aligned for success.

What does your organization need to know to introduce and implement the Enterprise Leadership Model? What are the expectations and best practices for everyone involved? How do the different players interact for organizational and personal success?

The pages that follow in this Field Guide provide an overview. First, though, it is important to understand that several key transformations are required before you can activate the Third Space.

The First Space

IF YOU HAVE NOT YET adopted the Enterprise Leadership Model, you are likely operating, along with most organizations, in the First Space *(see fig. 1)*. Hierarchy and the vertical chain of command dominate decision-making, implementation and governance. Miscommunication, a disengaged and disillusioned workforce, high turnover and burnout are commonplace. Change management is frequently unsuccessful.

The Second Space

ORGANIZATIONS MUST implement two parallel transformations to enter the Second Space, where team members are actively engaged in the pursuit of institutional success and organizations are equally committed to the growth of their people. The first transformation, in which we banish

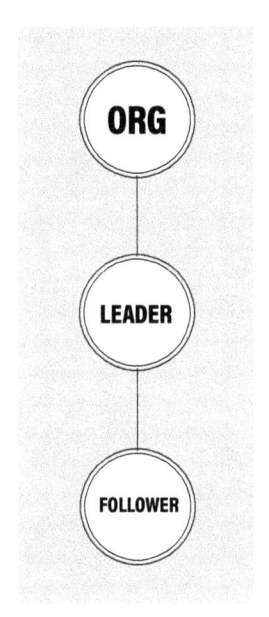

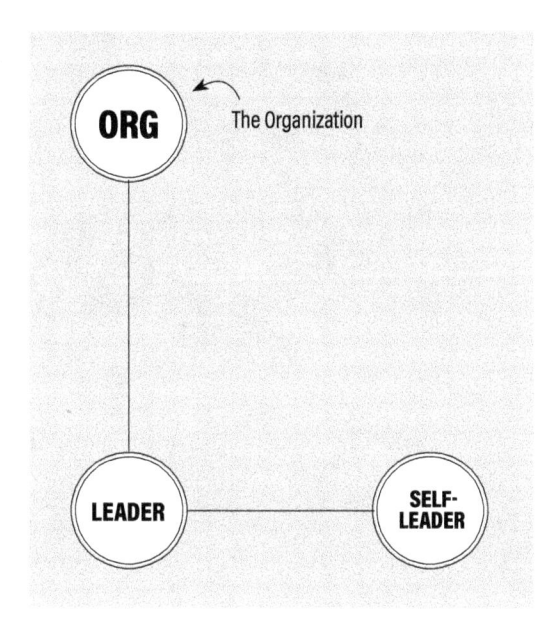

Fig. 1 The First Space

Fig. 2 An initial step into the Second Space

the term "follower," occurs throughout the organization, while the second takes place in the department currently known as "Human Resources."

Transformation #1

THE MISCOMMUNICATION prevalent in organizations is a result of the Tower of Babel effect, which is described in more detail in Chapter 2. Like a children's game of "telephone," messages morph as they are passed down the line. Important details are lost; entire messages can be distorted. To address this, leaders and team members alike require a clear view of the organization, which must stop filtering important communications about strategy and change *(see fig. 2)*.

Clearly communicated, broadly disseminated change management reduces employee anxiety and increases engagement. Team members gain a better understanding of business strategy, corporate structures and new projects. Followers become Self-Leaders, who are empowered and encouraged to ask questions and provide feedback in pursuit of organizational success. Self-Leaders actively want to improve. They are more likely to accept, or even volunteer, for new projects and responsibilities in order to learn and advance their careers.

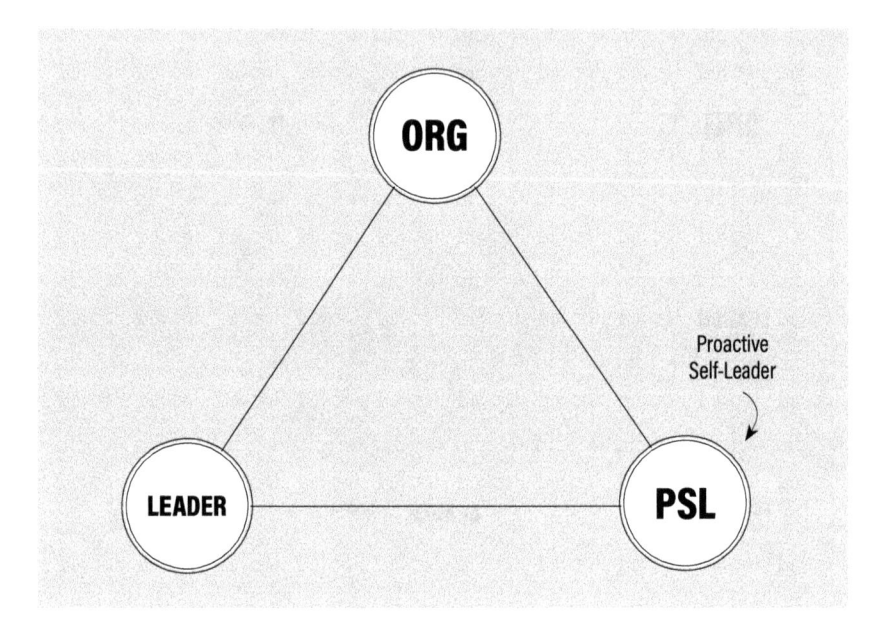

Fig. 3 Transformation #1 in the Second Space

Being a self-leader is a step in the right direction, but it is not sufficient.

In the Enterprise Leadership Model, team members accept personal responsibility for the success of the organization. They want their projects to succeed, not simply because it may help their careers, but also because they take pride in their work and believe in the organization's purpose.

In practice, how do team members do this?

One of the most essential components of leadership is proactivity — looking to the horizon and actively working to achieve a vision. Self-Leaders adopt this same practice. They ask themselves, "What can I do today to support the organization to be successful?" They take initiative, rather than waiting for assignments, and become Proactive Self-Leaders. With this step, Leaders and Proactive Self-Leaders are equidistant from the Organization. They are working together for its success *(see fig. 3)*.

There are two ways to accomplish this step and foster proactivity: through proclamation or purpose.

An organization can proclaim that the Enterprise Leadership Model is part of its culture and that every individual is expected to be proactive. Organizations must explain what this means and how to implement it, namely the expectations and best practices for each role.

The shift to proactivity and personal responsibility can also happen

THE MODEL

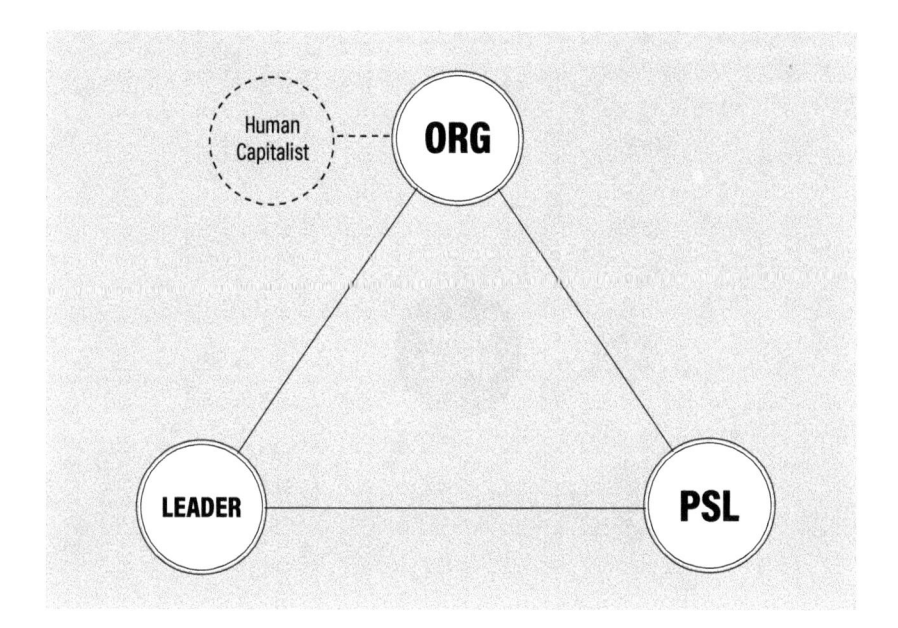

Fig. 4 Transformation #2 in the Second Space

organically when team members embrace an organization's purpose. Purpose-driven organizations stand for more than profits, sales and services. To this end, the purpose must be authentic and should guide all decisions made by the entity.

Transformation #2

MANY COMPANIES and leaders say, "People are our most important asset," yet their practices do not reflect this. Instead, employees are managed as resources, while HR professionals spend their time fighting fires, reconciling hiring numbers and managing a myriad of administrative issues like vacation days, salary increments and security access.

As ELM organizations drop "follower" from their lexicon, so too must they banish the term "human resources." To fully enter the Second Space, organizations transform their HR departments into divisions that think strategically, embody corporate culture and are focused on creating value, namely "Human Capital."

Human Capitalists are business partners, consultants and strategists who support the growth of people. They are best placed to represent the Organization *(see fig. 4)* — to embody its purpose, mission and values and

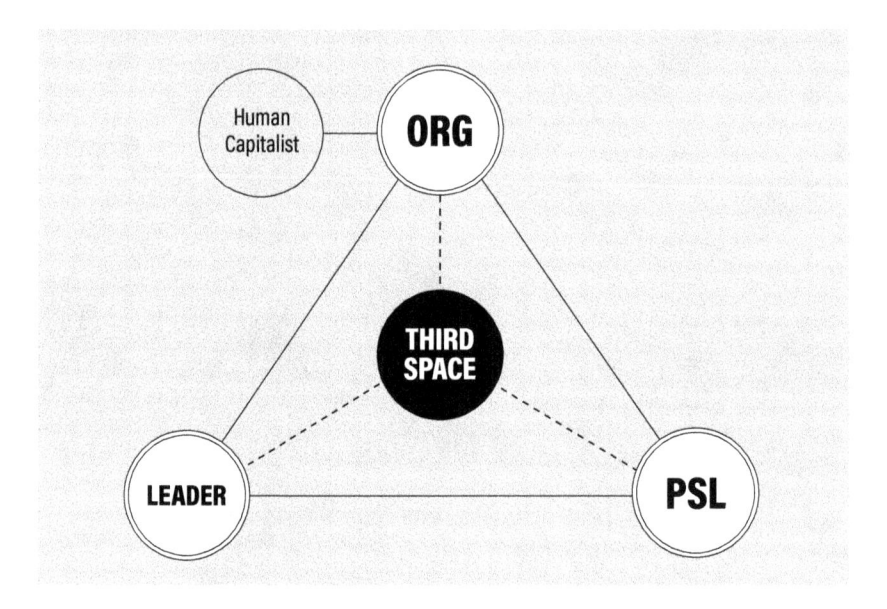

Fig. 5 The Third Space

ensure these principles are integrated throughout its people processes, from recruitment through training, staffing and performance management.

This shift from Human Resources to Human Capital, which occurs in tandem with the creation of Proactive Self-Leaders, is one of the most fundamental transformations of the model. It can be driven from above through proclamation or from below by qualified people professionals who demand change and a seat at the senior leadership table.

The Third Space

THE TRANSFORMATIONS of the Second Space are essential building blocks of the Enterprise Leadership Model. Working in the Second Space empowers and engages team members, while creating an environment that grows people and embeds an organization's values throughout its people processes.

Misunderstandings and misalignment can still occur in almost every entity, though, and an organization's entry into the Second Space does not prevent this. Hierarchy makes it difficult, if not impossible, to avoid or quickly rectify areas of misalignment. To do this, companies must take a further step, into the Third Space *(see fig. 5)*.

The Third Space is a nonhierarchical, psychologically safe space for

THE MODEL

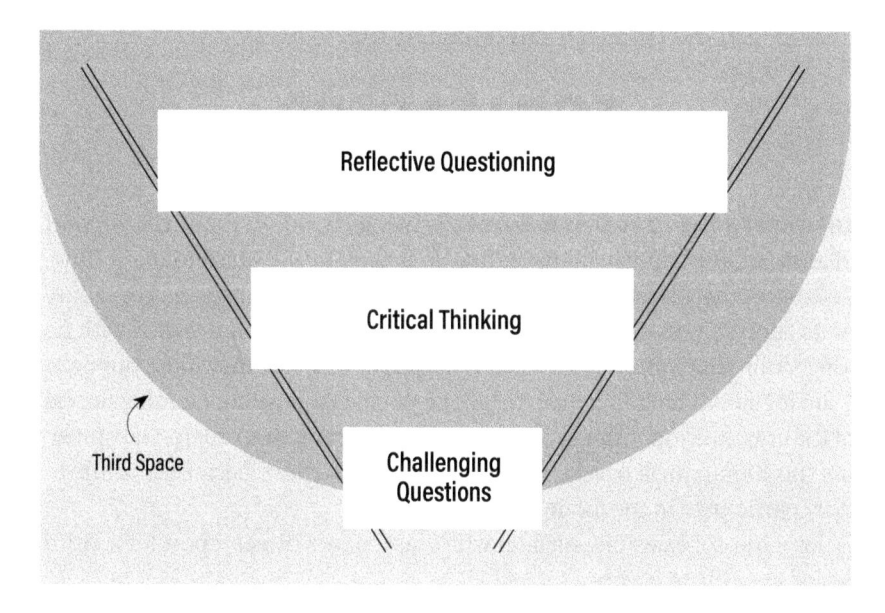

Fig. 6 The Funnel of Understanding

resolving issues, fostering understanding and achieving hyper-alignment.

Third Space discussions are like a funnel with broad questions at the top and specific action points at the bottom *(see fig. 6)*.

This "Funnel of Understanding" starts with reflective questions that are intended to elicit thoughtful replies and allow new possibilities to emerge. As the dialogue progresses, questions are designed to promote critical thinking and challenge participants to refine solutions. By the time they exit the funnel, team members are not only aligned around solutions, they also understand and have agreed upon the steps required for implementation.

THE PROCESS OF ACTIVE LISTENING — which requires being present, withholding judgment and reflection, as well as seeking clarifications and restating a speaker's key points to ensure alignment — is an essential component of Third Space discussions (and a good practice to apply to all communications).

Any member of the team can call a Third Space meeting and, within the funnel, any participant can pose questions to others, regardless of their rank and role. Third Space discussions may take time initially, but the payoff once alignment is achieved is clear.

At times, organizations need to slow down in order to speed up.

THE FIELD GUIDE

FOR LEADERS

THE ENTERPRISE LEADERSHIP MODEL is like a tripod. Without the support of each leg, the tripod will topple and your camera will crash to the ground. Leaders occupy a unique position in this model and the success or failure of its adoption rests heavily on their shoulders. Leaders are tasked with no longer thinking from a hierarchical perspective. Instead, they must empower team members, enabling them to take personal responsibility for the success of the organization. After a career of giving and receiving orders, transforming this hierarchical psyche requires a conscious effort, because a failure to fully participate in the model can destroy it.

Imagine, for example, a leader who is asked by a direct report for a Third Space meeting to clarify a project.

"I've found myself hesitating," the direct report says. "I'm not sure if we're properly aligned. Can we hold a Third Space meeting to discuss it?"

"I've already explained this to you," the leader replies. "This is easy. Why don't you get it?"

In the face of such an attitude, will the direct report ever request a Third Space meeting again? Not likely.

All too often, leaders worry that if they allow direct reports — or worse, employees further down the pecking order — to question them, their authority will be eroded. Quite the opposite is true.

Enabling Proactive Self-Leaders to pose questions, in the right way, within the framework of the model, contributes to greater engagement and productivity, while reducing leadership stress and enhancing leaders' capability to think strategically. Team members' respect for leadership increases, while a leader's authority remains constant. Leaders are still responsible for hiring, developing people's careers and dismissing, if necessary. What changes is a leader's expectations of team members because, in the Enterprise Leadership Model, everyone has personal responsibility and is equidistant from the Organization.

How to Be a Leader in the ELM

LEADERS ARE TASKED WITH fostering an environment that encourages proactive self-leadership so that team members are motivated and engaged to work together for the success of the organization.

To this end, leaders are responsible for:[1]

- Creating a safe environment for innovation and change
- Focusing on the future
- Aligning performance
- Developing new leaders
- Celebrating individual and team success

Expectations of an ELM Leader

- Takes personal responsibility for the success of the organization
- Understands and can articulate an organization's purpose, mission, vision and values and how these relate to specific areas of work
- Supports team members to be Proactive Self-Leaders
- Actively supports team members' work
- Looks forward to being challenged
- Available for Third Space discussions, when requested by colleagues
- Utilizes the Third Space to identify solutions and foster alignment
- Understands that hierarchy and ego have no place in the Third Space
- Actively practices and hones skills on the Leadership Driving Range *(see Chapter 3, p. 79 to learn more about the LDR)*

Best Practices for Leading in the ELM

Alignment and Influence[2]

- Inspire members to take greater responsibility
- During team meetings, if you sense that your team is not aligned, schedule a Third Space meeting with the relevant members as soon as possible

Coaching

- Be a "Leader-Coach"[3]
- Effectively challenge and coach team members
- Demonstrate a passion for growing the capabilities and capacities of colleagues
- Support Proactive Self-Leaders to grow within the organization

- Actively listen to your colleagues — paying attention to facts, values, feelings and worldview — in order to fully understand *(refer to Chapter 4, pp. 126-129)*

Empathy[4]

- Exercise Empathetic Leadership by seeking to understand team members' feelings, thoughts, opinions and needs
- Watch for signs of burnout

Feedback[5]

- Provide affirming feedback, as well as adjusting feedback for areas that require improvement or a different approach:
  - → Banish the words "positive" and "negative" from your feedback vocabulary. No one likes to receive negative feedback.
  - → Avoid providing "sandwich feedback," i.e., short praise, followed by a critique, then an affirmation to "keep up the good work." Team members only remember the stuff in the middle.
  - → Affirming feedback encourages habits that you would like to see repeated, while adjusting feedback provides guidance on how to improve work performance
- Watch how your team members perform and identify opportunities to provide feedback frequently and in a timely manner.
  - → Do not wait until an appraisal meeting to share feedback. (When feedback is delayed, a PSL may well reply, "If you had told me sooner, I would have made the required changes sooner.")
  - → Position feedback within the context of Situation, Behavior, Impact and Intention:[6]
    - ◇ Describe the specific situation where a behavior occurred
    - ◇ Describe the observable behavior
    - ◇ Explore the impact of the behavior
    - ◇ Ask the PSL about their intention
- Ensure that feedback is focused and relevant to a team member's role and professional goals
- Make clear linkages to provide context as to why the feedback is important

- Do not do all the talking. Actively listen to a PSL's questions and concerns
- Follow up to ensure action on the feedback is taken

Transparency

- Be transparent about organizational change
- Share your work so that Proactive Self-Leaders can contribute and support you

10 Ways to Challenge and Support Proactive Self-Leaders

ONE OF THE PRIMARY TASKS of a Leader is to enable team members to be Proactive Self-Leaders. As a Leader, you must challenge and support team members to:

1 Fully participate in the Enterprise Leadership Model
2 Understand what it means to take personal responsibility for the success of the organization and how to do this
3 Participate actively in team meetings and enjoy the process of interacting with leaders
4 Ask questions
5 Be curious, exercise initiative and support innovation
6 Receive feedback and learn from failure
7 Take responsibility for their personal and professional development
8 Be accountable
9 Receive recognition and celebrate individual and team success
10 Request Third Space meetings, without hesitation, whenever needed

Questions that Leaders ask PSLs

WITHIN the Enterprise Leadership Model, there are two places where Leaders and Proactive Self-Leaders interact: in the Third Space, where hierarchy does not exist, and along the base of the tetrahedron, where it does. Different types of questions are required in each environment. Along the base of the model, leaders should pose coaching questions to encourage team members to determine whether they are actively taking personal responsibility for the success of the organization. Examples of such questions include:

- How is your work supporting the purpose/mission/vision of the organization?
- What are your responsibilities (for this project, for our department's work)?
- What is the current state of the project? Describe your progress.
- What is the deadline? When will you accomplish this?
- What should I expect from you on *(insert day or date)* when you meet your deadline?
- How can we do better? How can we improve the process and outcomes?
- What support do you need from me?

The key in any organization is to produce. The tasks that you are required to do have to be done. These questions are intended to encourage PSLs to "think big" and set high expectations of themselves and what they can achieve.[7] In a similar vein, as leaders challenge PSLs to expand and grow, they also pose career-related questions to gauge the PSL's goals and encourage them to consider the skills and training needed to get there.

Leadership During a Time of Change

ORGANIZATIONS are in an almost constant state of flux. New projects, management reshuffling, external events all create uncertainty. During these periods, you can never over-communicate. A lack of communication creates anxiety among all team members, including other Leaders, Proactive Self-Leaders and Human Capitalists.

At the same time, leaders must also understand that no matter how hard they try to explain change, their communication is rarely heard precisely as intended, simply because everyone is different. It's important to have conversations about how change impacts individuals, as well as what it means for teams and organizations.

Best Practices During a Time of Change

1. Recognize that misunderstandings will happen
2. Communicate change as broadly as possible, in both big and small meetings
3. Be on high alert to listen for misunderstandings and areas of misalignment
4. Remember that Proactive Self-Leaders are purpose-driven. Their energy and time spent at work must link back to an organization's mission, vision and goals.
5. Be fluent in how to use the Third Space to achieve hyper-alignment and open to requests for Third Space discussions, as often as needed, when requested by any member of the team, be it another Leader, a Proactive Self-Leader or a Human Capitalist

Interacting with Human Capitalists

- **Recognize** the multiple roles played by human capitalists and leverage their experience as strategic business partners, internal consultants, executive coaches and repositories of organizational culture
- **Understand** that human capitalists are privy to information about team dynamics, project progress and anxieties related to change, based on their discussions with a leader's direct reports and other colleagues
- **Enable** and support human capitalists to institutionalize the Enterprise Leadership Model in the organization and to introduce the model to new team members
- **Schedule** regular conversations with human capitalists to strategize and discuss personnel and business issues
- **Welcome** suggestions, and make requests, regarding issues and skills to be practiced on the Leadership Driving Range

REMEMBER THIS

Every Leader is also a Proactive Self-Leader. COOs report to CEOs, chief executives report to Board Chairs, corporate boards report to shareholders. While leaders are responsible for enabling proactive self-leadership among team members, they must also exhibit proactive self-leadership when interacting with their bosses.

THE FIELD GUIDE

FOR PROACTIVE SELF-LEADERS

THE SECOND LEG of the ELM tripod consists of Proactive Self-Leaders. As with Leaders, PSLs must fully support the model; if not, it crashes to the ground.

But, as an employee, why should you want to be a Proactive Self-Leader? The short answer is: if you care about your career, this is the path to take. Becoming a Proactive Self-Leader will future-proof your success in an organization. It enables you to exert responsibility in your area of work.

Being a Proactive Self-Leader demonstrates that you:

(a) want to be engaged — actively engaged — in the organization
(b) expect your work to benefit the overall organization, not just your own division, and to be aligned with the organization's purpose
(c) are available to support your boss
(d) are willing to challenge the system, in a productive manner

By exhibiting a desire and determination to be involved, PSLs become someone that organizations and leaders can count on, and in the process, this enhances their reputation.

Some employees are natural Proactive Self-Leaders; others make a conscious decision to play this role. In either case, the key is to actively take personal responsibility for the success of the organization, every day and in every work action. Possessing an understanding and belief in the purpose of an organization — its raison d'être — and linking this purpose to every project paves the way for proactive self-leadership.

15 Expectations of a Proactive Self-Leader

1. Takes personal responsibility for the success of the organization
2. Understands and can articulate an organization's purpose, mission, vision and values, and how these relate to their areas of work
3. Asks for clarification when it is not clear how an area of work relates to an organization's purpose, mission, vision and values

4 Demonstrates initiative. Asks, "How can I help?" Does not wait for assignments.
5 Forges a connection between contribution and personal purpose
6 Assumes responsibility for their own personal and professional development and interacts on a regular basis with Human Capitalists
7 Demonstrates curiosity
8 Is actively involved in change
9 Challenges and supports leaders, as well as other PSLs
10 Participates actively in team meetings
11 Celebrates individual and team success
12 Actively supports the Work-Life integration of colleagues
13 Understands when to call Third Space meetings and utilizes it to identify solutions and foster alignment
14 Recognizes that hierarchy and ego have no place in the Third Space
15 Performs well and is successful in their current role

Best Practices for PSLs

THE ACTIONS that ground a Proactive Self-Leader, and ensure their success, start with an understanding of the term itself. What does it mean to be proactive? How does a Proactive Self-Leader exercise personal responsibility for the success of the organization? When does a PSL call for Third Space meetings and how do they act when they are held?

Proactivity

- Start each workday by asking yourself, "What can I do today to support the organization's success?"
- Ask your boss how you can support their work. What can you take off their plate?
- Look for opportunities to engage with leaders and other team members, always keeping in mind the objective of supporting the company's purpose, mission, vision and values
- Take responsibility for your personal and career growth. Continually look for opportunities to learn, train, improve and grow. Request access to training programs and resources when they do not appear to be available.

Exercising Personal Responsibility

- Think strategically. What is your next course of action? Ask, "What if? What if I did that … "
- Keep the organization's purpose, mission, vision and values in view, as well as the objectives of current projects and initiatives. Ask, "What do I need to do today to get to that horizon?"
- Take responsibility for your actions. Be accountable to yourself, your colleagues and the organization.
- Take responsibility for the actions of others, when doing so will have a positive impact on the company
- Think on your feet. Innovate. Consciously consider the best outcomes on a daily basis.
- Seek alignment

Alignment and Influence

- Memorize the organization's purpose, mission, vision and values (and if you don't know them, ask a Human Capitalist)
- Create a Personal Professional Vision Statement and a Statement of Values
- Ensure each work task — as well as your professional vision — is aligned and contributes to the organization's mandate and goals
- Participate actively during team meetings and ask questions to ensure there is alignment
- If you sense that you are not aligned, schedule a Third Space discussion
- Learn methods to influence leaders and colleagues in a positive manner[1]
- Inspire your peers to take greater responsibility
- Take the initiative to meet periodically in the Third Space to confirm alignment and discuss how to keep personal and professional vision and values aligned with work

The Third Space

- Engage in dialogue in the Third Space to build reciprocating, interdependent, collaborative relationships
- Have the confidence to call a Third Space meeting. This is a hallmark of a Proactive Self-Leader.
- Develop the ability to ask reflective, non-hierarchal questions
- Be comfortable asking the first question in the Third Space. Do not wait for a leader to go first.

PROACTIVE SELF-LEADERS may be leaders in their own right, with colleagues reporting to them. They are also leaders-in-training, aspiring to rise through the ranks. The price of admission to the next level is success in their current role. If you are a Proactive Self-Leader, the best practices that follow will help you achieve professional success and ensure the success of the organization.

Courage & Confidence

- Recognize that expectations of a Proactive Self-Leader are greater than those of a "follower." Accepting responsibility for the success of the organization necessitates accepting greater expectations for performance as well.
- Ask for assignments to be clearly communicated and be willing to question instructions
- Challenge leaders with the constructive use of affirming and adjusting feedback

Empathy

- Exercise effective listening to understand team members' feelings, thoughts, opinions and needs[2]
- Support your colleagues and watch for signs of burnout

Feedback

- Seek feedback and learn from failure
- Be at ease receiving feedback from leaders, human capitalists and other members of the team
- Act upon feedback, when provided

- Anchor feedback, both received and given, within the context of taking personal responsibility for the success of the organization
- Provide affirming feedback to leaders, when appropriate, to show appreciation for actions and policies that have a positive impact on you and the organization, as well as adjusting feedback when you believe a different approach is required
- Position feedback within the context of a specific situation *(what happened)*, observed behavior *(what they said or did)* and the impact on you *(what you thought or felt in reaction to the behavior)*[3]

Personal Growth

- Develop personal career vision and work values. Commit them to memory and share with your leader(s)
- Be receptive to being a coachee
- Recognize that coaching can come from multiple parties, including Leaders, Human Capitalists and even other Proactive Self-Leaders
- Begin the process of learning to be a Leader-Coach and learn techniques for asking open-ended questions

Transparency

- Share your work with leaders and other members of the team to ensure alignment and so that they can support you
- Ask for clarification the moment you hesitate about what to do next in order to ensure that time and resources are not wasted
- Share concerns with leaders and human capitalists regarding changes taking place in the team and organization

Questions that PSLs ask Leaders

ALONG THE BASE of the model, where hierarchy still exists, Proactive Self-Leaders interact with Leaders in a sort of reciprocal dance. PSLs ask questions in order to:

- **Determine** how they can best take personal responsibility for the success of the organization and, in the process, support other team members and leaders
- **Challenge** leaders, again with the aim of ensuring organizational success
- **Learn** how to grow their careers

At the same time, leaders pose questions to PSLs to coach them and to ensure that project outcomes are achieved.

Key Questions to Take Personal Responsibility for Success

- How can I support you (this week)?
- What do you think is the most important thing I should focus on this week?
- I have x-number of things I'm working on over the next several weeks. How do you suggest I prioritize them? What else do you think I should be doing?
- Here are three things I'm doing to advance this project. Is there a fourth?
- I'm working on an issue. This is my solution. What do you see as a solution?
- I'm struggling with an issue. This is what I'm trying to do. What else do you think I should be doing?

In response to these questions, a leader may often answer with a question. Consider the following:

PSL: I've been focused on expanding sales in the Midwest, but the returns are not high enough yet. What else should I do?

LEADER: What have you tried so far? Walk me through what you've done to move this project along.

PSL: Here's what we've already tried. What else do you think we should do?

LEADER: What other possibilities are there?

As a Proactive Self-Leader, you need to be coachable. This requires actively listening and considering a leader's answers. At the same time, the best leaders often guide their team members to a solution, rather than dictating one of their own.

Key Questions for Career Growth

POSING QUESTIONS about your career — to leaders and human capitalists — not only provides an opportunity to learn, it also obliges an organization to provide you with a clear path for growth. If not, and assuming you are a high-performing Proactive Self-Leader, they risk losing you to a competitor.

- What else do you think I should be doing in my role to be successful?
- What should I do differently to be more successful in this role?
- Based on my work to date, are there areas of expertise in which I need to become more proficient?
- What projects can I work on to expand my learning and development in specific areas, like project management, finance, etc.?
- What do you see as the time frame for my career development?
- What do I need to do next year to exceed expectations?
- If I do that and exceed expectations, what possibilities exist for me in the company?
- If I continue to do well, where do you see me in 12–18 months?

Challenging Leaders

PROACTIVE SELF-LEADERS may challenge leaders to interact with them, to explain strategies or decisions, to ensure alignment and to share possible solutions to issues that may be different from the leader's decision. However, challenges must always come from the standpoint of taking personal responsibility for the success of the organization. A challenge must be based on an issue, not personalities or ego. While PSLs are expected to have the courage and confidence to challenge leaders — and leaders in this model expect, and even encourage, challenges — Proactive Self-Leaders should frame, and preface, these challenges with respect. The approach is "soft," not direct.

What Not To Say

- "Why are we doing this?"
- "I don't think we should do that."
- "Your decision does not make sense to me."
- "I have a better idea. What we should be doing is . . ."

The questions and statements above are likely to put a leader on the defensive and will not result in a productive dialogue. That doesn't mean, though, that there is not a way to address the same issues from the standpoint of a Proactive Self-Leader.

What To Say and What to Ask

- "I would like to better understand why we are going in this direction."
- "Please help me understand how you came to that decision."
- "Help me understand this so that I can understand your decision-making better."
- "Could you please clarify my responsibility on this project?"
- "What actions should I take to deliver on this part of our strategy?"

Leaders are responsible for ensuring that their team is hyper-aligned and has the resources needed to achieve their goals. This second set of questions and statements tells a leader that the PSL is not aligned, but would like to be. Challenging a leader around alignment says, "I want to make sure what I'm doing is correct." A deeper explanation of the issue at hand, by the leader, is then needed to ensure that all members of the team expend their energies in the right area.

Suppose, though, that a Proactive Self-Leader does not agree with a decision made by a leader. Given that the leader still has the authority to dismiss or sideline members of their team, how can a PSL reasonably broach such an issue? How can they encourage a leader to reconsider their decision? In such circumstances, consider this approach:

> *"I've been thinking about this issue. Could I provide you with some alternative solutions?"*

A typical leader may think, "No. There's no need for this. I've already made a decision." But a Leader who leads Proactive Self-Leaders will think, "Multiple minds are better than one. I have talent on my team. I need to make the most of it." They will realize that the PSL thinks they have a better solution and instead of replying "no," will say, "Sure, go ahead. Let's think about a better alternative. Come back to me with ideas, along with a budget."

One exception to this approach, within the Enterprise Leadership Model, is when a project is already too far down the line to amend. In these situations, a leader will welcome the suggestion but note that, in this instance, it is too late to change course.

Challenging a Leader: An Example

A RADIO STATION constructs a studio with a small adjoining room for producers. There is a window between the two so that presenters and producers have a clear line of sight to signal each other. The multimedia team complains, though, that there is a glare off the glass when they are filming. To solve this problem, the leader commissions a large poster with the station's logo to cover the window. "Issue solved," he thinks. However, production processes and quality are compromised by the decision. The presenter and producer can still text via an app or speak via the control panel, but there are times when visual cues are more effective.

In a company that has adopted the Enterprise Leadership Model, how could this situation be addressed?

SCENARIO ONE

PSL: *(a producer)* The new window cover isn't working. I have a better idea. We should install a curtain or blinds that can be opened or closed.

LEADER: *(on the defensive)* The logo is great for multimedia. Use your phone or laptop to message the presenter.

SCENARIO TWO

PSL: I understand the glare from the window was affecting our Facebook Live streams. Could I provide you with some alternative solutions?

LEADER: *(who has yet to fully adopt the ELM)* We already have a solution. Why are you raising this now?

PSL: I'm concerned about our broadcasts. There are instances — like when the computer system freezes or we're having trouble connecting to a guest on the phone — when it's best if I can see the presenter to signal them.

LEADER: We opted for a cost-efficient solution because budget is an issue. Plus, the multimedia team likes being able to pan from the logo to the host.

PSL: Perhaps there are other solutions that could meet everyone's needs? Could we explore this?

LEADER: Alright, please get back to me with your ideas and the costs.

In the first scenario, the leader is resisting criticism and is not open to suggestions; the matter is already closed. In the second scenario, while the leader is initially hesitant, they realize the PSL is coming from a position of wanting to achieve success. As a result, they become more open to alternative suggestions.

Interacting with Human Capitalists

TWO KEY TERMS define a Proactive Self-Leader's relationship with Human Capitalists: proactivity and reciprocity.

A PSL cannot sit back and complain that an organization does nothing to grow their capacities and career. They have a responsibility to be proactive, to go to Human Capital to request training and discuss opportunities for career growth.

At the same time, this relationship is reciprocal. The Human Capitalist has a responsibility to approach PSLs to hold these same conversations. For example, when a PSL is promoted, a Human Capitalist may suggest specific areas of training relevant to the new role.

When to Meet with a Human Capitalist

- To discuss career advancement and areas for improvement
- To request training
- To be trained on the Leadership Driving Range
- When facing uncertainty around change or big picture issues, like an organization's purpose, mission, vision and values
- To request ideas, resources and suggestions regarding strategies and business projects

- If personal issues — outside the office or with other team members — are affecting your work

Keep in Mind

- Human Capitalists represent the Organization and they are your business partners. They are stewards of corporate culture and a source of unbiased understanding of an organization's purpose, mission, vision and values, which means they are well placed to provide an unfiltered view of change-related issues.

- In companies that have adopted the Enterprise Leadership Model, human capitalists are certified internal executive coaches. They can assist PSLs and leaders to hone their skills on a broad range of management and work-related issues.

- Welcome suggestions, and make requests, regarding issues and skills to be practiced on the Leadership Driving Range. If a human capitalist approaches you to suggest training, do not take offense. It does not mean that you are doing a bad job, but rather that you are being given an opportunity to grow.

- Be at ease interacting with human capitalists. Discussions can be confidential, when needed, and are designed to enhance your contribution, engagement and success.

REMEMBER THIS

Proactive Self-Leaders are often leaders in their own right. If not, they are leaders-in-training. Perform to the best of your abilities in your current role and avail yourself of training resources to continually grow and improve.

THE FIELD GUIDE

FOR HUMAN CAPITALISTS

HUMAN CAPITALISTS represent the Organization and underpin the Enterprise Leadership Model. The shift from Human Resources to Human Capital is one of the most fundamental transformations of the model.

When Human Capitalists are proactive and working effectively, it is as if the entire model is in motion; Human Capitalists make things happen. By actively listening and holistically observing operations throughout an organization, Human Capitalists break down silos. They look for synergies, notice conflicts and call Third Space discussions to promote alignment and resolve issues. They are constantly thinking about how to meet an organization's current and future human capital needs.

A Human Capitalist is a business partner, consultant, strategist and steward of corporate culture who supports the growth of people. Human Capitalists play a critical role promoting high levels of engagement in the organization and developing Proactive Self-Leaders.

Human Capitalists are also the only people in a company who can play all three roles in the Enterprise Leadership Model simultaneously; they are likely Leaders and Proactive Self-Leaders too. If you are a Human Capitalist, take note: you need to know this field guide, inside and out, including the expectations and best practices of each position in order to perform successfully.

This is a big ask. But when starting out in the field of human capital, do not think you need to master every skill immediately. Your organization will put processes into place to help you grow into the role. In addition, within the Human Capital department, there will be specialists. Some human capitalists may become experts in change workshops, while others will focus on coaching or strategic planning.

15 Expectations of a Human Capitalist

1. Takes personal responsibility for the success of the organization
2. Understands, articulates and is passionate about an organization's purpose, mission, vision and values, and reinforces these core tenets throughout the organization
3. Has a comprehensive understanding of an organization's strategy and operations

4   Is an internal business partner who provides the support, resources and guidance needed for business teams and the organization to be successful
5   Thinks strategically about human capital growth and challenges
6   Understands the Enterprise Leadership Model and supports its implementation throughout the workplace
7   Ensures that team members are hyper-aligned
8   Is a certified internal executive coach
9   Facilitates organizational change, strategic planning and leadership development workshops
10 Knows how to measure and foster high levels of employee engagement
11 Distinguishes between challenges that can be met by a human capitalist and those that require the input and guidance of other team members
12 Acts with positive intent and weaves this spirit into the fabric of the organization
13 Promotes the development and growth of Leaders and Proactive Self-Leaders
14 Respects confidentiality
15 Promotes an internal client-centric culture

HUMAN CAPITALISTS differ from human resource professionals in many ways. Top of the list is mindset. They focus on nurturing and growing people's careers by ensuring there are sufficient resources, training and coaching opportunities; creating the right positions for organizational success and filling them with the right people; and ensuring that individuals and teams are hyper-aligned.

When a human capitalist takes personal responsibility for the success of the organization, they become an organizational consultant and internal business partner. They must think strategically. Even if there are specialists within the organization, the human capitalist poses questions to uncover systemic issues and spark solutions.

Learn the Process of Consultancy

ASKING THE RIGHT QUESTIONS to determine an organization's strengths and stresses is fundamental to being an organizational consultant. In this role, human capitalists pose questions to uncover systemic issues and facilitate discussions to remove the impediments that prevent success.[1] An overarching question is, "Are the organization's current systems the best ones to support its strategy and growth?"

Consultancy questions may include:

- Why are decisions taking so long?
- Why are there silos? Why are people not interacting across departments and teams?
- Is our current organizational structure the right one for success?
- Do we have the right rhythm and frequency of meetings?
- How often should we activate the Third Space?

As issues surface, the human capitalist shares their findings with senior leaders, then activates the Third Space to discuss and identify solutions.

How to be a Stellar Business Partner

- **Develop** your business acumen. Understand what an organization does, how it does it and what resources are needed to ensure success.
- **Gather** information. Hold regular discussions with everyone in your division to understand their pressures and progress. Look outside your department and industry to notice trends and learn from others.
- **Facilitate** dialogue. Activate the Third Space, in both individual and group discussions, to overcome difficulties, break down silos and foster hyper-alignment.
- **Build** relationships. Know when to coach and when to have talent conversations to grow team members' competencies and careers.

In the story of Cascade Trading, Kathy Thomas demonstrates that she is a stellar business partner by understanding the snack department's dual mandate to increase profits and sell more nutritious products. In the face of initial opposition, she suggests that the department hire a nutritionist and a sustainable sourcing manager, positions that had not been previously considered. Kathy realizes these additions will help the snack division realize its purpose and that this, in turn, is linked to higher levels of employee engagement, increased sales and overall success.

As a human capitalist, you can be a stellar business partner by developing your business acumen, asking questions and actively listening to the answers, thinking about the impact and implementation of new corporate targets and policies on teams and departments, and building the relationships needed for success.

Coach for Success

AS A HUMAN CAPITALIST — responsible for nurturing talent, growing careers and ensuring hyper-alignment — you must master a series of coaching skills and create a curriculum of topics for Leaders and Proactive Self-Leaders to practice on the Leadership Driving Range.

You should become certified in at least two disciplines. There are many possibilities, but regardless of which ones you choose, become steeped in the understanding of what it means to be a business coach.

Be prepared for leaders who ask you to coach members of their team — to assist under-performers or perhaps help plan for career progression — as well as team members who raise issues about their leaders. Keep your ear to the ground, so that you notice and can address issues quickly, by calling for Third Space discussions or offering coaching, whichever is appropriate.

In this regard, there are a number of coaching-related abilities that a human capitalist needs to master.

Coaching Skills

- Build trust
- Ask broad, open-ended questions to unlock new avenues of thinking
- Listen carefully and recognize that your next question often lies within the coachee's answer to the question you have just asked
- Implement, interpret and clearly explain diagnostic tests, including personality and 360-degree tests
- Differentiate between issues that require ad hoc coaching (1-2 sessions) versus those that demand longer-term support
- Challenge team members to open up, acknowledge issues and develop solutions

- Provide regular follow-up support, when required.
- Articulate a coaching process — with a distinct beginning, middle and end — that will create momentum for change in the coachee.

Modules for the Leadership Driving Range

THE LEADERSHIP DRIVING RANGE is a safe space where internal certified coaches lead team members through specific, work-related scenarios so that they can practice and hone their skills.

If your organization does not already have a set of LDR modules (perhaps under a different name), you should develop at least a dozen sessions, then add more to your library as the need develops. Initial topics could include:

- Conducting Talent Conversations
  (with sub-modules on performance and potential)
- How to Provide Affirming and Adjusting Feedback
- Articulating Purpose, Mission, Vision and Values
- Aligning Performance
- Activating and Operating in the Third Space
- Influencing Methods and Techniques
- Transitioning to a New Role: The First 90 Days [2]
- Conducting Team Meetings
- Understanding Workplace Paradoxes
- Leadership Agility
- Supporting Proactive Self-Leaders
- Empathetic Leadership
- Being a Leader-Coach

A typical LDR module runs 30-45 minutes and consists of role-playing as well as a brief overview of related principles and best practices.

Best Practices for Human Capitalists

Alignment and Influence

- Conduct regular discussions with leaders (your internal business partners) about their teams
- Survey employees to determine whether teams are aligned and operating efficiently
- Share issues with leaders in a manner that promotes understanding and encourages resolution
- Facilitate Third Space discussions when misalignment is present
- Organize strategic planning and change management workshops to foster alignment
- Be aware of all major changes occurring within an organization. Understand the anxieties associated with change and conduct workshops and Third Space discussions to address them.
- Break down silos to promote alignment. Conduct discussions about how teams and divisions can better interact.
- Be proficient in methods and techniques for influence[3]

Business Acumen

- Develop a comprehensive understanding of the organization, including:
  - → What it does
  - → How it does this
  - → Strategies for operation and growth, including the vision and rationale behind them
  - → How revenue is generated and accounted for
  - → The challenges and pressures faced by the organization and its leaders
  - → Issues articulated in its annual report and other strategic documents
- Grow the human capital to meet these needs. Determine what personnel and resources are required for the organization to be successful.
- Produce evidence-based, data-driven business cases with insights and proposals

- Be curious. Follow trends inside and outside the industry, focusing on issues that could impact a company's business and its people.
- Prepare for disruption. Watch for potential new competitors and innovation that may affect human capital.

Coaching

- Certified as an internal executive coach, with proficiency in at least two diagnostics
- Facilitate conversations with both Leaders and Proactive Self-Leaders to address challenges in the workplace
- Suggest frameworks to approach these challenges and work through each stage of the chosen framework with the appropriate colleagues and internal business partners
- Train team members to ask good questions, actively listen and respond with empathy
- Understand business partners' roles and the requisite skills needed to excel. Provide coaching in these areas on the Leadership Driving Range
- Challenge team members around specific areas of performance

Courage & Confidence

- Join and actively participate in discussions at the senior leadership table
- Be willing to challenge the status quo
- Be comfortable accepting challenges from team members regarding personal development opportunities and organizational purpose and values
- Support and challenge Leaders and Proactive Self-Leaders to take equal responsibility for the success of the organization
- Ask Leaders: "When is the last time you activated the Third Space?" and if there is a gap, ask why
- Ask PSLs: "When is the last time you asked your leader, 'How can I support you this week?'" and if there is a gap, explore why
- Challenge leaders when there are retention or workplace issues

Empathy

- Ensure resources, tools, processes and systems are in place to identify and support employees struggling with business and personal issues
- Train colleagues to listen effectively to understand team members' feelings, thoughts, opinions and needs

Exercising Personal Responsibility

- Take personal responsibility to create and sustain the Enterprise Leadership Model within the organization
- Hyper-alignment begins with you. You have the authority, responsibility and tools to intervene when misalignment is present.
- Acknowledge that you have responsibility to Leaders, Proactive Self-Leaders and the Organization itself
- Grow people to make the organization a success

Feedback

- Teach team members how to provide affirming and adjusting feedback and encourage the use of this system
- Actively solicit feedback from team members

Mindset

- Human capital growth, not human resource management
- Represent the whole organization by embodying and promoting its purpose, mission, vision and values. Always keep this in view, even if you have a specific area of responsibility.

Organizational Culture

- Build programs to foster organizational purpose, mission vision and values
- Support the connection between purpose and proactive contribution
- Understand that team members must embrace a cultural shift and new standard of norms for the Enterprise Leadership Model to be successful
- Support the adoption, understanding and implementation of the Enterprise Leadership Model by embedding it in all people processes,

including recruitment, hiring, onboarding, training, strategic development, operations assessment and conflict resolution

- → During recruitment, provide an overview of the Enterprise Leadership Model and define what is expected of Leaders and Proactive Self-Leaders
- → Train leaders how to present the model and pose questions about it to prospective employees during the interview process
- → During onboarding, reinforce how employees operate within the model
- → Encourage team members to exercise proactive self-leadership
- → Provide team members who do not exercise proactive self-leadership with opportunities to more comprehensively understand and apply the Enterprise Leadership Model or leave the organization

- Cultivate an understanding within the organization of a Human Capitalist's role and responsibilities
- Define, articulate and recognize stellar employee performance. Know what it looks like, what it doesn't, and what is not acceptable

Proactivity

- Engage the most senior people in an organization to ensure that the right leaders and workforce are in place to realize its purpose and vision for the future
- Start each workday by asking yourself two questions: "What do I need to do today to support better alignment within the organization?" and "What do I need to do today to support the organization's success?"
- Discuss strategic and human capital needs with business partners and other team members on a regular basis
- Ensure processes are in place so that your time is focused on planning for the future, not "fighting fires"

Supporting PSLs

- Actively partner with Proactive Self-Leaders to support their personal and career development
- Share resources and provide coaching sessions on the Leadership

Driving Range to enable team members to excel in their areas of responsibility and advance their careers

- → When a PSL is promoted, provide a shortlist of skills required for success in the new role and invite them to practice these skills with you on the Leadership Driving Range
- → Ensure that training grants, e-learning resources and workshops are available to support team members' growth

- Quickly recognize when team members are not performing up to standard and offer coaching, training and/or other required support to get them back on track

The Third Space

- Master the techniques of the Third Space — including reflective questioning, critical thinking, challenging questions and active listening (the Funnel of Understanding) — and ensure all team members are properly trained in this practice
- Reinforce when the Third Space should be used and remind Leaders and Proactive Self-Leaders about the ground rules *(see Chapter 4, p. 114)*
- Facilitate Third Space meetings, when the model is newly adopted in your organization, until team members are comfortable and competent holding these discussions independently
- Be willing to moderate Third Space discussions, when requested
- Call a Third Space meeting, or encourage team members to do so, any time you notice a lack of alignment
- Follow up with Leaders and Proactive Self-Leaders, in the days and weeks after a Third Space discussion, to determine if they are hyper-aligned and whether additional discussion is required

Transparency

- Be transparent about organizational change
- Ask questions to uncover and understand issues
- Trust, but verify

REMEMBER THIS

Senior leaders, such as the Chief Human Capital Officer, are expected to have a strong understanding of the process of consultancy, business partnership and coaching, in addition to acting as stewards of organizational culture. They do not need to be an expert in every discipline, as long as they know who within their department plays these roles. At the same time, junior members of the team cannot be expected to be proficient in every aspect of being a human capitalist, but they do need to be given opportunities to acquire these skills as they grow their careers.

THE FIELD GUIDE

FOR THE ORGANIZATION

SUCCESSFUL IMPLEMENTATION and adoption of the Enterprise Leadership Model requires the full support of everyone involved. Leaders, Proactive Self-Leaders and Human Capitalists all have a role to play, but the success of the model also depends upon the organization itself.

Organizations are like living, breathing entities. They grow, age and mature. They can even die, though your goal is normally to prevent their expiration (except in cases of an acquisition). Like its brand, an organization is constituted by all of its actions and operations. It has a culture, history and standard of norms. It also has a "brain," which is an amalgamation of the senior leadership team.

If the organization, and the senior leadership team working on its behalf, do not actively champion the model, through actions and words, the model may wither and die, like so many failed archetypes and initiatives before it.

Expectations of an ELM Organization

IF YOU WISH TO CREATE an environment where employees are valued and engaged, where purpose is paramount and team members are proactive and hyper-aligned, then you must ensure that the organization is fully behind the implementation of the Enterprise Leadership Model. In practice, this means:

- Developing the requisite systems and structures
- Dedicating time and sufficient resources
- Clearly communicating that the Enterprise Leadership Model is an integral component of the organization's culture

ELM adoption requires a mindset shift …

- Stop expecting leaders to be solely responsible for the success of the organization
- Recognize the importance of Proactive Self-Leaders and Human Capitalists
- Foster an authentic sense of organizational purpose

- Encourage all team members to be proactive and forward-looking

... as well as resource deployment to:

- Support human capital development
- Equip human capitalists to become internal certified coaches
- Develop the Leadership Driving Range
- Train leaders and those responsible for bringing new people into the organization to speak with confidence about the enterprise leadership corporate culture
- Ensure that every member of the organization understands the expectations associated with their role and how to use the Third Space

Organizations need to develop, promote and sustain a culture in which team members are enrolled in the Enterprise Leadership Model and can comfortably say, "We are an enterprise of Proactive Self-Leaders, Human Capitalists and Leaders who lead Proactive Self-Leaders. We activate the Third Space to achieve hyper-alignment. And we take personal responsibility, every day, for the success of the Organization."

For New Adopters

THE NUMBER-ONE thing to recognize when adopting the Enterprise Leadership Model is that organizational change does not happen overnight. Organizations need to allow 12–18 months for a transformation of this magnitude to be adopted, understood, embraced and internalized.

Team members must also be given the space to practice and fail. Their first attempts at Third Space discussions may not go according to plan; leaders may jump back into their hierarchical roles too quickly or participants may be too eager to rush to a solution in the Third Space.

Leaders — and the senior leadership team — must understand the imperative of "slowing down to speed up." There will be times when leaders are tempted to say, "We're too busy. The deadlines are too tight. We don't have time for a Third Space meeting. I'm just going to tell people what to do." But unless you take the time, organizational change breaks down. Your teams then risk being misaligned, projects will actually take longer to be realized and the results may not be optimal.

Checklist for New Adopters

- Have we dedicated resources to introduce and implement the change?
- Are we providing opportunities for Proactive Self-Leaders and Human Capitalists to accept personal responsibility for the success of the organization?
- Have we explained the Field Guide and discussed how it applies to our work?
- Are we clearly communicating the organization's purpose, mission, vision and values?

Best Practices

- Invest in human capital systems that support the model
- Develop and provide workshops to discuss the Field Guide for:
  - → Leaders who lead Proactive Self-Leaders
  - → Proactive Self-Leaders
  - → Human Capitalists
  - → How to activate and operate in the Third Space
- Be clear about the expectations of everyone involved
- Recognize that implementing proactive self-leadership requires a cultural shift
- Hire people who believe in the model and realize that those who do not accept it should leave the organization

This process may sound simple, but it will take time for leaders to fully realize that they must set hierarchy aside in the Third Space and support Proactive Self-Leaders as they exercise their responsibility for the success of the organization.

The Mindset Shift:
Obtaining the Buy-in of Junior Team Members

WHILE THE ENTERPRISE Leadership Model requires a mindset shift and new actions to be taken by every member of an organization, the adjustment may be particularly challenging for junior and mid-career employees. While they generally like the idea of a nonhierarchical safe space where their opinion is valued as highly as everyone else's, it can be difficult for them to believe that this space actually exists.

"The natural tendency of junior colleagues is to treat the meeting as a manager review," explains Mayu Arao, SK-II's vice-president for Japan. "But if they treat Third Space discussions like a performance assessment, this doesn't work."

Arao notes that it is almost as if leaders are telling their subordinates, "Let's be friends." It can be difficult to accept.

"There's always a fear of opening up," adds Arao's former boss, Sandeep Seth. "No matter what you say, in a big organization, people often believe they need to have all the answers before engaging management. They're worried they will sound stupid otherwise."

Human Capitalists have a large role to play here to set the right tone, while Leaders must also make a conscious effort to establish an atmosphere of trust.

Experience, though, is the best teacher. When Proactive Self-Leaders realize there are no repercussions for opening up, asking questions and sharing challenges, the Third Space culture will propagate itself.

Best Practices

- Be clear about why the organization is embracing the model. Explain how it can eliminate misunderstandings, heighten alignment, boost efficiency, increase engagement and enable teams to achieve their goals more quickly.
- Share real examples of projects that have run smoothly and others that have gone around in circles. Explain how the Enterprise Leadership Model has made a difference in these cases.

For Existing ELM Companies

1. Training New Employees

Employee turnover is a fact of life in any organization. People move on, they retire, switch jobs, take gap years and are asked to leave; new hires are constantly being made. The average annual employee turnover rate is 15-20 percent, possibly higher, depending upon the industry and region.[1] Organizations with high levels of employee engagement that also pay close attention to career advancement — such as those that adopt the Enterprise Leadership Model — may cut attrition rates in half. Still, that means there are a lot of new team members who need to understand the fundamentals of the Enterprise Leadership Model.

Best Practices

- Introduce recruits to the Enterprise Leadership Model during the hiring process
- Hire people who want to work in an ELM culture
- Conduct ELM workshops, for employees at all levels, within the first 30 days of onboarding

2. Measuring the Success of the Model

Organizations cannot simply provide training, then walk away. It is important to solicit feedback on a regular basis to determine if the model is being implemented and how it is working. Human capitalists should present the results of these surveys throughout the organization.

Best Practice: Conduct monthly pulse surveys to garner feedback

Possible Pulse Survey Questions

- Did you have a Third Space meeting this month? If *no,* why not? If *yes:*
    → How many Third Space meetings did you have?
    → On a scale of 1-10, how easy was it to call the meeting?
    → On a scale of 1-10, how beneficial were they?
- Do you clearly understand the objectives and next steps of your current projects?
- Have you discussed your work with colleagues from other departments who are working on the same initiative?

- Have you asked your team leader how you can support them this week?
- Have you met with your boss or a human capitalist in the past six months to discuss career growth?

3. Making a Commitment

All parts of the organization must make a sustained commitment to ensure that the Enterprise Leadership Model is embedded in the organization's culture and continues to be practiced. If not, you risk hearing, "Oh, we did this a few years ago, but we're not really using that anymore."

Keep in mind that the ELM and other leadership models are not mutually exclusive. Any system of leadership — servant leadership, transactional leadership, situational leadership, you name it — can fit inside the Enterprise Leadership Model. Regardless of the system chosen, the organization still needs Proactive Self-Leaders, Leaders who lead PSLs and Human Capitalists, as well as a safe, nonhierarchical Third Space to discuss issues, resolve conflicts and achieve alignment.

Best Practices

- Include ELM metrics in team members' Key Performance Indicators (KPIs) and performance appraisals to gauge whether they understand and apply the model
- Create and deploy tools, such as ELM Codes of Conduct, that should be reviewed annually by Leaders, Proactive Self-Leaders and Human Capitalists
- Communicate ELM success stories in the organization's annual report, share ELM tips and advice in internal newsletters and be willing to discuss ELM issues in town hall meetings
- Ensure that change management is communicated at multiple levels, in groups big and small

4. Fostering Proactivity with Purpose

At the heart of the Enterprise Leadership Model is a belief that proactivity should not be confined to the C-suite. Proactive Self-Leaders take personal responsibility for the success of the organization, and in the process, workplace engagement soars, leaders receive much-needed support and organizations prosper.

But how do you promote proactivity? Organizations can proclaim it from above. This works, but even better is to be a purpose-driven organization. People are motivated by purpose and they will take action to support it. For this to succeed, an organization must ensure that:

(a) its purpose is authentic, not just words on a website

(b) everyone within the organization knows the purpose

(c) everything the organization does — all its operations, plans and strategies— link back to and are consistent with the purpose

Many leaders have lost the ability to reflect on an organization's identity and purpose. It feels like there are just too many things to do in the day. When their team members become Proactive Self-Leaders, though, time opens up for strategic thinking.

Best Practices

- Revisit the organization's purpose, mission, vision and values annually. Do they resonate with team members and day-to-day operations?
- Establish systems that allow for contemplation, including workshops and Third Space discussions about purpose
- Produce reminders of the organization's purpose, such as physical cards and purpose-related pulse surveys
- When new policies, strategies and projects are introduced, ask, "Are these consistent with our purpose, mission, vision and values?" and "Are our actions arbitrated by purpose?""

5. Resourcing and Listening

When an organization asks every member to take personal responsibility for its success, it is more important than ever to ensure that every department is adequately resourced. Without sufficient personnel, time and resources, teams become shackled and discouraged. There is perhaps no better way to undermine the model than to expect excellence yet ignore resource constraints.

When obstacles occur, team members have a responsibility to flag them, regardless of their rank within the organization. The same goes for situations in which they believe the organization is not living up to expectations or adhering to best practices.

Best Practices

- Continually monitor resource deployment to ensure that teams have what they need to succeed
- Provide mechanisms for feedback, actively listen and take adequate steps to address issues

Guidelines for Operating in the Third Space

ACTIVATING AND OPERATING in the Third Space is simple. While there are a few guidelines and rules to follow, they are not complex. Any organization can adopt a Third Space culture; any member of the organization can activate the Third Space.

The initial transition to the Third Space will require patience and practice. At first, a human capitalist may facilitate discussions, but team members will become comfortable discussing issues in the Third Space independently over time.

Most important is to remember that the Third Space is a place and process, devoid of ego and hierarchy, to discuss issues, promote understanding, develop solutions and foster hyper-alignment, so that all parties are working together and in the same direction. It is a psychologically safe space where individuals can speak freely without fear of adverse consequences.

The first part of any Third Space discussion is to establish why the meeting has been called. It's up to the team member who requested the meeting to share the issue at hand in a succinct manner. Consider this to be a "Third Space elevator pitch" that is two minutes or less.

The most common follow-up then is to ask each participant for their understanding of the issue. "What is your understanding of the project?" Every person in the meeting should have an opportunity to reply, without interruption. Leaders may be tempted to interject with comments like "That's not what I said" or "You misunderstood me," but if they do, they should be reminded — most likely by a human capitalist — that there are no right answers, nor does a leader's opinion carry more weight in this Third Space discussion than anyone else's. The initial goal is for each individual to understand the perceptions of the others.

Third Space questioning follows a process — the Funnel of Understanding — that begins with broad-based reflective questions to enable team members to gather data so that they can make better-informed decisions. Gradually, the questions become more targeted until participants have agreed and are aligned on the objectives, next steps, deadlines and outcomes. More details about reflective questioning, critical thinking, challenging questions and active listening can be found in the second half of Chapter 4. Our friends from Cascade Trading, meanwhile, engage in Third Space discussions in Chapter 5 and in the subsequent section, Third Space Dialogues.

As with any conversation, it is essential that the right people participate. If there is a misalignment, for example, between marketing and logistics that has financial or budgetary implications, the issue can only be addressed if there are representatives from marketing, logistics and finance in the room.

Mastering the Third Space will take time and effort. Practice calling and holding Third Space discussions regularly. They will not always be successful, so be prepared to fail and learn from these failures. Within six months, your team will be good at operating in the Third Space. After one year, it will feel easy, and within 18 months, the time you have taken to "slow down to speed up" will definitely yield dividends as your organization operates at hyperspeed.

THE FIELD GUIDE

TOOLS & RESOURCES

Measuring ELM Impact

TO GAUGE the success of the Enterprise Leadership Model in your organization, at any given point in time, here are several metrics for your reference:

Employee engagement

A classic measure of employee engagement is Gallup's 12-question survey:[1]

1. Do I know what is expected of me at work?
2. Do I have the materials and equipment I need to do my work right?
3. At work, do I have the opportunity to do what I do best every day?
4. In the last seven days, have I received recognition or praise for doing good work?
5. Does my supervisor, or someone at work, seem to care about me as a person?
6. Is there someone at work who encourages my development?
7. At work, do my opinions seem to count?
8. Does the mission/purpose of my company make me feel my job is important?
9. Are my co-workers committed to doing quality work?
10. Do I have a best friend at work?
11. In the last six months, has someone at work talked to me about my progress?
12. This last year, have I had opportunities at work to learn and grow?

These questions are not meant to simply be a survey, but also to start conversations between the organization and its team members, discussions which can occur in the Third Space.

Retention

Closely linked to employee engagement are retention figures. Most large organizations calculate this percentage regularly — if you are not, you should. Turnover may initially spike when the Enterprise Leadership

Model is introduced, as employees who do not wish to accept personal responsibility for the success of the organization and leaders who do not want to give up the perks of hierarchy leave the organization. However, as the model is adopted and becomes part of your organization's culture, retention levels will rise.

Alignment

The Center for Creative Leadership has a tested framework for measuring and addressing Direction, Alignment and Commitment.[2] Survey questions measure whether:

- Work is aligned across a group
- The combined work of different individuals fits together
- Team members are coordinating their work effectively with each other and the group overall

Pulse Surveys to track Second Space and Third Space adoption

Many tools are available online, or within HR platforms, for conducting pulse surveys. It's important to survey team members at least once a month. Keep the surveys short and alternate between polls that focus on the Second Space (to gauge proactivity and human capital metrics) and those that track the Third Space. Examples of pulse survey questions can be found in *The Field Guide for the Organization, pp. 192-193*.

Sample ELM Codes of Conduct

TO DEMONSTRATE an organization's commitment to the model and reinforce its expectations of employees, consider drafting ELM Codes of Conduct for every team member. Remember that individuals often hold more than one role — they can be a Leader and Proactive Self-Leader, or even a Human Capitalist, Leader and Proactive Self-Leader — so they may need to acknowledge more than one ELM Code of Conduct.

TOOLS AND RESOURCES

TEMPLATE #1

A Leader's ELM Code of Conduct

I AM A LEADER who leads Proactive Self-Leaders. I accept personal responsibility for *[insert organization's name]*'s success and will work to create a safe environment for innovation, change and growth.

I affirm that I have read and understand our organization's ELM Manual, which includes a list of expectations and best practices for leaders. Notably, I agree to:

- Challenge, support, inspire and coach team members to become Proactive Self-Leaders who fully exercise their responsibilities to ensure organizational success
- Understand and articulate *[insert organization's name]*'s purpose, mission, vision and values, and how these relate to projects within my areas of responsibility
- Provide clear communication
- Welcome questions and accept challenges to my decision-making processes
- Actively listen to team members and be respectful and considerate of their views
- Utilize the Third Space to discuss issues, identify solutions and foster alignment
- Accept requests from my team for Third Space meetings
- Develop new leaders
- Celebrate individual and team success

In addition, I recognize the multiple roles played by Human Capitalists and will leverage their experience as strategic business partners, internal consultants, executive coaches and repositories of organizational culture. I welcome invitations to discuss issues and hone my skills on the Leadership Driving Range and will also proactively request coaching and training sessions.

Click here to acknowledge.

TEMPLATE #2

A Proactive Self-Leader's ELM Code of Conduct

I AM A PROACTIVE SELF-LEADER who accepts personal responsibility for *[insert organization's name]*'s success. I affirm that I have read and understand our organization's ELM Manual, which includes a list of expectations and best practices for Proactive Self-Leaders. Notably, I agree to:

- Work for the achievement of the organization's purpose, mission, vision and values
- Perform well and be successful in my role
- Start each workday by asking myself what I can do today to support *[insert organization's name]*'s success
- Support the work of my department's leaders by regularly asking how I can assist them
- Ask for assignments to be clearly communicated and be willing to question instructions to gain clarity
- Challenge leaders in a productive, non-confrontational manner
- Understand how to constructively provide affirming and adjusting feedback
- Demonstrate initiative and curiosity
- Actively listen to team members and be respectful and considerate of their views
- Speak openly, honestly and respectfully
- Actively participate in team meetings
- Ensure that my work is aligned with that of my colleagues and with the organization's purpose, mission, vision and values
- Utilize the Third Space to discuss issues, identify solutions and foster alignment
- Be proficient in posing reflective, critical-thinking and challenging questions to foster understanding and alignment in the Third Space
- Celebrate individual and team success
- Seek feedback and learn from failure

I also assume responsibility for my personal and professional development. To this end, I welcome invitations to discuss issues and hone my skills on the Leadership Driving Range and will proactively request coaching and training sessions from *[insert organization's name]*'s Human Capitalists.

Click here to acknowledge.

TEMPLATE #3

A Human Capitalist's ELM Code of Conduct

I AM A HUMAN CAPITALIST who accepts personal responsibility for *[insert organization's name]*'s success. I affirm that I have read and understand our organization's ELM Manual, which includes a list of expectations and best practices for Human Capitalists. In this role, I agree to:

- Be a steward of organizational culture who is passionate about [insert organization's name]'s purpose, mission, vision and values and can articulate and reinforce these core tenets
- Support the growth of people throughout the organization
- Learn and practice the process of consultancy and be a stellar internal business partner
- Develop Proactive Self-Leaders and promote high levels of employee engagement
- Coach for success

In this regard, I understand that I must:

- Think strategically about *[insert organization's name]*'s human capital needs
- Develop a comprehensive understanding of the organization's business
- Build programs to foster *[insert organization's name]*'s core tenets and support the link between purpose and proactive contribution
- Master the techniques of the Third Space and reinforce its use within the organization

I am responsible for growing the knowledge, skill sets and opportunities for team members throughout the organization. I will be an advocate for the Enterprise Leadership Model within *[insert organization's name]*. Hyper-alignment in the organization begins with me.

Click here to acknowledge.

Third Space Dialogues

Examples & Sample Questions

AS YOUR ORGANIZATION flexes its ELM muscles, you'll begin to identify more and more situations where Third Space dialogues can foster alignment, resolve conflict and serve as a valuable tool to foster success. Whether it's to discuss strategy, jumpstart wayward projects or break down silos, the Third Space provides a model for addressing issues, devoid of ego or rank, in a productive and safe manner.

Remember, the framework is simple: start with broad reflective questions *(Top of the Funnel)*, engage in critical thinking *(Middle of the Funnel)* and proceed to Challenging Questions *(Bottom of the Funnel)*. Throughout the discussion, anyone can ask anyone else a question, but everyone must actively listen to each other. Before wrapping up, each discussant should recap their understanding of the issue, as well as any requisite next steps and deadlines.

To help guide you with Third Space discussions, you will find several examples in the pages that follow. While we may use different formats — the scripts of a play, lists of questions — the goal is the same: to share question areas and ideas that you can deploy in your organization when approaching similar topics.

Career Conversations

THE "CAREER CONVERSATION" is a discussion that Leaders and Proactive Self-Leaders should have at least once a quarter to consider accomplishments, key leadership challenges and individual development plans. These one-on-one discussions should take place at all levels throughout an organization. In traditional, hierarchical entities, the career conversation typically occurs during the annual review and goes something like this:

LEADER: As you know, every six months, our HR system prompts me to schedule a review with you. Over the past half year, I've noticed that you're doing these things well ... and these are the areas where I think you need to improve.

ACTIVATE THE THIRD SPACE

DIRECT REPORT *(Nods and replies):* OK, thank you.

There is very little back-and-forth in these conversations; they are monologues without any deeper understanding of the context and issues faced by the assessee, and their infrequent nature often leaves team members thinking, "Why didn't you tell me this earlier? I would have made adjustments." Millennials and Zoomers, in particular, expect timely input on their performance and promotion opportunities.

In a Third Space career discussion, a Leader recognizes that they do not have all the answers because, simply put, they are not with the direct report all the time. The discussion flows in both directions and, unlike in hierarchical organizations, no one is on the defensive.

Remember, though, that the "price of admission" to a career conversation is performance. If a team member's work misses the mark, a performance improvement discussion is required instead.

To illustrate a career conversation in the Third Space, consider the following scenario: Cascade Trading CEO Mark Leicester is meeting with Penelope (Penny) Neubronner, the company's property development president.

Mark begins the discussion with a "powerful opening statement" about the purpose of the meeting.

MARK: Come on in, Penny. I'm really looking forward to this opportunity to chat with you in the Third Space about your career. There are a number of things you've been involved with over the past quarter that are going very well. I'd like to congratulate you on these and discuss them with you. There are also a few areas I think you can work on which are going to be very important for your career and future leadership opportunities.

PENELOPE: Thanks, Mark. I always appreciate these discussions with you. Even though the external environment has been challenging, it's been a good quarter for the property division.

Mark initiates the Top of the Funnel discussion with a Reflective Question. After Penelope replies, she and Mark engage in more broad-based questioning to explore her performance and expectations.

MARK: Penny, tell me, **what do you think you've done well this past quarter and what have been your major challenges?**

PENELOPE: The three areas where my team and I have had the greatest success over the past quarter are: one, the launch of the new residential development in Farrer Park. As you saw, the take-up numbers were quite high and the price-per-square-foot was near the upper end of our expectations. Two, our sustainability team has put together new designs for a green office building that should reduce energy consumption by as much as 20 percent. I've been leading this project. And three, we are moving forward with the finance department on a proposal to enhance Cascade Trading's land bank. We're still working on the numbers, but we should have a more defined strategy to share with you by next month.

As for areas where I could improve, I think my last presentation to the board could have gone better. They were not as engaged as I would have liked. We are also facing some employee retention issues in the property division, particularly among junior members of the team. And pricing of future projects is becoming more challenging, given the uncertain inflationary environment.

Mark, let me ask you, **what have you seen me do well and where do you think I need to focus in order to improve?**

MARK: You know, Penny, I agree with every one of the things that you mentioned that you are doing well. I've watched as you've led the property division. The latest launch has undoubtedly gone well, and I'm pleased to see new sustainability designs. These will be extremely important if we are to compete successfully on upcoming projects. As for the land bank report, I've read the interim reports and it is progressing on schedule. Keep up the good work.

As for the challenges, I agree with you regarding your board presentation and pricing issues. As for employee retention at the junior staffing level, this is an issue that we are witnessing across departments, and we will work together over the next six months to implement changes to address this.

At this point, Mark reflects. They could discuss Penelope's challenges in more depth, but he realizes he still needs more information about her career plans. The more data he has, the better he can respond to her issues. So, instead of moving to the middle of the funnel, Mark asks another broad, reflective question.

MARK: We can discuss presentations and pricing in more detail in a bit, but first, based on our conversation, **where do you see yourself in one or two years?**

PENELOPE: Mark, my top priority is to add value to the organization and to be of greater assistance to you, the board and all our stakeholders. Looking ahead, my personal goal is to grow my capabilities as a leader and be well-positioned for more senior leadership responsibility down the line, whatever that may be.

After Mark and Penelope have established the areas of Penelope's work that are being done well and those where changes are needed, they move to the middle of the funnel with Critical Thinking, bridging questions to explore these issues in more detail.

MARK: As we've noted, your team has had a very good quarter, and I believe that this is thanks, in part, to how well you have inspired your team. **How would you do more of this?**

PENELOPE: There are three factors. Over the past couple years, I think we've all seen that purpose is a great motivational tool. Within the property division, we have defined purpose as "creating innovative, sustainable and inviting properties for home and work," which syncs well with Cascade Trading's overall purpose. At the same time, we are implementing processes that allow for greater input from all levels of the department. Our bonus structure and employee rewards program have also proved to be very popular; the keys to rewards are to offer outings or gifts that people really want — like a villa for the weekend by the beach — and to ensure that the awards process is fair and transparent. Going forward, I can build on all three of these tiers.

MARK: That's excellent, Penny.

PENELOPE: Mark, we talked earlier about presenting to the board and we both agreed that I can do better in this area. I've seen you make presentations many times and I'm always impressed by them. **If you were me, what would you do differently? What would be the first steps you would take?**

After Mark and Penelope discuss this, Penelope poses another bridge question to Mark, which provides him with an opportunity to offer additional mentoring.

PENELOPE: I've shared my career goals with you, Mark. To achieve them, **what do you think are other areas that I need to strengthen?**

MARK: Your team is cohesive, so you're doing well on that front. But I think you need to develop more bench strength. If not, you know we're not going to let you go anywhere! There should be at least two people in your department in the running to succeed you, and I don't think we've seen this yet. The second area where I'd focus is to develop a stronger relationship with your peers. You're working well with Finance, but I haven't seen a lot of interaction with other departments. **What are your thoughts about this? And if you agree, what do you think are the steps that need to be taken?**

After discussing these areas, Mark moves the Third Space discussion to the Bottom of the Funnel with a Challenging Question.

MARK: Penny, let's talk a bit more about bench strength. Prioritize for me: **what is the first step you will take to address this issue?**

PENELOPE: I have several people in mind. My first step, though, would be to confer with my business partner in Human Capital, then I would request a career conversation with each candidate, much as we are doing here today, to discuss this with them. There is also someone from Finance that we've worked closely with, who has shown a strong interest in property development. I think she has good leadership potential in this area. If Human Capital agrees, I'll speak with Oscar in Finance to see if he is OK with me approaching a member of his team.

MARK: That's smart, Penny. It's a sound plan. You want to consider different scenarios before word gets out. In fact, I'd suggest you take some time on the Leadership Driving Range to practice some mock career conversations before directly engaging members of your team.

PENELOPE: Thank you, Mark. I'll sign up for some time on the LDR with Human Capital this week, then update you when I've identi-

	fied candidates and have scheduled meetings with them.
MARK:	Before we wrap up, two things: first, are there any additional resources or support that you need from me in order for the property division to be successful?
PENELOPE:	Well, we're having an offsite retreat next month and it would be great if you could join us for a couple sessions.
MARK:	Sure, I'd be happy to do that. Please check my schedule with Sheryl and we'll arrange it. It'll be a great opportunity for me to mix with more members of your team. Penny, before we wrap up, let's recap. **What are your next steps and when will you take them?**

And with this last question, Mark and Penelope exit the Third Space. They discuss and take note of her action items, ensuring that they are aligned going forward.

DIALOGUES

The Team Discussion:
Assessing a New Project or Initiative

WHENEVER an organization is planning to embark on a major initiative, a Third Space discussion is advisable to chart the best course and ensure that all teams are working together in the same direction.

SCENARIO: Cascade Snacks is considering a new initiative to expand into North America with a line of healthy energy bars that would pit it against some of the biggest players in the sector. A collaboration with one of the largest sporting organizations in the United States, the Amateur Athletic Union, is envisioned to launch this multimillion-dollar project.

This discussion takes place one year after the conclusion of our story in the first part of the book; by this time, all members of Aaron's team are well acquainted with the Enterprise Leadership Model and how to conduct discussions in the Third Space.

PARTICIPANTS: Aaron Chua, the president of Cascade Snacks; his senior leadership team, comprised of Carlos Reyes (VP), Selena Tan (Sales), Jennifer Yacob (Marketing), Ajay Singh (Operations) and Jake Williams (Finance); and the department's Human Capitalist Business Partner, Kathy Thomas.

Aaron begins the discussion with a "powerful opening statement" about the purpose of the meeting.

AARON: Thank you, everyone, for coming together today for this Third Space discussion. As you know, we are exploring the best way to expand Cascade Snacks into the United States. This is a major undertaking — one with substantial risks, but also significant upside for Cascade Trading — so we need to ensure that we are all on the same page regarding the nature of the initiative, the objectives and desired outcomes, as well as our individual responsibilities and timelines.

I've asked Kathy from Human Capital to join us, as she is our business partner. Kathy, good to see you. Carlos, to set the stage, could you please provide a brief summary of the proposal?

CARLOS: Thank you, Aaron. Everyone, in front of you, please find a background document outlining the draft proposal. This is the same one that I shared with you by email. It's an initiative to capture significant market share in the United States by partnering with one of the most powerful and popular youth sports organizations in the US. The proposed budget is on page 5. *(Carlos initiates the Top of the Funnel discussion with a broad Reflective Question.)* To begin the discussion, I'd like to ask each of you, **"What are your thoughts on this project?"**

SELENA: Expanding to more markets has always been part of Cascade Snacks' plans. And there's no bigger market, no bigger opportunity than the US. However, that said, taking a targeted approach, like we're looking at doing here, makes a lot of sense.

JENNIFER: I agree. Sports are hugely popular in the US and focusing on youth will provide a great foothold. It should be a relatively low-cost way of expanding into new markets — much more cost-effective and easier to implement than, say, if we were partnering with a professional sports association like the NBA. Plus, healthy, low-sugar, or even no-sugar, energy bars align well with our mission statement.

AJAY: Americans are definitely sports-crazy, no doubt about that. The timing to enter the US is also good for us. Over the past 18 months, Cascade Snacks has hit, and exceeded, all of our major Asia-Pacific targets. While we certainly should not let up in this region, our division has the resources and expertise to broaden its business.

JAKE: Snack foods is an extremely competitive sector in the US. Margins can be slim. While there are a number of players in the energy bar segment of this space, the margins are higher and the overall market is still growing. So, energy bars make sense, and if we are going down this route, partnering with an athletics association is a smart approach.

CARLOS: AAU has 700,000 members and 150,000 volunteers. That's fantastic access. They have more than 40 sporting programs across the United States, so we might need to narrow down our partnership, at least in the initial stages. We'll essentially be targeting teenage athletes and their parents. If we can get their buy-in, if they like our product, well, then we are well on our way.

KATHY: Expanding to the US along these lines is in sync with Cascade Trading's purpose, mission, vision and values. From a human capital perspective, I can see several synergies with other units of the company that are already operating there.

AARON: It looks like we have a good consensus around expanding our business into the US and starting with energy bars and sports. Let's talk more about the proposed partnership with AAU. **What are the pros and cons of doing this?** Let's start with the benefits, then we can discuss the challenges after that.

After the team discusses the benefits and drawbacks of the project, Jake poses the next question.

JAKE: Alright, everyone, I have another broad question for us to consider. It's an important one to check whether we are all talking about the same thing: **what is your understanding of this project?**

CARLOS: We are going to rebrand our existing line of energy bars for the US market and distribute them in partnership with the country's largest amateur sports association. The bars will be available for sale on AAU's website and at sporting events.

AJAY: We've identified three production hubs that have the right expertise: one in Port Coquitlam, outside Vancouver; another in Idaho and a third in Chicago. Depending on the launch date, we may want to ship some product from our Philippines' factory.

KATHY: What's the proposed agreement with AAU? Is it a revenue share?

SELENA: I thought the proposal was sponsorship. We provide 50,000 energy bars, free of charge, for distribution to players at their games, and in return, Cascade Snacks, or our energy bar brand, is recognized as AAU's official energy bar. The website sales should be a revenue share.

AARON: Is there a minimum spend on the website? Are these bulk sales to teams or retail? We don't have a track record for direct-to-consumer sales.

CARLOS: AAU's other partners offer retail sales, but usually with a minimum purchase of $20-30.

JAKE: We have a choice on how to deliver on this — AAU has an online distribution partner, so we would just need to stock their warehouse. There will be additional fees, of course. Alternatively, we could work with Cascade Trading's US fast-moving consumer goods unit. They should be set up for this.

JENNIFER: Going back to something Carlos said earlier, are we rebranding these energy bars? I thought we were sticking with our High Energy brand.

AARON: It appears there are a few top-level issues that we need to sort out. One, is this sponsorship, revenue share or both? Related to this, what is our exposure in terms of initial outlay? Two, do we want to sell direct to consumers via the AAU website, and if so, how do we implement this? And three, are we planning to rebrand an existing product, create a new line of energy bars specifically for the US market or sell our products, as is, in the US? Let's take each of these in turn.

After going around the room several more times to discuss different interpretations and details, Aaron's team arrives at a common understanding of this breakthrough project. Before proceeding, though, they explore whether other solutions may also help them achieve their goals.

KATHY: In addition to the AAU, **are there other strategies or tactics we should consider when entering this market?**

JAKE: I'm not sure if you've been following the "Name, Image, Likeness" discussions in the US? The AAU will give us access to high school students, but we could also make inroads at the university level through NIL sponsorships.

CARLOS: Isn't that really expensive? Some of the contracts are six figures.

JAKE: Only if we're working with basketball and football players at major universities. NIL applies to all sports, for both men and women attending universities, big and small. If we sponsor athletes who play softball, volleyball, lacrosse, etc., the cost is likely in the low hundreds per athlete. This could be a great way to market our products.

JENNIFER: I have another idea. Have you seen how F1 broke into the US market? For years, Americans had no interest in it, only in NASCAR races. But F1 launched a successful Netflix series that really fueled viewer interest. Now, I'm not suggesting a whole Netflix series — that would definitely be out of our budget and take too long — but could we explore brand placements in an appropriate Netflix series or in content on other platforms?

As the team discusses additional approaches for gaining market share, they agree to develop some ideas in more detail, while keeping others in view for the future. Before moving further down the funnel, Carlos poses one more broad question.

CARLOS: **What is the perfect outcome for this initiative?**

AJAY: Without question, the US has the potential to become one of Cascade Snacks' largest markets. Ideally, we start with energy bars, but then after gaining more traction, greater brand recognition and establishing our production and distribution centers, we can expand further.

JAKE: If we put some numbers on it, approximately 20 percent of Americans exercise every day. That's 66 million people. More than $4 billion worth of energy bars are sold in the US every year. The market is relatively fragmented. There are a number of players, like Kellogg's and Clif Bar, but no one has a dominant monopoly. Clif Bar grosses $500 million per year. Given the potential reach of the AAU partnership, I'd say that a perfect outcome would entail Cascade Snacks matching that figure within three years.

SELENA: We need to keep profitability in mind too. There will be a significant outlay during the first year as we distribute free snacks. Ideally, we will recoup this investment within 18 months.

JENNIFER: Let's not forget brand value either. The AAU and possibly NIL partnerships will increase Cascade Snacks' brand value. We can track this in social media and customer loyalty surveys.

KATHY: In a perfect world, within two years, Cascade Snacks will be recognized across the US as the provider of a breakthrough energy bar known for its fantastic taste, healthy nutritious energy boost and sustainable production.

Taking note of the desired outcomes, Aaron and the team advance the discussion in the direction of actionable outcomes with a series of Critical Thinking questions — What is the best timeframe to begin this project? What is the overall timing for the project? How will budgets be established? — and then turn to the issue of project leadership.

AARON: This is a major initiative for Cascade Snacks. **Who should be the project lead?**

AJAY: I would like to put my hand up for it, Aaron. I've been studying the production and distribution centers. I have experience growing our channel partnerships and I worked with Carlos on the draft proposal. I understand the importance of this project for the company and am ready for the task.

JAKE: There's a member of my team, Kianna, who played college ball in Kentucky and on an AAU team before that. She's one of my star performers, and I think her athletic experience will be a great asset here.

KATHY: Perhaps we could consider joint leads for this initiative? Ajay and Kianna could work together.

AARON: What are your thoughts on this, Ajay?

AJAY: There's a time when I would have said "no," but this is an all-hands-on-deck project, and I understand what Kianna will bring to it. Together, we'll ensure it's a success.

JENNIFER: As we move forward, **how will we make sure that we remain aligned?**

To move from alignment to action, the meeting participants progress to the Bottom of the Funnel, where they entertain a series of Challenging Questions, such as where to find the data needed to advance the project, how to assess if the project is not going according to plan and who will be responsible for bringing the group back together to discuss issues.

CARLOS:	Alright, let's think about our next steps. **What do we need to do first?**
SELENA:	We need to finalize a proposal that we can take to AAU.
AJAY:	And have some internal guidelines for our negotiations with them.
CARLOS:	We also need to set up a meeting with the right people at AAU to move this along quickly.
KATHY:	I believe there are a few new hires that we'll need to make in order to implement and promote the project.
JENNIFER:	We should put together or acquire a list of potential players for Name, Image and Likeness sponsorships, along with statistics about their market reach and cost.
JAKE:	Let's not forget production. Once partnerships are approved, we'll need to quickly ramp up our product distribution.

After some discussion, the Cascade Snacks team prioritize the next steps and discuss who will be responsible for each action.

The Bottom of the Funnel

BY THE END of most meetings, participants are often tired, they may be in a rush for their next appointment or need to get back to work. Typically, just before concluding, leaders ask their team members, "Any questions?" Invariably, few, if any, hands go up, and the meeting is concluded. Alternatively, before wrapping up, some leaders offer a brief summary of their own.

But do you really think everyone understands their next steps? Likely not. This is why it's important to set aside ten to fifteen minutes at the end of every Third Space discussion to ensure alignment. Initially, these discussions may go slowly, because participants assume leaders will let them off the hook if they do not answer correctly at first. However, over time, people will listen better and these end-of-meeting discussions will go more quickly.

These are hierarchical, base-of-the-model, bottom-of-the-funnel discussions. Here's an example that picks up where we left off in the story of Cascade Trading.

AARON: Alright, everyone, this has been a great discussion. We've made some real progress today. I realize it's late, but let's go around the table now to summarize. Ajay, since you and Kianna are the new project leads, let's start with you.

AJAY: My first step is to meet with Kianna. After we delineate our individual and mutual leadership responsibilities, we'll prepare a project matrix and action plan, then update the team. We'll do that by Thursday. Kianna and I will also plan bilateral meetings with the various team leads, and I will liaise with the factories and develop an operational plan, so that we're ready to hit the ground running and score some quick goals.

JAKE: Ajay, I can see you're already on board with the sports metaphors! That's great. As for me, I will revise the P&L scenarios based on today's discussions. There are a few price and cost inputs missing, but we can make some initial assumptions until we have that data.

AARON: Great. What's the timeline for this?

JAKE: I can share it with the team by next week.

AARON: I'm meeting with Mark and the senior leadership team on Friday. Can you send me a preliminary update by Thursday?

JAKE: OK, sure.

AARON: Thanks, Jake. Anything else on your action list?

JAKE: Oh, yes, I will also meet with Kianna today to brief her about the project, ensure that she is willing to play a leadership role and then introduce her to Ajay.

AARON: Thanks, Jake. Carlos?

CARLOS: There are several areas where the project proposal needs to be updated. I'll start work on this, then liaise with Ajay and Kianna to make sure I've captured the points correctly. I'll also meet with Jake so he can see if there are any ramifications for the scenario planning.

AARON: Anything else?

CARLOS: I'm not sure. I don't see any other action items in my notes.

AARON: Who's going to produce the plan for direct-to-consumer sales via the AAU website and social media channels?

SELENA: That's on my list. But I believe, Carlos, you had some ideas about that as well, which you could help me with.

CARLOS: That's right. I did. I do. I'm happy to liaise with you about that and reach out to some potential partners as well.

AARON: What's a reasonable timeline for this?

CARLOS: Selena and I can update the team in two weeks at the next project meeting.

AARON: Alright, thank you, Carlos. Jennifer over to you.

JENNIFER: We are going to conduct focus group tests of the product in five US markets, using the existing brand name and two alternate names that we discussed here today. The first round of tests, based on the name alone, can take place next week. A subsequent round, with sample energy bars, will be a week later. My team is also going to prepare an initial marketing plan based on the AAU proposal as well as a version that factors in Name, Image and Likeness sponsorship.

AARON: Thank you, Jennifer. Selena, what's on your action list, in addition to the direct sales plan?

SELENA: As this is a new geographic market for Cascade Snacks, there's a lot of work to be done to build up our sales network. This will depend, in part, on which markets within the US we debut in. My first action point is to find out where the AAU is strongest and then target these areas.

KATHY: There are several team members from other business units who may be able to assist with inputs and other project information. I will confirm this and update Ajay and Kianna by next week. We also discussed two new roles to assist with the rollout. I will liaise with Selena, Carlos and Aaron to determine the job scopes and start the recruitment process.

AARON: Thank you, everyone. On my part, as I mentioned, I will be updating the senior leadership team on Friday. I'll also be supporting each of you by blocking two hours on my calendar every Thursday for any discussions you might need to advance this project. This has been a good meeting. I look forward to the next one in two weeks.

Additional Scenarios

WHETHER YOUR ORGANIZATION is revisiting its purpose, mission, vision and values or assessing the pros and cons of a possible acquisition, the Third Space provides a psychologically safe space, devoid of rank or ego, to discuss issues. Here are possible questions to help guide you in a variety of scenarios.

For each discussion, questions are divided into three parts: Top of the Funnel *(Reflective Questions)*, Middle of the Funnel *(Critical Thinking / Bridging Questions)* and Bottom of the Funnel *(Challenging Questions)*. You do not need to ask every question in each section.

Participants gather data at the top of the funnel. Bridge questions generate discussion about the current state of affairs and the types of actions for the organization to take moving forward. Challenging questions at the bottom of the funnel determine individual responsibility for these actions. Each stage of the funnel refines the discussion until alignment is reached and clear action points established.

Remember to practice Active Listening; if you do, subsequent questions will be found in the answers to previous replies.

#1 Big Picture Discussion: Purpose

Top of the Funnel

- Why do we work here?
- What do you think are the original roots of the organization's purpose? How were they derived?
- What is your understanding of the organization's purpose?
- Why is purpose important for our organization?
- How does this purpose benefit the organization?
- How do you think other stakeholders view our purpose, both inside and outside the organization?
- Why is the organization's purpose important to you?
- If you could amend the current wording of the organization's purpose, what changes, if any, would you make?
- What are the differences between the organization's purpose and its mission, vision and values?

Middle of the Funnel

- Why is living the purpose important for the organization?
- Is the organization's purpose integrated throughout its operations and strategies? How?
- If we amend the purpose, how would this impact the organization's operations and strategies?
- Are there elements of the organization's purpose that are difficult to understand?
- Why do you think this purpose was developed?
- How does the organization's purpose guide you at work?
- What is the best way for you to start working with the organization's purpose in mind? (Prioritize the steps that you could take.)
- If you are unclear, where would you go to obtain a better understanding of the organization's purpose?

Bottom of the Funnel

- What three things would you do to further integrate the organization's purpose into your work?

#2 Big Picture Discussion: Strategy

Top of the Funnel

- What is your understanding of our current strategy (for the organization, business unit and/or team)?
- How was our current strategy developed? Why?
- Why is this strategy important for the organization?
- Why is our strategy important to you?
- How does the current strategy benefit the company? What elements of our strategy are working?
- How do you think other stakeholders, such as our customers and partners, view the organization's strategy?
- How do you see the current strategy being played out (from an organizational, business unit and/or team perspective)?

Middle of the Funnel

- How did you participate in the development of our current strategy?
- What is not working in our current strategy? Why is this the case?
- Are there elements of the strategy that are difficult to understand? If so, which ones, and why?
- Do you think our strategy needs to change? If so, why, and how would you change it?

Bottom of the Funnel

- How does your work or your team's work impact the organization's overall strategy?
- How is your team executing against the current strategy?
- What would you change about the strategy in the coming years?
- What specifically would you change about the current strategy?
- How would you or your team want to be involved in developing the strategy in the future?
- How could you gain a better understanding of the organization's strategy? Where could you go?
- What are the best ways for you to work with the current strategy in mind?

#3 Organizational Change

Top of the Funnel

- What is your current understanding of the changes the organization is requesting of your business unit or team?
- What are the expected benefits of these changes?
- Why are these changes important?
- Who benefits from these changes?
- Where do you see your team members in the transition?

Middle of the Funnel

- What needs to take place for these changes to be effective?

- How is this similar or different to other changes made by the organization?
- How has the organization communicated these changes to you and your team?
- How could this communication be more effective?
- When do you expect to see the benefits of these changes?
- In a perfect world, when can we expect these changes to be fully implemented?

Bottom of the Funnel

- What do you and your team need to do to support these changes and the transition process?
- What process is required for you to implement these changes?
- When can you begin this process?
- What support do you need from the organization?
- How would you approach resistance to these changes?

#4 Breaking Down Corporate Silos

Top of the Funnel

- Why is the organization set up the way it is?
- What is your understanding of the term "corporate silo"?
- How is breaking down silos beneficial for the company?
- What is difficult about working across silos?
- What are the barriers to breaking down silos?

Middle of the Funnel

- What in your experience makes working across silos difficult?
- In your role, are there benefits to working across silos?
- What can you do to work across silos more effectively?

Bottom of the Funnel

- What are your first steps to begin working more effectively across silos?

#5 Stalled or Wayward Projects

DISCUSSIONS ABOUT PROJECTS that are off course, over budget or behind schedule can invariably be contentious. In these situations, Third Space participants must pay special attention to their tone, inflection, attitude and even body language in order to create and maintain a safe space for an issues-based discussion.

Keep in mind that questions in the top of the funnel are intended to gather data and enable a full understanding of each team member's perceptions. Why do they think about an issue in the way that they do?

When posing questions, be sure to use the 1st person plural ("we") rather than the 2nd person "you" and to avoid any questions that may seem accusatory. For example, ask "what is *our* understanding of the project?" or "why are *we* behind schedule?" rather than "why did *you* spend money on this?" or "why are *you* behind schedule?"

An important follow-up question is often "what else?" This two-word query encourages respondents to think more deeply and deliberately. Initial replies to any question generally consist of the first points to come to mine. Ask "what else?" two or three times and you are likely to get to the real issue.

Top of the Funnel

- What is our understanding of the project?
- Why are we behind? Why is the project not on schedule?
- What are the major issues that we are facing in this project?
- Why didn't we recognize these problems earlier?

Middle of the Funnel

- When did we notice that the project was not working?
- What does being on track look like?
- What steps can we take to put the project back on schedule?

Bottom of the Funnel

- Who will be responsible for each step that's needed to get the project back on track?
- What will be the first actions taken?
- What are the deadlines to do this?

#6 Mergers & Acquisitions

THE THIRD SPACE is a useful forum for discussing M&A activities. Discussions can take place within a single department, across senior leadership teams or even between two organizations.

If the discussion is between an acquiring company and its acquisition target, the primary goal is to establish the reasons for the deal and potential benefits to each party. Once each side more accurately understands the other, they are in a better position to negotiate a mutually advantageous deal.

M&A Scenario One

Discussion between two organizations prior to completion of a deal.

In the early stages of discussion between two organizations, gathering data is the most important issue. While we provide Critical Thinking and Challenging Questions, participants may decide to remain at the top of the funnel, then return for additional Third Space discussions if negotiations progress.

Top of the Funnel

- What is your understanding of the proposed merger/acquisition?
- What are the reasons behind this merger/acquisition?
- How will it benefit each party?
- What additional information do we need to understand this better?

Middle of the Funnel

- What are the best- and worst-case scenarios?
- What will be the result of the merger/acquisition in practical terms?
- Why is a merger/acquisition needed?
- What would be the way forward?

Bottom of the Funnel

- What are the next steps?
- When should we meet again?

M&A Scenario Two

Senior Leadership Discussion to assess a proposed deal.

Top of the Funnel

- Why is this acquisition important for us?
- What is our current relationship, if any, with the acquisition target?
- Which parts of our company will benefit the most from the proposed acquisition? (Which will benefit the least? Will any suffer from it?)
- Why wouldn't we proceed with this acquisition?
- Is this an investment or a takeover?

Middle of the Funnel

- Which parts of this acquisition concern you the most?
- If this is an investment, what percent stake would benefit our company the most? Why?
- What other information do we need to make a decision?

Bottom of the Funnel

- How will we overcome those concerns?
- Who will get this info for us?
- What are the next steps?

M&A Scenario Three

Post-Acquisition Third Space Discussion within a department.

Top of the Funnel

- What is your understanding of the acquisition?
- Why is this deal important for the organization?
- How will this acquisition benefit our department?

Middle of the Funnel

- What questions do you have about how the acquisition will impact our department?

- What are the hurdles within our department that need to be addressed in order for the acquisition to be a success?

Bottom of the Funnel

- What steps are required by our department to maximize the success of the acquisition?
- Which actions should we prioritize first?
- What is the timeline required for this?

#7 Personal Conflict

THIRD SPACE DISCUSSIONS about personal conflict are most likely to take place between two or three people. Imagine a scenario, for example, when competition for a promotion interferes with effective collaboration in the workplace.

Top of the Funnel

- How did this conflict start?
- What are the issues facing us here?
- Why does this conflict persist?
- How do you see these issues impacting others in the organization?

Middle of the Funnel

- What is the best outcome going forward?
- How will we resolve this issue?

Bottom of the Funnel

- What specific changes will each of us make?
- If this conflict is not resolved, what should happen?

Frequently Asked Questions

1. What is the Enterprise Leadership Model?

The Enterprise Leadership Model is a transformative process to foster high levels of employee engagement, facilitate clear internal communication and ensure that team members are hyper-aligned with each other on every project as well as with the organization's key tenets — its purpose, mission, vision, values and strategy. The model recognizes that there are three distinct parts of any organization — Leaders, Proactive Self-Leaders and Human Capitalists — who have responsibilities to each other as well as to the overall organization and that there are crucial times when they work most effectively together in a nonhierarchical environment.

2. What is a Proactive Self-Leader?

Proactive Self-Leaders are team members who accept two distinct, but overlapping, sets of responsibility — an overall responsibility for the success of the organization that starts with their current position, plus a responsibility to support their leaders and teams. Proactive Self-Leaders believe in an organization's purpose. They regularly demonstrate initiative and have a growth mindset, which leads them to accept new projects and challenges and to take charge of their own personal and professional development.

3. What is a Human Capitalist?

Human Capitalists are internal business partners, consultants, strategists and stewards of corporate culture who support the growth of people within an organization. Within the Enterprise Leadership Model, Human Capitalists represent the organization by embodying and promoting its purpose, mission, vision and values.

4. What is the difference between Human Resources and Human Capitalists?

Human resource professionals and human capitalists have very different mindsets. HR is a traditional administrative function that manages employees like resources and aims to deploy them in ways that are most effective for the organization. Human capitalists, on the other hand, nurture and grow people's careers by ensuring there are sufficient resources, training and coaching opportunities. They create the required positions for organizational success and fill them with the right people. They ensure that individuals and teams are hyper-aligned. Human capital consists of skills, knowledge, experience, networks and health. Just as finance departments are responsible for growing money, human capitalists are responsible for growing people so that they succeed and flourish together with the organization.

5. What is the First Space?

The First Space is classic top-down organizational structure. Hierarchy and the vertical chain of command dominate decision-making, implementation and governance. This is the "I say, you do" style of leadership. Miscommunication, a disengaged, disillusioned workforce, high turnover and burnout are commonplace. Change management is frequently unsuccessful. If you have not yet adopted the Enterprise Leadership Model, you are likely operating in the First Space.

6. What is the Second Space?

In the Second Space, Leaders and Proactive Self-Leaders are both actively engaged in the pursuit of institutional success. In return, Human Capitalists are equally committed to creating conditions that enable every team member to grow.

Internal communication, particularly around change management, is no longer hierarchical in order to minimize misunderstandings and misconceptions. Human Capitalists — who represent the organization's purpose, mission, vision and values — embed these tenets throughout people processes. Leaders recognize that success is predicated on working more collaboratively with their direct reports and peers alike and that they have a responsibility to coach their team members.

7. What is the Third Space?

The Third Space is the apex of the Enterprise Leadership Model. It is characterized by the suspension of hierarchy; respectful, issues-based communications; and hyper-alignment. Silos are broken down. Team members work in sync on projects and strategy, which are, in turn, aligned with an organization's purpose, mission, vision and values.

Misunderstandings routinely occur in almost every entity, even for those operating in the Second Space. Only by suspending hierarchy and entering the Third Space can organizations quickly rectify areas of misalignment.

The Third Space is a nonhierarchical, psychologically safe space in which discussions are held to resolve issues, foster understanding and achieve hyper-alignment. Third Space discussions can be held in specially designated rooms, in online forums or anywhere, simply by mutual agreement.

8. Does hierarchy exist in the Third Space?

No.

9. Does hierarchy still have a role to play in corporate organizations?

Yes. While all team members are equidistant from the Organization in the Enterprise Leadership Model, hierarchy still exists at the base of the model in several key interactions between Leaders and Proactive Self-Leaders.

First, leaders can still hire and fire team members. Together with Human Capital, they are responsible for setting KPIs, conducting performance reviews and determining salary levels and bonuses. Leaders also have the final say on budgeting decisions, though nonhierarchical discussions should inform this process.

Second, renewal and employee engagement — is classically hierarchical as leaders guide more junior members of the team.

Third, hierarchy is needed during a crisis, particularly when urgent action is required, but team members do not know how to proceed. During crisis situations, team members naturally lean toward leaders with experience and welcome instruction.

Most leaders act as if their businesses are constantly under threat. They need to recognize that organizations, and the people within them, cannot live in crisis mode 24/7. On top of that, traditional leadership systems only work well if leaders have earned the trust and respect of their teams during non-crisis times, and the best way to do this is to foster nonhierarchical communication.

A leader's authority within the Enterprise Leadership Model is the same as before, but the leader's expectations of their direct reports have shifted as Proactive Self-Leaders accept personal responsibility for an organization's success.

10. How about setting deadlines and providing performance appraisals? Aren't these strictly hierarchical functions?

No, not if they are done well. Asking a direct report when they can accomplish a key deliverable creates ownership and is much more effective than giving a deadline. Leaders can still persuade or support a team member to accomplish something faster, but this is part of a discussion, not a direct order.

Effective performance appraisals are also a collaborative process. The person being appraised is first asked to assess their accomplishments and challenges during the previous quarter or half-year. Leaders then provide feedback and share specific examples along with points of agreement, disagreement and further elaboration. The end of this discussion remains hierarchical as the leader must provide the final assessment of whether a direct report meets or exceeds expectations.

11. Can I start having Third Space discussions in my company right away?

No. If your organization is still operating in the First Space or has not completed the transition into the Second Space, it is not ready for Third Space discussions. Team members must also understand the Funnel of Understanding and how to pose questions in the Third Space. If your organization attempts to enter the Third Space prematurely — in an atmosphere where hierarchy is prevalent, individuals are managed as resources and team members have not been taught the process of having an effective dialogue — your discussions will not succeed, as they lack the foundations for success.

12. How do we create Proactive Self-Leaders and Human Capitalists?

The first step is for organizations to recognize: one, communication can no longer be strictly hierarchical and, two, every team member is capable of playing a greater role by accepting ownership and personal responsibility for the organization's success. Breakdowns in top-down communication lead to anxiety, missteps and delays. Clearly communicated, broadly disseminated change management addresses these issues and creates higher levels of employee engagement.

The next step is for organizations to create an environment that fosters and encourages proactivity. This occurs organically in purpose-driven organizations, where team members take action and demonstrate initiative because they believe in the organization's raison d'être, the reason why it exists, and they can see how this purpose is embedded in the organization's mission, vision, values and operations.

Similarly, the transformation from human resources to human capital can be driven from below by professionals who strive to play a more strategic role.

The creation of Proactive Self-Leaders and Human Capitalists can also be proclaimed from above, when organizations adopt the Enterprise Leadership Model and share the expectations and best practices associated with each role with every team member.

FREQUENTLY ASKED QUESTIONS

13. When should we have Third Space discussions?

Regardless of the topic, if you are looking for issues-based solutions, here are five clues that it is time to hold a Third Space meeting:

- A project is behind schedule
- A project is not proceeding as planned
- Team members are not working well together
- Team members do not appear to be working on the same thing
- Any member of the team hesitates about what to do next

Each of these clues signals a lack of clarity and alignment that can be addressed and rectified in the Third Space.

Third Space discussions will surface new ideas and generate the support needed to foster success. Holding a Third Space discussion at the beginning of a project will avoid delays down the line.

14. Can anyone lead a Third Space discussion?

When an organization adopts the Enterprise Leadership Model, it can be helpful to designate a person or team to initially facilitate Third Space meetings; this is usually a Human Capitalist, who is well-versed in how to manage nonhierarchical, issues-based discussions. Anyone in the organization can call for a Third Space meeting; similarly, any team member can ask the first question.

15. What can we achieve in the Third Space?

Third Space discussions are based on a transfer of understanding between participants, which leads to hyper-alignment. In the process, they develop empathy, engagement, a heightened sense of ownership, improved relationships and a recognition that every team member, no matter their rank or role, contributes to the growth and success of the organization.

16. What are the four ground rules for the Third Space?

1) The Third Space is not your space. It's not my space. It's the Third Space, a place that fosters alignment and understanding.
2) Hierarchy does not exist in the Third Space. Rank does not matter. The Third Space is an issues space.
3) Anyone can call a Third Space meeting and every participant has the opportunity in the meeting to lead the discussion.

4) Discussions are advanced through issues-based questioning. Questions are multi-directional; any question that a leader asks a team member, a team member can also ask of the leader.

17. What is the Funnel of Understanding and what type of questions can we ask in the Third Space?

Third Space discussions are built on dialogue to achieve a common understanding. This dialogue can be pictured as a funnel. At the top are big, broad, reflective questions to examine issues from a variety of angles and to foster alignment. Questions become sharper and more targeted as we apply critical thinking to the issue. At the bottom of the funnel are challenging questions to produce actionable next steps and deadlines. Throughout the discussion, participants must actively listen to each other. While the specific questions posed in the Third Space will vary based on the topic under consideration, the types of questions — beginning with broad questions and working toward more focused ones — remain the same.

18. What is Active Listening and why is it important?

Active Listening is a practice to thoroughly absorb, understand and retain what is said by another person. It requires being present, withholding judgment, consciously listening, restating what you've heard, seeking clarifications and summarizing a speaker's key points. Active Listening is a back-and-forth process. It shows up in dialogue as an acknowledgment that I hear what you say. Active Listening techniques can be applied to any communication, but they are particularly essential to discussions in the Third Space, which are designed to foster hyper-alignment.

19. Why is it important to set aside 10 minutes for a recap at the end of every Third Space meeting?

Most meetings end with the assumption that people have a common understanding of what has been discussed and agreed upon and what they need to do to implement it. However, this is often not the case. Toward the end of any meeting, people are ready to leave and there's a tendency to rush. Afterward, meeting participants gather and ask each other, "Did you catch what our boss said? What did you get out of that meeting? What do I need to do?" To avoid this scenario, and save yourself headaches down the road, set aside ten minutes at the end of every project meeting and Third Space discussion to ask, "What are your next steps?" Allowing each participant the time to answer this question is a key step on the path to hyper-alignment and action.

20. What is the Leadership Driving Range?

Like any skill, leadership is not innate. It must be practiced. The Leadership Driving Range is a safe space that exists within the Human Capital department for Leaders and Proactive Self-Leaders to practice and hone their skills. LDR modules focus on specific, work-related scenarios — such as how to conduct meetings or provide feedback — and are led by internal certified coaches. Leaders should spend time every month on the LDR to maintain and sharpen their communication and management skills.

21. My company has already adopted a leadership model. Why do we need a new model? Will we need to shift away from our current model in order to implement this one?

The Enterprise Leadership Model is like the string theory of organizational leadership. You do not have to drop your existing model. The ELM supports any leadership style. It builds on other models by providing a holistic paradigm that mobilizes and embraces the entire workforce, not just the upper echelons. Every team member in an ELM organization has a personal responsibility for the success of the organization. This not only takes a weight off leaders' shoulders, it provides a framework to cultivate high levels of engagement, clear communication and hyper-alignment in a fast-moving, hyper-competitive world.

Suggested Reading

There are a number of works that have influenced my thinking over the years. I regularly reference many of these; you may wish to do the same.

- Bill Pasmore, *Leading Continuous Change: Navigating Churn in the Real World,* 2015
- Brene Brown, *Dare to Lead,* 2018
- Cal Newport, *Deep Work: Rules for Focused Success in a Distracted World,* 2016
- Center for Creative Leadership (CCL), *Ideas into Action Guidebooks.* A very useful series with advice and insights on topics ranging from accountability to talent conversations. Refer to shop.ccl.org/usa/books/ideas_into_action_guidebooks.
- David Whyte, *The Heart Aroused: Poetry and the Preservation of the Soul in Corporate America,* 1994
- James Kousner & Barry Posner, *The Leadership Challenge: How to Make Extraordinary Things Happen in Organizations,* 5th edition, 2012
- Jim Collins, *Good to Great: Why Some Companies Make the Leap and Others Don't,* 2001
- John Kotter and Dan Cohen, *The Heart of Change: Real-Life Stories of How People Change Their Organizations,* 2012
- John Kotter, *Leading Change,* 2012
- Ken Blanchard, Thad Lacinak, Chuck Tompkins and Jim Ballard, *Whale Done! The Power of Positive Relationships,* 2002
- Margaret J. Wheatley, *Leadership and the New Science: Discovering Order in a Chaotic World,* 1992
- Marshall Goldsmith, *What Got You Here Won't Get You There: How Successful People Become Even More Successful,* 2007
- Michael D. Watkins, *The First 90 Days: Proven Strategies for Getting Up to Speed Faster and Smarter,* 2013

- Michael J. Marquardt, *Leading with Questions: How Leaders Find the Right Solutions by Knowing What to Ask,* 2014
- Patrick Lencioni, *The Five Dysfunctions of a Team*, 2002
- Peter Senge et al, *The Dance of Change: The Challenges to Sustaining Momentum in a Learning Organization,* 1999
- Richard Koch, *Financial Times Guide to Strategy: How to Create, Pursue and Deliver a Winning Strategy,* 1995
- Robert Cooper and Ayman Sawaf, *Executive EQ,* 1998
- Warren Bennis, *On Becoming a Leader,* 1989
- William Isaacs, *Dialogue: The Art of Thinking Together,* 1999

Acknowledgements

The Enterprise Leadership Model took sixteen years to develop, refine, practice and articulate. Along the way, I am indebted to friends and colleagues who have challenged and encouraged me. Their support provided me with the courage to write and publish a book, which I sincerely believe has the potential to transform the way in which 21st-century organizations communicate and operate, to become hyper-aligned in the pursuit of purpose and success. In particular, I would like to acknowledge:

- **T Raja Kumar,** a dynamic, introspective professional whose desire to be an even better leader set me on a path that led to the development of the Enterprise Leadership Model.

- **Ira Chalaff,** the author of *The Courageous Follower: Standing Up To and For Our Leaders.* Intrigued by his ideas, I contacted Ira, out of the blue, in 2006. If he had not answered my email — and subsequently invited me to speak at a national conference on followership at Claremont McKenna College, supported by the Drucker School of Management and Kravis Leadership Institute — I may never have formulated the concept of Proactive Self-Leaders.

- **Cresswell Walker,** author of *Sail the 7Cs,* collaborated with me when we were first venturing down the path of Enterprise Leadership. He helped draft an early version of the Field Guide, then decided to sail around the world — twice.

- **Eva Au,** an accomplished leader and wise strategist, who encouraged me to drop the term "follower" from my lexicon, and her colleague **Steve Vass,** a constant advocate and source of support who has always been enamored with my magnetic models.

- **Yeardley Smith** and my son **Ben Cornwell** run the L.A.-based production house Paperclip Ltd. They were one of the first companies to adopt my ideas and credit them with the successful production of six movies, and counting, plus the globally recognized podcast, *Small Town Dicks,* now in its ninth season.

- **Sandeep Seth** is an innovator and early adopter of the Enterprise Leadership Model. He has been a joy to coach and I am immensely grateful for his foreword to this book. The ELM would not have succeeded at SK-II if not also for the full support of **Mayu Arao,** a warm, friendly leader with a keen eye for strategy and implementation. Many thanks as well to **YoeGin Chang** and **Shuqi Fu,** who shared their insights, and to SK-II's former HR director, **Won Xue Ling.**

- **Stephanie Nash,** by any measure, is a human capitalist par excellence. She is an internal business partner, consultant, strategist, coach and steward of corporate culture, who supports the growth of people. I am grateful for her time and openness to share insights and anecdotes. Her experience and expertise clearly highlight that the time is ripe for a sea change in organizational development from human resources to human capitalists.

- My love **Tina Cornwell** is generous, quick to support friends and a natural-born skeptic. She forced me to better articulate the details of the model, then successfully applied its concepts. Tina is a leader who draws out the best in the people around her, me included.

- The world-class athletes **Brent Barnes** and **Greg Burns** are no strangers to the quest for perfection, nor are **Rob Whittaker** and **George Quek,** my colleagues at the Center for Creative Leadership. They actively listen and have challenged me to refine the model to a point where it can be easily applied in any organization.

- Over the past two and a half decades, the very successful F&B entrepreneur **Mike Hadley** has been an amazing source of support and has constantly challenged my thinking. **Steve Stine** and **OB Wetzell** join me in weekly Round Ice Cube discussions. Steve is a mensch and challenger; his soon-to-be-published book will change the world. OB is a master builder and project manager who has been a constant sounding board for all things important.

- The tremendously talented serial entrepreneur **Joe Ranieri.** Not only did he convince me that I needed to publish my ideas, he also connected me with the writer who made it happen.

- **Steve Morris,** one of the best facilitators I know, offered me an opportunity that launched my coaching career.

- My channel partners, the Center for Creative Leadership and **Lee Hecht Harrison.** LHH offered me one of my first coaching jobs, then an opportunity to train and certify leaders as coaches in their exec-

ACKNOWLEDGEMENTS

utive results-based model. CCL's five decades of research has set the bar for how leaders can best support their teams.

- All the incredible coachees whom I have had the honor to work with over the years. Your willingness to authentically share your deepest challenges, struggles and visions of success have contributed immeasurably to my understanding of organizational development.

- **James Eric Jones,** an art director whose way with words is as skillful as his designs.

- Finally, to **Michael Switow,** my co-writer, without whom this book would have never taken form. His challenging questions and insistence that we tell a story have brought my concepts for modern organizational communication and leadership to life.

Notes

FOREWORD

1   P.12 | The terms "hipsters, hackers and hustlers" were reportedly coined by the designer Rei Inamoto, the founding partner of I&CO.

2   P.12 | Andy Ellwood, "The Dream Team: Hipster, Hacker, and Hustler," *Forbes*, 22 August 2012.

INTRODUCTION

1   P.18 | Gallup, *State of the Global Workplace: 2021 Report*, p.2.

2   P.18 | Paul Petrone, "How to Calculate the Cost of Employee Disengagement," *LinkedIn Learning Blog*, March 2017.

3   P.18 | Among the bestselling business books of 2021-22 are Chip Heath and Karla Starr's *Making Numbers Count* and Gallup's *First, Break All the Rules*.

CHAPTER 1: RETHINKING HIERARCHY

1   P.33 | Robert S. Gibbons and John Roberts, *The Handbook of Organizational Economics* (Princeton University Press, 2013) presents an overview of theoretical and empirical studies of hierarchy, while annual surveys by Gallup and Mercer document the costs of traditional leader-follower modes of organization.

2   P.33 | See, for example, Peter Gray, "How Hunter-Gatherers Maintained Their Egalitarian Ways," *Psychologytoday.com*, 16 May 2011. Refer to psychologytoday.com/sg/blog/freedom-learn/201105/how-hunter-gatherers-maintained-their-egalitarian-ways.

3   P.34 | Gray, *Psychologytoday.com*, 16 May 2011.

4   P.34 | Peter Gray, "Play Theory of Hunter-Gatherer Egalitarianism," in *Ancestral Landscapes in Human Evolution*, edited by Darcia Narvaez et al, pp. 192-215 (Oxford University Press, 2014).

5   P.35 | See *Deloitte*, "Decoding Digital Leadership," 2016.

6   P.37 | The *Deloitte Global Millennial Survey 2020: Resilient generations hold the key to creating a "better normal"* can be viewed online at deloitte.com/millennialsurvey.

CHAPTER 2: PROACTIVE SELF-LEADERS

1   P.51 | Michael Hammer and James Champy, *Reengineering the Corporation: A Manifesto for Business Revolution* (Harper Collins, 1993).

2   P.52 | I first published this argument in an article written with Cresswell Walker: "Top-down is out, partnership is in," *The Straits Times,* 8 August 2009, p. R9.

3. P.55 | Henry Mintzberg, "The Fall and Rise of Strategic Planning," *Harvard Business Review,* January-February 1994.

4   P.56 | Adrian J. Slywotzky and Karl Weber, *The Upside: The 7 Strategies for Turning Big Threats into Growth Breakthroughs* (Crown Business, 2007).

5   P.56 | Jim Kouzes and Barry Posner detail these practices in their book, *The Leadership Challenge: How to Make Extraordinary Things Happen in Organizations,* which was first published in 1987.

6   P.58 | Diana O'Brien et al, "Purpose is everything: How brands that authentically lead with purpose are changing the nature of business today," *Deloitte,* 15 October 2019.

7   P.58 | "Putting Purpose to Work: A study of purpose in the workplace," *PwC,* June 2016.

8   P.58 | Jennifer Robison, "The Future of Your Workplace Depends on Your Purpose," *Gallup,* 24 May 2019.

CHAPTER 3: HUMAN CAPITALISTS

1   P.64 | David Green interviews Dave Ulrich, "The Role of the HR Business Partner in a Digital Age" (podcast), Episode 11, 27 August 2019

2   P.75 | "HR satisfaction survey 2018: what's working life like for your peers?" *People Management,* 24 May 2018.

3   P.77 | *Gallup,* "State of the Global Workplace: 2021 Report," p.2.

4   P.77 | Eduardo Briceño, *TEDx Manhattan Beach,* "How to get better at things you care about," November 2016.

NOTES

5   P.79 | McKinsey first launched a 9-box potential-performance matrix in the 1970s to assist General Electric prioritize investments. The concept has since been adapted for human resources and talent management.

6   P.80 | Geoff Hash, "Human Resources: The Engine or the Roadblock to Your Growth," *NativeBusiness,* 9 July 2018.

7   P.81 | See for example, "The Essential Clayton Christensen Articles," *Harvard Business Review,* 24 January 2020.

8   P.81 | David Garrison, "Most Mergers Fail Because People Aren't Boxes," *Forbes.com,* 24 June 2019.

9   P.89 | Grab and Uber used to compete directly until Grab acquired Uber's southeast Asia operations in March 2018.

10   P.90 | *Boku,* "Mobile Wallets Report 2021." boku.com/resources/news/download-our-2021-mobile-wallets-report.

CHAPTER 4: THE THIRD SPACE

1   P.98 | The energy savings associated with cool paint is based on a real client testimonial from St. Mary's Village in Australia. For more information, see skycool.net.au.

2   P.112 | The anecdote about the "Bitcoin Exchange" is based on a true story, though the name of the company has been changed to protect its privacy.

3   P.112 | "Direction + Alignment + Commitment (DAC) = Leadership," *Center for Creative Leadership.* Refer to ccl.org/articles/leading-effectively-articles/make-leadership-happen-with-dac-framework.

4   P.115 | Ronnie Littlejohn & Qingjun Li, "The Concept of Dialogue in Chinese Philosophy," *Educational Philosophy and Theory,* 2020.

5   P.115 | William Isaacs, *Dialogue and the Art of Thinking Together* (Crown, 1999), p. 19.

6   P.115 | David Bohm, *On Dialogue* (Routledge, 1996), p.26.

7   P.116 | While it's difficult to find the original source for this quote, former US President Barack Obama cited Thích Nhất Hạnh in a speech during his first visit to Vietnam in May 2016. See obamawhitehouse.archives.gov/the-press-office/2016/05/24/remarks-president-obama-address-people-vietnam

8   P.121 | Source: *Oxford Languages* (formerly *Oxford Dictionaries*).

9   P.125 | Herminia Ibarra and Anne Scoular, "The Leader as Coach," *Harvard Business Review,* November-December 2019.

10 P.126 | Carl R. Rogers and Richard E. Farson, *Active Listening,* 1957. (Republished by Mockingbird Press in 2021).

11 P.127 | The linguist Paul Frommer created the *Na'vi* language for Avatar, using Maori as a base and inspiration. Cameron and Frommer hoped that Avatar fans would embrace *Na'vi* with the same passion as Star Trekkers who converse in Klingon.

12 P.127 | *Center for Creative Leadership,* "Listening to Understand." See ccl.org/leadership-solutions/leadership-topics/listen-to-understand. See also Michael H. Hoppe, *Active Listening: Improve Your Ability to Listen and Lead* (CCL, 2006).

13 P.131 | At the time of the attempted acquisition, ESR-REIT had assets worth S$3.2 billion, while Sabana REIT's properties were valued at S$900 million.

14 P.132 | Larry Bossidy recounts this story in *Execution: The Discipline of Getting Things Done,* a 2002 best-selling book co-authored with Ram Charan.

THE LEADER'S FIELD GUIDE

1   P.161 | These leadership responsibilities build upon the work of James Kouzes and Barry Posner. See for example, Kouzes and Posner, *The Leadership Challenge: How to Make Extraordinary Things Happen in Organizations,* which was first published in 1987. The book's sixth edition was released in 2017.

2   P.161 | The literature on Leadership and Influence is rich. See, for example, Gary Yukl's perennial classic *Leadership in Organizations,* which was first published in 1981, or Terry Bacon, *Elements of Influence: The Art of Getting Others to Follow Your Lead* (Amacom, 2011).

3   P.161 | For more information on how to be a Leader-Coach, refer to Sharon Ting and Peter Scisco, *The CCL Handbook of Coaching: A Guide for the Leader Coach* (Jossey-Bass, 2006).

4   P.162 | Learn more in "Empathy in the Workplace: A Tool for Effective

NOTES

Leadership," a *Center for Creative Leadership* white paper by William A. Gentry, Todd J. Weber and Golnaz Sadri, April 2007.

5   P. 162 | For more insights on providing feedback, see Glenn Leibowitz, "6 Ways Truly Effective Leaders Deliver Feedback," *Inc.com,* or Sloan R. Weitzel, "Feedback that Works," *Center for Creative Leadership,* September 2000.

6   P. 162 | To learn more about SBI, see *Center for Creative Leadership,* "Use Situation-Behavior-Impact (SBI)™ to Understand Intent" and "How to Give the Most Effective Feedback," both of which were published in November 2020.

7   P. 164 | A useful model for questions that leaders can ask team members is RACSR (Relationship, Assessment, Challenge, Support, Results). See Sarah Stawiski, Maggie Sass and Rosa Grunhaus Belzer, "Building the Case for Executive Coaching," *Center for Creative Leadership,* 2016.

THE PROACTIVE SELF-LEADER'S FIELD GUIDE

1   P. 168 | To learn more about influence techniques, see Gary Yukl's list of Proactive Influence Tactics in Harold Scharlatt and Roland Smith, *Influence: Gaining Commitment, Getting Results* (CCL, 2001).

2   P. 169 | For more better listening techniques, see Art James and Dennis Kratz, *Effective Listening Skills, McGraw-Hill Education* (McGraw-Hill Education, 1995) or *Mindful Listening* (HBR Emotional Intelligence Series, 2019).

3   P. 170 | Situation-Behavior-Impact (SBI) is trademarked by the Center for Creative Leadership. Learn more about SBI in *Feedback that Works* by Sloan Weitzel (Center for Creative Leadership, 2011) and "Use Situation-Behavior-Impact (SBI)™ to Understand Intent," ccl.org.

THE HUMAN CAPITALIST'S FIELD GUIDE

1   P. 179 | To learn more about how to "empower employees for broad based action," see John P. Kotter, *Leading Change* (Harvard Business Review Press, 2012), Chapter 7.

2   P. 181 | Michael Watkins has written a series of leadership books including *The First 90 Days: Critical Success Strategies for New Leaders at All Levels* (Harvard Business School Press, 2003).

3 P. 182 | Another excellent resource to learn about influence techniques is Harold Scharlatt and Roland Smith, *Influence: Gaining Commitment and Getting Results,* 2nd ed. (Center for Creative Leadership, 2014).

THE ORGANIZATION'S FIELD GUIDE

1 P. 192 | For employee retention and turnover statistics, see: *SHRM,* "2016 Human Capital Benchmarking Report;" *Apollo Technical,* "19 Employee Retention Statistics That Will Surprise You" (2022); *Aon,* "Technology Companies Report Hiring Slowdown in Asia Pacific" (2019); *E-days,* "Employee Turnover Rates by Industry Comparison."

TOOLS & RESOURCES

1 P. 197 | "Gallup's Employee Engagement Survey: Ask the Right Questions with the Q12 Survey," gallup.com/workplace/356063/gallup-q12-employee-engagement-survey.aspx.

2 P. 198 | Survey questions can be found at ccl.org/insights-research/direction-alignment-and-commitment-assessment. See also Cynthia McCauley and Lynn Fick-Cooper, *Direction, Alignment, Commitment: Achieving Better Results Through Leadership* (CCL, 2015).

About the Authors

BILL CORNWELL is an expert in the art of asking questions. An executive coach to C-suite leaders, Bill's ground-breaking work developing the Enterprise Leadership Model is transforming the way organizations communicate, connect and grow in a hyper-competitive world. As the managing director of Cascade Consulting, he has coached and facilitated transformative workshops for leaders from organizations, big and small, including the Development Bank of Singapore, Estee Lauder, Exxon Mobil, Ford Motor, Procter & Gamble, Sanofi and public sector agencies. Recognized for creating the space for leaders and teams to feel confident with each other, Bill is a performance coach who enables professionals to overcome challenges, turn "awareness into action" and reach their full potential.

MICHAEL SWITOW is the managing partner of Switow Media LLP, a top-tier editorial consultancy that develops content for multi-media platforms, produces intelligent panel discussions from scratch and provides full-service book coaching and book development programs. Michael's commentary and financial reports have been featured across leading news platforms, including the Associated Press, NPR's *Morning Edition,* PRI's *The World,* Singapore's Money FM and Hong Kong's TVB. Michael earned a master's degree from Princeton University's School of Public and International Affairs. His first book, *Taming the Mouse,* recounts how a small Hong Kong theme park fought for survival and thrived in the face of competition from Disneyland. He is the founder of ONE (Singapore), a charity dedicated to Making Poverty History.

Printed in the USA
CPSIA information can be obtained
at www.ICGtesting.com
LVHW010529210923
758806LV00001B/90